STUART BLANCH: A LIFE

Dick Williams has combined 40 years of parish ministry with 30 years of diocesan communications work. Ordained in 1956, he served in parishes in Hull and Canada before coming to Liverpool diocese in 1964. He is married with three children. Previous titles include *The Gospels in Scouse* (with Frank Shaw, first published by Gear Press), *Godthoughts* and *Godfacts* (both published by Falcon), *Prayers for Today's Church*, *More Prayers for Today's Church* and *Prayers for Today's World* (published by Kingsway). He has broadcast on BBC Radio 4, Radio 2 and the World Service.

To Susan – wife, friend and helper

Stuart Blanch:
A Life

DICK WILLIAMS

SPCK

First published in Great Britain in 2001 by
Society for Promoting Christian Knowledge
Holy Trinity Church
Marylebone Road
London NW1 4DU

British Library Cataloguing-in-Publication Data

A catalogue record for this book is available from the British Library

ISBN 0-281-05412-6

Designed and typeset by Kenneth Burnley, Wirral, Cheshire.
Printed in Great Britain
by Bookcraft, Midsomer Norton.

Contents

The plate section will be found between pages 116 and 117.

Acknowledgements

I am deeply grateful to Lady Blanch for generously making available a large, rich and previously unstudied body of material from the family archive and for her unfailing encouragement and support. The help of so many members of her family has also been invaluable. I acknowledge with gratitude an afternoon spent with the late Mr Ronald Blanch, Stuart's then surviving elder brother, to whom I owe my account of Stuart's early childhood. My wife and I greatly appreciated the hospitality of Lord and Lady Coggan and their willing response to many questions and I gladly acknowledge my debt to Margaret Pawley's excellent biography of Lord Coggan: *Donald Coggan: Servant of Christ* (SPCK, 1987). I was also heartened by encouragement from Lord Runcie and Lord Jacobovits. Lord Habgood and Lord Sheppard were generous in time given to interviews and I greatly valued their reflections. Bishop John Bickersteth read an early draft of some sections of the book and added support and counsel to his personal recollections. The section on Rochester Theological College would have been threadbare indeed without the remarkable help of the Revd Alan Robson. As Stuart's former vice-principal, he contacted 60 former students in order to write the memoir, which he made freely available to me. I also gratefully acknowledge access to records held at the Borthwick Institute in York, to cathedral records at St George's, Jerusalem, to library facilities at the Ecumenical Institute, Tantur, at Liverpool Cathedral, and at Liverpool Hope University College.

I am grateful to Mr David Blunt, Canon Raymond Lee, Bishop James Roxburgh, and my wife for reading the manuscript and offering helpful observations. And in the travel and travail of the overall enterprise my deepest debt is to my wife Susan for support and enablement at every level.

A great number of people have helped provide material for this book and I am indebted to them all. I hope that those who are not mentioned here by name will also accept the personal thanks which is their due.

Acknowledgements

Sir Lindsay Alexander, Mrs Dorothy Atkins, the Revd R. W. Bailey, the Rt Revd Clifford Barker, Canon Dr Geoffrey Barnard, the Rt Revd Gordon Bates, Mrs Jennet Blake, Mr David and Mrs Dorothy Blunt, Mr Leslie A. M. Brannan, the Revd Dr Leslie Bruce, the Revd Margaret Cundiff, Mrs Joan Calcutt, Ms Alice Chappell, the Revd Norton H. Callard, Mr F. Patrick Cook, the Ven. Eric Corbett, Mr Brian D. Dagnall, the Revd Peter R. Davies, Miss Peggy Dunn, Canon Bob Evans, Canon Malcolm Forrest, Mrs Elsie Floyd, Canon Sydney Goddard, the Revd Norman Goodacre, Mr Stanley and Mrs Joan Green, Mr Douglas Hall, Mrs Joyce Hall, the Rt Revd Michael Henshall, Mr Ernest M. Hickin, the Revd John Higham, Canon John G. Hunter, Canon Geoffrey Hunter, Mrs Betty Jasper, the Rt Revd Samir Kafity, Mr Joe Kelly, the Revd Robert (Bob) Lewis, Sir Douglas Lovelock, Mrs Mary McMaster, OBE, the Rt Revd Morris Maddocks, Mrs Patience Markby, the Revd Peter Markby, Mr Malcolm J. McLaren, Mr John Miles, Mrs Brenda Miles, Canon John Morris, Canon Richard and Mrs Susan Page, Mr John Pimm, the Revd Paul Rathbone, the Revd Gruffydd N. Rees, Mrs Phyllis Richardson, the Revd Paul N. Rimmer, the Rt Revd Dr Anthony Russell, the Rt Revd Dr R. David Say, Dr A. and Mrs Freda Speirs, Mrs Josie Smith, the Ven. L. Stanbridge, Mrs Margaret Taylor, Mrs Elizabeth Tow, Mrs Yvonne Townsend, Canon Douglas R. Vicary, Mr Stephen S. Watson, Deaconess Sybil J. Webb, Mr Gordon and Mrs Margery Wise, Canon David Woodhouse, Canon Michael Wolfe, Canon Simon Wright.

Photo acknowledgements: J. G. Hunter, *Daily Express*, *Holderness Gazette*, *Liverpool Daily Post and Echo*, *Yorkshire Press & Gazette & Herald*, *Yorkshire Evening Post*.

Preface

I first met Stuart Blanch in 1966 at a clergy chapter meeting held near Liverpool's famous Pier Head. My last meeting with him was during his own final visit to Liverpool on 11 November 1993 when he came to open the fine theological library now housed in Liverpool Cathedral. That day has left a graphic memory of him standing between the ranks of books and somehow summoning them to life. Between those two occasions I had been rector of the Liverpool parish in which he had lived, had begun there to be his part-time press and radio officer, benefited from the warm hospitality of Bishop's Lodge, witnessed his role in landmark mission and ecumenical developments, and, during his years at York, been press officer for the Northern Consultation for Mission in which he played a leading part. My research therefore has had the background of many memories over many years.

The invitation to write this biography was a great honour. It has also been a daunting one. I have, however, received warmest help and encouragement on every hand, and crucially from Lady Blanch who entrusted me with her husband's diaries, journals, unpublished manuscripts, lectures, sermons, personal study notes, broadcast recordings, and their five-year wartime correspondence; in total a very large and personal archive of great richness and depth. For this and much else I am grateful indeed.

A biographer should not, I think, presume to make judgements about his subject. His task is to tell the story, so far as that is possible. The question is how to do it. In approaching the task I have been guided by some of Stuart's own words. On page 115 of his book *Encounters with Jesus* he writes: 'I have . . . for the greater part of my career, been involved in public life . . . but I know that this outward life which seems to dominate us most of the time, was nothing like as important as events, perceptions and impressions in my inner life which shaped and controlled my feelings and attitudes.' This observation laid down an important marker for me. It suggests that if he had written his own story he would have required of himself an account of that inner life. On the same page, however, he provides a second guideline, saying of St Mark that 'history for him was the outward expression of the activity of God in the human soul'. Although Stuart Blanch had a remarkably rich interior life it found an equally remarkable outward expression in his concern for others, and – as in the title of another of his books – it was a concern 'for all mankind'. These thoughts have helped shape this biography. Knowing what to leave out has been a problem and much detail has necessarily been omitted, but amid the events in his lifetime I have tried to let him speak for himself.

There are of course many other voices. Of the huge number of letters received by Lady Blanch following Stuart's death in 1994 I was able to read more than 400, and in my research I have received almost a hundred contributions. The overwhelming impression was of many witnesses agreeing together about a man who combined formidable endowments of intellect and imagination with genuine humility in a way which was plainly the fruit of prayer. Humility was not a mask, it was the man. It did not obscure his talents, it made them shine. In times of worldwide ferment in church and society Stuart guarded the springs of living water, unblocked its wells and made clear its connections with issues of the day. He was a true bishop.

Although there were memorial services in York Minster, Liverpool Cathedral and Oxford it was somehow fitting that his funeral, like his baptism, was in a small country church – his baptism performed by the local vicar, his funeral conducted by a former domestic chaplain. Equally fitting is a charitable foundation set up in Liverpool for an annual lecture in his memory where distinguished speakers are invited in their own way to guard the springs, unblock the wells and make connections with issues of the day. In its way I hope this book, whatever its shortcomings, may also do the same.

DICK WILLIAMS

Foreword

Reading through this biography of Stuart has been a strange experience for me, rather similar, I imagine, to the experiences that dying people are supposed to have. One is confronted by one's mistakes! But Dick Williams has done a wonderfully thorough and accurate job and, moreover, has contributed a useful survey of the C of E's history over the past sixty-odd years. How he managed to decipher Stuart's diaries, I do not know. Stuart's writing was never easy to read. But Dick has done it and thereby enabled us to know some of Stuart's inner thoughts.

However, Stuart's desire to serve God, while wholehearted, was not the whole person. He loved sport, played soccer, cricket, tennis and squash at school and continued to play squash until he was too old for it. At Eynsham, once we had tamed the jungle that was our garden, we created a tennis court on the lawn. It had some hazards – a pear tree in the wrong place and a yucca plant whose leaves had sharp points! But we had great fun. We also had wonderful birthday parties for our children, organized by Stuart, involving treasure hunts; and he told fascinating stories to our children at bedtime, stories involving a family of animals who lived with us.

Stuart always took his day off and we went walking somewhere – Delamere Forest when in Liverpool and the North Yorkshire Moors when in York. In the evening we would play a game together, Scrabble or Bezique or Mah-jong. Best of all was life at the little cottage in Marloes, Pembrokeshire, which we managed to buy. This was our own home – not a tied house – and we all loved it. Cricket on the beach, swimming and picnics, walking round the coast, talking with the friends we had made down there, watching the sea birds, boating. The Church seemed far away! One day the people of Marloes asked me to open their fête in aid of Marloes Church. I dressed for the occasion, but the rest of the family came in their holiday gear, so we had the comic spectacle of Stuart in his leather shorts being presented with a buttonhole to wear and no jacket to fix it to!

These were happy times which we treasured, time to be with our family, to relax and to enjoy all the beauty of God's creation. I tackled our garden while Stuart tackled some of the necessary repair jobs. We were fortunate to have fifty years together, but I miss him very much. His sense of humour was a great help. Little did we know the sort of life that God was going to call us to, and the last ten years without Stuart, Susan or Alison, have been difficult ones. I hope this book may help you to understand the strange ways in which God sometimes works. May he bless you as you read.

BRENDA BLANCH

~ 1 ~

Genesis:
Introduction and Early Years

INDIA

Bombay, 23 September 1944: 'India! – glorious, pillared mansions behind green trees, lying next to the most pitiable poverty; bullock carts with their yokes smooth and "easy", tiny wizened children and old men carrying phenomenal loads and those who have hired them stalking majestically ahead . . .'

These words, scribbled by Stuart Blanch on a single-sheet fold-over aerogramme, say almost as much about him as about India. The flash of lyrical description linked to a verbal cartoon going to the heart of what he saw is typical of his skill as a correspondent. There was much of the poet in him. His inner and outer worlds were woven closely together and one was often the sounding board of the other.

Since the beginning of a biography is not necessarily about the start of its subject's life, I have not begun with Stuart Blanch's birth on a Gloucestershire farm, nor with the idyll of his early years, nor the tragedy that ended his childhood. I begin, as he might have begun himself, with some quotations requiring explanation.

Some of the threads that link the beginning and end of his life are perceptible in the letters he wrote from India at the age of 26 and 27. Like many people of his generation, he was for a number of years doing things he didn't want to do in places where he didn't want to be, but nevertheless finding this to be the time of his life in which he came to know beyond doubt what he wanted to be and to do. It was a long and arduous process, lit with great joys and shadowed with dark moments, and it was spanned by the growing relationship with his wife Brenda. The letter from Bombay was part of their remarkable and prolific correspondence. From their first evening out together in September 1941 to his return from India in February 1946, they coped with wartime separation by writing to each other several times a week.

1

They were married on 10 July 1943, almost halfway through those years, but saw little of each other until the spring of 1946. A four-day honeymoon preceded his travel to Canada for aircrew training and his return brought only a few more days together before the passage to India. Unbroken throughout, however, was their correspondence. In it they shared their growing experience of a Christian faith they had discovered in different settings, but at much the same time. The correspondence, like the relationship, helped lay the foundations of a remarkable ministry.

Years later, two months after Stuart was consecrated Bishop of Liverpool, he was pondering the sources of his faith. On 25 May 1966 he had been reading the story of Samson and made the following entry in his new five-year diary: '"The spirit of the Lord began to stir him in Mahanehdan between Zorah and Eshtaol" (Judges 13.25). . . . What strange hidden portent was given him that he should become aware of powers at work in him? When was my Mahanehdan?' I don't think it was in India – we shall search for it elsewhere. But India was where his thoughts of ordination became the settled conviction of a calling, and where he began to discover some of the links between inner discipleship and public ministry.

On 23 September 1944 he had just disembarked from a crowded troopship en route for Calcutta and RAF aircrew duties as a navigator. His posting came a year after the creation of South East Asia Command with its Unified Eastern Air Command based at Calcutta. Much of the air work was to get goods into China and to survey the movement of Japanese troops and supplies. Stuart flew as a navigator–wireless operator in Dakotas of Transport Command. There was a very great deal of flying to do. From January 1945 troop and cargo planes were each clocking up 220 flying hours per month. Pilots were being required to fly between 150 and 200 hours per month, and radio operators 300 hours. Questions of censorship precluded much reference to his duties but he did give Brenda this glimpse of daily work: '. . . we sail about the countryside, pitched about over spiky hills, looking down upon mile after mile of jungle, watching for the spiral of dust that marks an aerodrome, seeing the fires that glint mysteriously on the hillsides as the dusk comes. These are times of isolation, almost of spiritual suspension.'

There was, however, another side of Air Force life, denied – as Stuart often reflected – to ground troops engaged in jungle, desert or European battlefields. After the perils and tedium of flight there were home comforts of a sort. He appreciated these. Waiting for the 1,200-mile train journey to Calcutta he wrote about his inner life in the barracks:

These have been days of spiritual quietness, of activity as regular and as rhythmic as the chiming of a great clock. . . . Early morning prayers in a cool, marble-floored chapel with birds flapping against the open windows, with the sound of work beginning in the room below until the last faint thanksgiving when mosquito nets are tucked in and the barrack floor is patterned by the camp lights outside. 'My God how wonderful thou art, thy majesty how bright, how beautiful thy mercy seat in depths of burning light'. . . . 'Religion is adoration'; I begin to understand dear old Baron Von H[ugel].

He also enjoyed the friendship and hospitality of some remarkable service chaplains, and his letters show the enormous importance of such men. Stuart would often be talking late into the night at the Calcutta home of the Revd Cecil and Mrs de Vall, with memories of many other similar encounters in England and Canada.

Given the impossibility of home leave, Brenda had a suggestion. She knew the writings of Amy Carmichael and had begun to correspond with her. She urged Stuart to visit her and the Christian community that she had founded at Dohnavur to care for orphaned children. Stuart used one leave to make the journey there. On meeting the now frail and aged Amy Carmichael, he discovered to his surprise that she had written both his and Brenda's names inside the back cover of her Bible as an aid to praying for them.

It was while at Dohnavur that Stuart was able to visit neighbouring villages. This was a moving experience that underlay and foreshadowed much pastoral visiting in England:

Murray [a minister at Dohnavur] had to visit a poor old Indian lady dying of consumption, with limbs no thicker than knitting needles; she is still sitting, just outside the doorway of her mud and thatched house, waiting for death and the neighbours stand helpless at the gate, watching. Afterwards we went into one or two of the houses – about as big as our kitchen, without light or ventilation, where men, women and children eat, sleep, quarrel, cook and work; in the corner is a parrot peering out through a hole in a basket, on the floor rice is drying, hung from the roof is a baby in a linen sling, a cat nestles against the wall and hens scratch in the doorway. The floor is of cow dung, renewed daily to keep away insects, but quite firm and clean, the roof is of palm leaf, dry as tinder and about as flammable. . . . No privacy, no room for prayer and reading save perhaps for a very small man in the rice tub with the lid on!

As well as foreshadowing his own pastoral visiting in later years, the final flash of humour speaks volumes of his own need for privacy and prayer.

At Dohnavur Stuart was also moved to write a little about the light and shade of his experience of mystery. The words echoed something of his past and spoke of experiences that would recur in days to come. They are words that, it might be argued, find a distant echo on his death bed:

> My hut is perched at the top of a flight of stone steps and the view from the verandah is through the tops of the trees; the wind is fresh and clean and the sun dances and dazzles on the leaves. By day a place of earthly delight but by night, so I have found, a lonely silent place which strips the mind and spirit of its trappings and holds them up naked to the eye of God. The precipice yawns at our feet again, as it has done before, and we look up from its depths, help-less, to the mercy of God and the homely companionship of His Son. Deep cries unto deep.

These were the days in which ideas of ordination became a sense of vocation. The thought was already there when he arrived in India, and on landing at Bombay he had made his first tentative enquiry. He wrote about it on 22 October 1944:

> I am in touch with Command Chaplain over here and am enquiring, amongst other things, about library facilities. He has sent me a few forms to fill up as a provisional ordinand. . . . Usual variety with five lines to say 'yes' in, and half a line to explain what caused you to decide 'to study for ordination'. The only crisp and truthful answer I could find for that was 'not my decision', but may amplify this curt rejoinder in a covering letter.

It was 18 months later before the die was cast – and then things happened quickly. In deciding to offer for ordination he was joining a distinctive gen-eration of clergy: those who had been to war and who knew the world and themselves in the light of that experience. They brought into the Church qualities that were to mark it to the end of the twentieth century and that it will continue to need in centuries to come.

As for all others, so for him there comes the question of his pathway to faith. How was it that a farmer's son, transplanted in childhood from rural Gloucestershire to London suburbia, uncertain of his beliefs as a young man and critical of the Church as he saw it, came to be what Lord Runcie would one day call 'a teacher of our faith beloved throughout the world', and what

Britain's former chief rabbi, Lord Jacobovits, would call 'a leading spiritual guide of our time'?

India has its place in this process and we shall return to it, but now it is time to visit Gloucestershire.

THE FOREST OF DEAN

Two brothers surnamed Blanch came to England from France in 1680. One of them went to London and settled in Chelsea. The other went to Gloucestershire and settled in the Forest of Dean. The Chelsea Blanches involved themselves in a coach-building business. The Gloucestershire Blanches applied themselves to the Forest of Dean coal industry and the rail network that came to serve it. These were the forebears of Stuart Blanch.

By the nineteenth century the family had prospered and made its mark, particularly in the railway business. By the twentieth century a variety of its associated jobs had been spread among family members, one of whom, William, had charge of the horses used in the coal industry's rail system. He was a man of erect, athletic carriage, with strong, pleasant features, a humorous mouth and generous moustache. At the turn of the century he married Elizabeth (Bessie) Yarworth, the daughter of a Forest of Dean butcher. Her photograph shows a strong face, clear eyes, determined mouth, and a brightness of spirit that perhaps found expression in her paintings. She was a keen artist and watercolours signed 'Bessie Yarworth' accompanied her into her new home.

Two sons were born before 1910, William (Will) in 1902, and Ronald (Ron) in 1908. Family life was close-knit, fun-filled and musical. From such a background William and Bessie moved into farming and took possession of Viney Hill Farm, near Blakeney. It was a courageous move, not without cost to family life. The farmhouse was well away from village communities and the neighbourly networks of earlier days, and Bessie in particular felt the lack of their support. Festive gatherings of friends and family ceased to be a normal feature of life and the years of the First World War brought hardships of their own. But they worked the farm successfully and did very much more than survive. Their third son was born into a successful and hardworking home on 2 February 1918. On 17 March, the day before the birth was registered, he was baptized at All Saints, Blakeney, with the name of Stuart Yarworth.

Like many parents of their day, William and Bessie must have wondered about the sort of world awaiting their son. Although nearing its end, the First

World War was setting new standards of horror for mankind and by March 1918 its outcome was still very much in the balance. The Russian Revolution, only six months old, had ensured Russia's withdrawal from a war begun, as they saw it, by capitalists. Thus German troops were released from their eastern front. Consequently the month in which Stuart was baptized brought news of a devastating 40-mile German advance in the west, with 80,000 allied troops taken prisoner. The shadow of war lay across the world. Certainly it embraced the Forest of Dean and doubtless shaped the prayers of the good vicar who held Stuart in his arms at the font and prayed that he would be Christ's faithful soldier and servant until his life's end.

CHANGING WORLD AND CHANGING CHURCH

The war ended before Stuart's first birthday, but by then his parents lived in a different world from that in which their elder sons were born. So did the vicar. World and Church were caught up in processes of far-reaching change.

The year 1918 is thought by some to mark the beginning of the modern world. For our purposes it is worth noting some of the changes that were to shape Stuart's early life and to stay with him to the end. Unquestionably there was far more to the experience of change than the political and economic turmoil of European countries and their colonies, or the plethora of international conferences, or the founding of the League of Nations, or the vast movement of people to new homelands. The scale and horror of what had erupted in an advanced civilization between nations with long Christian traditions raised questions for the multitudes. These were not only the concern of governments, they were embodied in the hosts of the returning servicemen and bereaved families who spread them through every level of society. Writers, artists, musicians, and philosophers struggled with the avalanche of sombre material invading their mental landscape. So too did theologians and churchmen. The world was digesting a nightmare.

For the churches the next few years brought to birth a range of initiatives that, however slowly, began to affect the shape of things to come. In 1918 the Archbishops of Canterbury and York formed a committee of enquiry into the evangelistic work of the Church. Among the many conundrums and causes clamouring for enquiry it is significant that they saw the need to think again about the root cause of human need and God's purpose in the face of it. In a world like this, what is the good news of Christ, what are its effects, and how can it be heard and shared?

Amazingly, the fruits of that particular process were not to appear until the end of the next world war. It was not until 1943 that Archbishop William Temple, then at Canterbury, convened a working party to pick up its threads and produce a report. The result was *Towards the Conversion of England*, which appeared in 1945. The lifetime of that particular process spanned the years between Stuart Blanch's baptism and his first enquiry about ordination. However, its most quoted statement, which was a definition of evangelism, was actually written at the start of the process in 1918. It was: 'so to present Jesus Christ in the power of the Holy Spirit that men shall come to put their trust in God through Him, to accept Him as their Saviour and serve Him as their King in the fellowship of His Church'. The year that brought that famous definition saw the birth of Billy Graham as well as that of Stuart Blanch.

In 1919, however, William Temple was also busy with other things that were to affect the life of Church and nation, one of which was the possibility of holding a general Christian conference to tackle social questions. These ideas bore fruit with the formation of COPEC (the Conference on Christian Politics, Economics and Citizenship), which had its first meeting in Birmingham in 1924. This has come to be seen as a watershed in the development of social teaching in the Church, prompting the then Archbishop of Uppsala to declare that 'COPEC has given a new word to the English language'. It was a pioneering ecumenical venture, but one in which the Church of England was a driving force. Social concerns, however, had already been active with the formation in 1918 of the Industrial Christian Fellowship.

Lay involvement in church government was also being called for and 1919 saw the Enabling Act which created the Church Assembly and parochial church councils. The voices and votes of lay men and women were being built into church decision-making processes. Meanwhile, for Roman Catholics 1918 was the year in which Rome recognized its churches and their localities in England as parishes rather than mission stations.

On the theological front it was in 1919 that Karl Barth published his work on the Epistle to the Romans. Liberal interpretations of Christianity, flowing from nineteenth-century thought and biblical criticism, had reached a high-water mark, but Barth's work gave startling academic endorsement for the view that God speaks on his own terms and in his own way, and must be heard. The scale and character of human sin and tragedy, placarded in every place by the horrors of war, had given notice of humanity's need for a God of love and judgement who is almighty and who speaks. Barth talked of faith as decision in the context of crisis and showed that Christianity was not the flowering of human virtue but a resurrection from the dead. The second edition, published in 1922, has been famously described as the bomb that burst in the playground of the liberal theologians.

Nevertheless, in 1921, the liberal Modern Churchmen's Union held its most controversial conference at Girton College, Cambridge. Here, anti-supernatural views of the faith were at full flood and Jesus was viewed as no more than a moral teacher. These fruits of pre-war liberalism were no match for the hour and it is significant that 1922 saw the setting up of a commission on doctrine in the Church of England. In that same year the Bible Reading Fellowship was formed, helping rank and file Christians to come to grips with Bible study in the home.

As the misery of war was followed in an unequal society by the misery of peace, the 1920s saw notable work by clergy, some of them colourfully Anglo-Catholic in style and conviction, in the great city slums. In various ways the local churches struggled to find renewal in faith and an effective ministry. Symptomatic of such endeavours was one effort in Stuart's future diocese of Liverpool where the 1926 Diocesan Congress, held in Southport, chose the theme of the Holy Spirit, and Liverpool Cathedral's congregation made its own attempt to understand things during the Depression by visiting dockland parishes in partnership with the university's department of social studies. The Archbishops also made some thoughtfully high-profile moves. During the national strike the Archbishop of Canterbury, Randall Davidson, himself intervened with an offer of mediation.

Evangelistic, theological, and social concerns were joined by a quest for changes in forms of worship. This was evident in the Church Assembly and in 1927 a revised prayer book was presented to Parliament and was there rejected. Questions of disestablishment swam into focus, and many parishes pressed on with some of the proposed changes anyway. A process of diversification was under way.

In 1928 the Church's foundation task of world mission was considered at the Jerusalem Missionary Conference and in 1929 the new Archbishops of Canterbury and York, Lang and Temple, issued a joint pastoral letter calling Christians to Bible study and prayer, to the preaching of the gospel, and to liveliness of worship. Significantly, William Temple combined high ecclesiastical office with a capacity for evangelistic preaching that was direct and appealing.

Other processes were at work that profoundly influenced the Church into which Stuart Blanch was introduced and in which he grew up. In 1937, when he was 19, the ecumenical Faith and Order Conference combined with the Life and Work Movement to form the basis of the World Council of Churches. And in 1938 the Church of England commission on doctrine, set on its way in 1922, published its report. Its emphasis showed a movement on from an earlier, and proper, concern to understand the incarnation within a rational explanation of the world. It was concerned now with a gospel of judgement and redemption.

The severe catechism for Christians posed by the First World War was finding its way to the threshold of some answers just as the world was on the brink of another catastrophe. However, the progress of Christian thinking in social concerns, epitomized by Temple's work, was laying foundations that would serve the nation well in the years following the Second World War.

For the young Stuart Blanch these things were part of the climate, process, and framework within which he became acquainted with the Church and eventually came to faith. And it would be in a world at war again that he would come to faith and find his vocation. All that, however, would have seemed a world away from day-to-day life at Viney Hill Farm in the years between Stuart's birth and the family's leaving of Gloucestershire.

IDYLL AND TRAGEDY

A puff of smoke drifted away unnoticed from a hedgerow. The sound of a gunshot hung on the air for a moment and was gone. The Gloucestershire countryside continued to look rich, verdant and untroubled, and on that spring day in 1923 most of the occupants of Viney Hill Farm were building up a hearty appetite for their meal. Mrs Bessie Blanch bustled about the kitchen, 21-year-old Will and 16-year-old Ron pursued their own tasks and, like everyone else, five-year-old Stuart was wondering why Dad was so late. As on so many days, Father had gone off with his gun to see if he could shoot a rabbit for the pot. Everything was normal.

Writing of his early childhood 60 years later, Stuart Blanch said:

Mine was, by any standards, a fortunate childhood, . . . surrounded by all the evidences of a singularly beautiful countryside, and insulated from the harsh and glaring unrealities to which many a city child is subjected. My life was bounded by the garden and the farmyard and the paddock. My memory, no doubt influenced by the recollections of others, is of long summer days and warm flagstones and the highly distinctive smell of the Scottish collie who was my inveterate companion. That was the beginning of my inner life, not just my outward existence, in which those first impressions were formed, impressions of a friendly world and comforting companionship. Long before I became a practising Christian and began to articulate my faith in words and concepts, I was the happy victim of circumstances which conspired to create an inner life of faith in the ultimate goodness of the universe and of the One who mysteriously abides within it and presides over it (*Living by Faith*, pp. 104–5).

These sentiments were frequently repeated in his later life. In an article written in retirement ('Experiencing the Divine'), he spoke of 'warm days on the flagstones outside the front door, the cows, the horses, the hens, the pigs. Memory conjures up the magic of it all. . . . Those early years gave me an inchoate experience of the divine which has never altogether left me, and has coloured my imagination ever since.'

Living on a farm far removed from other children of his age, and by the margin of 11 years the youngest son, Stuart had fewer than most of childhood's usual playmates. He had little opportunity to share his secrets, tell his stories or – in play – act out his fantasies with children of his own age. He was, however, well provided with companions of another sort, first among which was a dog – a cross-bred collie named Rover. When he and Rover first kept company, family snapshots show the dog towering over the toddler as he sat on the grass. Gradually their relative dimensions were exchanged and Rover was at his heels. But most of the time was spent in eye-to-eye contact, shoulder-to-shoulder camaraderie. And then there were the pigs, some of which Stuart regarded as his own. Pigs free of the sty are clean enough, and Stuart's pigs pottered about the farmyard and basked in whatever sunshine providence might afford – as did Stuart. One day, when he was out of sight and failed to respond to a call from the house, Ron was sent to look for him. An educated guess led him to the pigs – among their somnolent sun-warmed bodies lay young Stuart asleep in equal bliss!

He must often have talked with his animal friends, certainly with Rover, as he was apt to do with Rover's many successors. In later years, visitors to Bishopthorpe were apt to find a relaxing Archbishop in animated chat with the dog of the day, for each of whom he would conceive what he once told a Lambeth Conference was 'inordinate affection'.

Stuart's formal education began at an early age, with walks through leafy lanes to the village school. At the end of the school day, though, he would bring home strange and startling tales of the day's adventures, calling for parental investigation. When it became clear that these vivid episodes were all in the mind, his mother took him to the doctor. That wise man advised her to let Stuart be. What many small boys do in play with others, Stuart had to do solo. Time would reveal the boundaries and cross-over points between fantasy and fact. Fantasy was wisely not repressed. The wells of the imagination were not blocked. But it was by no means a lonely childhood, for he loved to attach himself to his father and mingle with the men on the farm. In later life, Stuart's calm urbanity was frequently shot through with a country-side charm and startling directness that owed much to farmyard life.

One other feature of his childhood that stood out in his brother Ron's mind was of Stuart's quite extraordinary devotion to his father. The mater-nal bond was strong and enduring, but for his father there was a deep and special affinity – one that Ron had encountered nowhere else and that dated from earliest days. At mealtimes, Stuart's high-chair would be placed at a point equidistant between his father and mother, but as soon as all were at table Stuart would inch his chair ever closer to his father's. And when Father came into the house, in the course of a working day, there would be a pan-demonium of entreaty from Stuart to be taken out with him to wherever he was working on the farm. It became a feature of life for Father, popping in briefly from farmyard or field, to peer cautiously round the door and enquire, 'Where is he?' before taking off his boots to tip-toe about his business in the hope of escaping unnoticed.

William Blanch attracted the warm affection of all his sons, for he was a quiet, harmonious man. Likewise, his relationships with those who worked for him, and with him, on the farm were sound and peaceable. Warmly regarded as a natural gentleman, he was a countryman through and through.

This was the background to that spring day in 1923 when William Blanch took his gun and went out into the fields to shoot a rabbit. It was all part of the warp and woof of familiar life. But this time his return was so long delayed that Will and Ron set out to look for him. Five-year-old Stuart, eager to pursue his father with his usual relentless devotion, thought he knew where to look. Running ahead of his brothers across a familiar field he cried out: 'There he is. I can see him. He's lying down.'

Ron remembered Will's voice calling out sharply: 'The boy! The boy!' They ran hard to try and reach their father before Stuart did, but in vain. Between them and the rising ground of the next meadow was a hedge and a ditch. There was a way through a gap in the hedge that their father had been taking when his gun had been triggered by a branch. The safety catch was faulty, the gun had discharged itself, their father was dead, and the five-year-old was the first to reach his side. As he fled from the scene of the tragedy to his mother in the house, it was Ron's task to get there before him to break the terrible news to their mother.

Quite how these moments and that day registered in the mind and spirit of a little boy one cannot know. Immediate contact with the bloodied body of the beloved father who had daily swept him up in his arms was an experience beyond imagining.

LONDON

Following the shock and in the course of their mourning, the family had to make plans and take drastic action. Will and Ron were not farmers; both aimed at careers in the city. So with no one to take over the running of the farm, a move was inevitable. Within the year, the family had left the farm and moved to London. As with most moves made necessary by bereavement, transplantation added another dimension to it. Loss of husband and father now also entailed the loss of well-loved countryside and – for Bessie – a well-defined and significant role in her local community. When their old home recently came on the market again some 80 years later, it was described as 'an imposing country period house with eighteenth-century origins'. Exchanging it and its surrounding open countryside for a semi-detached house in Norwood could only have reinforced the shock of bereavement.

The move, however, was not without incident. The first stage of the journey, by pony and trap, was to an overnight stay at an uncle's house. Here Rover escaped. They knew where to look for him, though, and there was a return journey for the older members of the family to collect him from the recently vacated farm. Rover, however, was not the only one to feel the loss of territory. London, to a five-year-old used to roaming fields and feeding his pigs, was another world and Stuart felt doubly bereaved. The decision to move, however, was clearly made with vision, courage, and resolve, and Ron remembered with gratitude the burdens assumed by 21-year-old Will in those critical months.

In London, young Stuart was to find a different world. He was also, by degrees, to discover some means of coping with this vast addition to the agenda of growing up. Writing in retirement he said:

There was little 'magic' about life in a London suburb, and we obviously had financial problems, though largely screened from my view. My mother, in addition to ill health, had her anxieties about the future, when inevitably my elder brothers would marry and move away. I recall a particular moment of tension in the household which prevented me from sleeping, when I reacted in an untypical way: I got out of bed and said the only prayer I knew – 'Our Father . . .' I heard no answering voice from heaven, but I felt better, reassured, no longer alone. I went to sleep. If the farm had given me an experience of the divine as the beneficent Creator, this incident gave me an impression of the Divine Father, replacing the father I had so prematurely lost.

The move to London meant a hunt for Stuart's new school. When one was located nearby, its imposing name – Canterbury College – caused family amusement. He seems to have settled in well, but the atmosphere of study was probably even more marked at home than at school. His immensely able elder brothers were both studying for degrees and professional qualifications while earning their living during the day – Will in the Inland Revenue and Ron in a bank. The 'semi' that replaced the farm was home to students who were ultimately to hold positions of national importance in income tax, banking, and the Church – Will at Somerset House, Ron as senior manager of Lloyds Bank. At home, though, their work patterns differed: Will liked to work late into the night; Ron preferred to go to bed early and rise to study. For Stuart, who got up for school as Ron left for work, and went to bed as Will settled to his studies, it meant that he saw very little of his brothers. But their influence was loving and profound, and their application to study sounded a tonal note throughout Stuart's schooldays.

Bessie Blanch was ambitious for her boys, and of course a parent's ambitions for a child can be a mixed blessing. At its best it can be a confidence-building inspiration and part of parenthood's special creativity. At its worst it can be selfish pursuit that deeply damages a child being forced into the wrong mould. It is particularly important for ambitious parents to know their children and learn from them who and what they are. There is a proper humility needed to match the proper pride so important to the relationship, and it is not the easiest of balances to strike. It seems not to have been the easiest of Bessie's achievements. For most parents, perhaps, the ambition for their young is directed towards their safe and healthy flowering into what it is in their nature to be. This was undoubtedly Bessie's ambition, but it was super-charged and linked to crossing the frontiers deployed by an unequal society. Stuart must have felt the power of his mother's ambition, and he could not have failed to have been influenced by his brothers' single-minded pursuit of excellence. Whatever dynamic this may have imparted, it was not in the sphere of drawing attention to himself. In the exercise of his gifts and responsibilities, Stuart was among the most modest of people.

Bessie was undoubtedly a devoted mother, but she was also fearful of losing her sons, a fear, no doubt, owing much to her husband's tragic death. The prospect of her son's marriages seems to have been a cause of anxiety rather than a blossoming of hope. And when Will and Ron in due course married and moved out, Stuart had to find his own way of supporting her with his love while at the same time finding his proper freedoms as a young man. He seems to have been quite successful in this and the local church played an important part in the enterprise.

CHURCH AND SCHOOL

One day the vicar, Canon Harold Montague Dale, called at the house. Stuart had had little contact with the Church up to then, and in his teens became a keen critic of much of church life. But from that day on, Canon Dale left in his mind an impression of godliness that comes only from a good and kindly person. This impression – not depending upon rational argument or inspired preaching – endured for a lifetime. The Canon had called to invite Stuart to join the choir, though his pastoral agenda in visiting a widow and her family was probably broader than that. Stuart – and Mother – agreed, and a fruitful link was formed.

Thus Stuart first became familiar with church life and worship at Holy Trinity, Tulse Hill. Opened in 1856 to meet the needs of the growing suburb, its handsome nave and gallery was built to accommodate 1,000 worshippers, its 88-foot spire commanding attention in the locality. There was a large and active congregation, and as Stuart began to sit in the choirstalls there was a lot for him to take in. Close to the choir were the Cleopatra chairs – made from the wooden casing that had supported the erection of Cleopatra's Needle on the Embankment. Just beyond them was the recently installed reredos which was part of a First World War memorial installed in 1920: in five panels it depicted an unusual range of saints in company with Christ, together with a nurse, a soldier, a sailor, and an airman, symbolizing the nations that had been allies in war. There was also a great sense of space imparted by the absence of pillars in the nave – fruit of a condition laid down by generous founding donor Jonah Cressingham, who had spent too many frustrating Sundays stuck behind a pillar in the church of his childhood.

Holy Trinity was the focal point of a strong community life, with a lively musical tradition, a large choir, and many clubs and societies. The home of organist and choirmaster Henry Findon Hall was equipped with a table-tennis table and the boys were always welcome there. In joining the choir, Stuart was entering a family of families with multifarious activities and interests. And so it was that he had his roots firmly in a local community when he won a scholarship to Alleyn's School in Dulwich. He was extremely fortunate in this, and the school had such a powerful influence upon his life that it is worth more than a passing mention.

When Stuart began in 1929 to catch his daily train to Dulwich, Alleyn's was prospering under R. B. Henderson, its headmaster from 1920 to 1940. Henderson was at the height of a remarkable career in which he became the first non-boarding-school headmaster to serve a year as chairman of the Headmasters' Conference, and he is reputed to be the first layman since the Reformation to be awarded a Lambeth BD. The weight of his personality clearly made a deep impression on his pupils. One old boy graphically describes his imposing presence: 'Invariably dressed in black coat and striped trousers, he always wore academic dress. Add to this a deep and resonant voice, and large gold-rimmed glasses to round off a balding head of grey hair, sharp grey-blue eyes and a nose which might have been called a snout, it was small wonder that he had his own way.'

He had his own way with Stuart when it came to discussing academic options with him and his mother. 'Classics,' said Henderson. Contemplating possible routes to gainful employment, Mrs Blanch may well have wondered about other subjects for Stuart. But Henderson said 'Classics', and Classics it was.

Henderson's aim was to make Alleyn's into a school that combined the good points of both boarding schools and day secondary schools. Though boys would benefit from living with their families, they were not to lose the time out of class that gave boarding schools the advantage of wider curricula, and of team games, music, and other leisure activities. The same old boy quoted above adds that 'Henderson had two other guiding lights – a deep religious faith and a strong belief that Western civilization was unmatched in the world, and that it stemmed from classical Rome and especially Greece.'

Teachers in the 1930s made for a 'heady brew'. Even in this galaxy, Henderson was not a remote figure and 'always thought of himself as a member of the teaching staff'. At the daily assembly

religious content was pushed well ahead of administrative convenience. Henderson himself took the service and the prefects read the lessons. . . . And Henderson had a Greek translation of the Bible at his desk and followed the reading every day. Every now and then a boy became a prefect of his house of the school and what amounted to an ordination took place: Henderson pronounced the sentences which left a lasting impression on every new prefect (as they were intended to) – 'To you, who are now made a Prefect of your House, a position of trust and authority is given. What you find to do, do with all your might, using your power to the good of your house.'

In due course Stuart became a prefect. Contemporary Douglas Hall says that this 'carried much kudos in those days – Stuart carried the role with characteristic humility'. And his gifts of fun and mimicry were alive and well, with Stuart doing a very good impression of the actor Robertson Hare whose quavering catchphrase 'Oh, calamity!' was renowned long before his later success as the archdeacon in television's *All Gas and Gaiters*.

Another contemporary, Leslie Brannan, later head of Classics and senior teacher at King Edward VI School, Lichfield, has other memories of Stuart. Being adjacent alphabetically, they were paired off in 1933 for the School Certificate French oral exam, with Stuart being questioned and Leslie ostensibly preparing the reading passage:

> The examiner's first question to Stuart was 'Quel age avez-vous?' Stuart was some time in deciding the answer before giving, in that voice of his that was already authoritative, a firm 'Non, monsieur!' . . . Our friendship ripened during the years we shared together in the Classical section of the sixth form. We shared a common joy in the game of cricket. . . . Stuart was no mean fast bowler. I have recollections of us vacating, via a window, the temporary library where we were supposed to be engaged in unsupervised private study in order to bowl a ball at each other in a far, unseen part of the school grounds.
>
> My chief recollection concerns our four-day walk together during the winter half term holiday of 1935. We took a train to Henley-on-Thames and set off cross-country in our cadet force boots for Cambridge, 100 miles distant. We had three bed-and-breakfast halts en route at half-a-crown [12.5p] a time, before reuniting with a number of Alleyn Old Boys who were at Cambridge colleges. I remember the first night particularly. In the dusk of an autumnal evening we stopped at Amersham and found a kindly landlady. Just before retiring Stuart produced a piece of string, one end of which he tied to a big toe and the other to the end of the bed. I was fascinated and puzzled. 'As a precaution against sleep-walking,' he said solemnly, and we retired. On none of the three nights did he sleepwalk and I was bitterly disappointed.

INSURANCE DESK

Schooldays were good days for Stuart. They co-ordinated and enlarged the powerful educational influences active in home, family, and church and richly endowed him for the years ahead. When eventually he went to university to study for ordination, his background in the Classics and knowledge of Greek gave him a flying start. Leaving school at 18, however, university was still ten years in the future. Family finances meant finding a job. Forty years later Stuart recalled this time in an interview with Linda Christmas for the *Guardian*'s Women's Page (15 December 1977): 'I originally intended to become a journalist, having read Classics at school, but jobs were scarce and journalism in particular was difficult to get into without contacts.'

His brothers thought he might have gone into banking like Ron, but even here the influence of R. B. Henderson was at work. The headmaster's links with employers seeking the kind of young men his school produced bore swift fruit, and one day in the summer of 1936 Stuart presented himself to the Law Fire Office, 114 Chancery Lane, WC2, to start work in insurance. Here he was greeted by Mr Steve Watson, 12 or so years his senior, who writes: 'I made him feel at home in the Accident Department' – a remark that no doubt would have drawn a dry comment from the new boy had he heard it.

Steve Watson describes the scene of the next few years:

The office had similarities with those of the legal office described by Charles Dickens in his novel *David Copperfield*, the only change, I think, being the use of a pen and nib instead of a quill pen. One wrote in near silence on a high desk after mounting an appropriately high stool. Good handwriting was *the* most important quality of several then needed to secure employment, and it could be remarked that the superb large inkstands, with two quill pens each, were still part of the furnishing of the entrance counters. Founded in 1845, the Board-room of Directors, all of them lawyers, was as attractive as that of the Life Assurance Company described by Charles Dickens in *Martin Chuzzlewit*. A full-length oil painting of the first chairman, Sir George Rose, above a large fireplace was the dominant feature, though the glorious chiming clock at the other end of this plainly important business-control room regularly and melodiously reminded one of passing time.

In his 1977 interview with the *Guardian*, Stuart said:

I recall catching a tram to Chancery Lane, a sixpenny ride lasting half an hour, and arriving early and walking through swing doors. I was given responsibility 'bang off'. I had to answer enquiries at the desk and on the telephone, and had my own batch of mail to handle. I remember answering a telephone request for insurance cover for a thatched cottage. Since the call came from a really important agent I had to accept the request, but it was too late to reinsure it. I had a sleepless night praying that the cottage did not burn down.

Starting pay was £90 per annum, rising to £100, provided necessary exams, mostly in law, were passed. Work therefore involved a correspondence course, and evening study at home: 'The job taught me a great deal, not just about administration, but how to deal with people from all walks of life. It opened my eyes to many unfamiliar things – great wealth for example. Men who had six cars insured at the same time, with one of them always wrapped round a lamp-post.' Stuart also read a great deal: 'Two or three books a week on the tram. Penguin paperbacks were just starting.' He also played soccer and cricket for the company on Saturday afternoons, as well as having piano lessons on Fridays, and attending weekday church choir practice and Sunday services. As a chorister he received 30 shillings per quarter. Although involved with the Church, he remained a stern critic of much that it stood for. Nevertheless, life at work brought him its own moments of spiritual significance. Writing in his book *Living by Faith* (pp. 104–5), Stuart spoke of an inner life of faith in childhood and how there were moments in the office 'which evoked cherished memories and revived recollections long since subdued by my own passion for rationality and my spirited resistance to religion'.

Steve Watson recalls how the four immediate colleagues formed a 'choir' to cheer themselves up when they were working late. Their 'very cheering' repertoire included 'Just a Song at Twilight', 'Here's a Health unto His Majesty', 'There is a Tavern in the Town', and 'Way Down upon de Swanee Ribber'. 'We even produced a record of Christmas music, recording on a dictaphone cylinder then being used for daily correspondence, and sent it to the typists' room one Christmas Eve. It was perhaps a grand finale to his brief insurance career. It certainly created a lot of happiness.'

Stuart seems not to have written about how he viewed the possibility of war, but after a few years in insurance he knew that he wanted a change of employment: 'When I did decide it was time for a change there were several alternatives: a commercial traveller selling guns, the sporting sort; an overseas bank, perhaps Singapore; the Civil Service Executive, but from 1,500 applicants only the first five got jobs; and the *Brixton Free Press*. And this is what I was going to do, become a cub reporter, when war broke out.'

A CHURCH AT WAR

It says much for Holy Trinity, Tulse Hill, that it retained Stuart's involvement and interest throughout his teenage years and early adulthood. These were years in which he became a keen critic of the Church in general, and in his book *Living by Faith*, he wrote about his 'passion for rationality' and 'spirited resistance to religion' at that time of life. But life at the church was a living stream and not a stagnant pond. The well-loved Canon Dale had been succeeded by Canon Edwards, who in 1938 was able to appoint a curate. And the curate was to have a radical influence on many young people, and notably on Stuart. It was a first position for the Revd Eric Atkins, but, at the age of 32 and with a science degree, he was a man of parts who was used to doing other things. One who knew him best, his wife Dorothy, said that 'he had a logical, well-ordered and well-stocked mind. Although firm in principle he was of a warm compassionate nature. He was a man of prayer.'

One youngster of the time, now Mrs Alice Chappell, recalls how Eric formed a youth fellowship which quickly grew in numbers:

> We had a service on Sunday afternoons in the church hall which was well attended. Various members, including Stuart, were encouraged to take part, either leading in prayers, reading a lesson and later giving a brief talk. Once a month we had an early morning service held mid-week in church at 7 a.m. called the Morning Watch – a lovely way to start the day. We had badminton evenings, and on most bank holidays we took part in a ramble to one of the many places in Kent or Surrey which were easily reached from Tulse Hill. . . . Many of us also taught in the various Sunday School classes. A Nativity Play was produced one year with Stuart playing the part of Joseph.

Such activities partnered life in the office and basic rearrangements of family life at home. There were the marriages of Will and Ron, and the subsequent removal of Stuart and his mother from the family semi to an apartment in a large Victorian house that was situated, perhaps symbolically, close to both church and vicarage.

Writing from the USA, Mr Ernest Hicken, a fellow chorister at the time, remembers the new home and recalls Mrs Blanch as a 'jolly little lady with a collection of her paintings signed Bessie Yarworth'. He added, 'as a tribute to Stuart's great patience I remember that he entrusted me, an embryonic engineer, with the attempted repair of their old Marconi wireless receiver; I never succeeded but never heard a word of complaint'. Another chorister of the day, Douglas Hall, recalls their regular visits to choirmaster Mr Henry Findon Hall's home where the table-tennis table gave an extra dimension to the term 'choir practice'. Stuart retained a taste for table-tennis well into his retirement years. One diocesan bishop recalls an enjoyable knock-about with the Archbishop on the eve of his consecration by Stuart in York Minster, and when former First Estates Commissioner Sir Douglas Lovelock called to see him in retirement in Bloxham, the visit included a game of table-tennis between them!

When war came, the youth fellowship was to prove its mettle in various ways, sharing with the vicar and others in conducting services in some of the public air-raid shelters. At one of these, it was recalled with amusement, a group of communists objected to such activity. It was put to the vote and the church folk got a rousing request to go ahead, with the vicar receiving hearty thanks 'for the entertainment' when they finished. Life in air-raid shelters was a widespread and common experience. One Sunday in 1940 the congregation was trapped in church during prolonged air-raids; these kept them there all night in the crypt shelter.

Inevitably the blitz brought its toll of local tragedy. Among the homes and families not spared was that of organist and choirmaster Henry Findon Hall. He and his wife, together with their daughter and her fiancé, all died when a bomb struck their house. Later, in the days of the flying bombs, the church itself was hit and on the following Sunday the services were held, as a parish publication puts it, 'in the debris'. That particular bomb fell very close to where Stuart and his mother had lived, but by that time they were both elsewhere.

Stuart's career in insurance ended before the bombing started. He remembered the day well: 'On the evening of 14 March 1940 I walked out through the office door for the last time. On the following morning, instead of my customary walk from Blackfriars to Chancery Lane, I took the tube to Uxbridge. I have had many long journeys in my time. This was the longest of them all – 23 stations clutching a broken-down suitcase with the few possessions we were permitted to take with us to the recruitment centre.'

$\sim$ 2 $\sim$

Exodus:
Leaving Home and Finding Faith

THE 'LONGEST JOURNEY'

March 1940 was a time of uneasy pragmatism in Britain. While the pattern of wartime life was gradually taking shape, the run-on effects of pre-war show business were still very much in evidence. In the alternative world of the cinema, Vivien Leigh had just won an Oscar for her role in *Gone with the Wind*, with Robert Donat similarly honoured for his work in *Goodbye Mr Chips*. But the 'phoney war' was ending, and America's attempts to secure peace negotiations with Germany were rapidly getting nowhere. And although the three-month-long Russo-Finnish War had just ended, 16 March 1940 brought Britain's first civilian death by air-raid in Scotland – the first of the 50,000 civilian deaths that were to follow.

It was on the eve of that grim day that Stuart joined the RAF. His daily paper would have told him that it was the day professional football restarted in wartime England, with the Second World War's first league matches being played in Birmingham. But he wouldn't have needed the newspaper to tell him that 15 March was the Ides of March. For the farmer's son, well groomed by home and school, disciplined by office procedures, and accustomed only to living at home and in the southern counties, life was transformed in a day. It would be six years before he would return to civilian life, and when he did the home he had left would no longer be there, nor would his mother, who was to die in 1944. It was a massive disruption, no doubt echoing something of his uprooting in childhood. But it was part of the common stuff of life and he knew it. Leaving home for Uxbridge on what he later called his 'longest journey', he took with him a new resolve to take belief in God seriously, and the few belongings in his battered suitcase included a Bible. The journey itself seems to have been a time of decision. Writing in his journal later, on 20 January 1943, he noted: 'I have thought often in the last few days that the decision I took on the train to Uxbridge was the decision to appear, not nec-essarily to be, on the side of God.' Given that to 'appear' to be on the side of God among raw recruits in an RAF barrack block was a fairly tough option, his faith was perhaps stronger than he thought. And indeed, as he concluded the journal entry just quoted, 'it was the road to Christ'.

The enlistment at Uxbridge of number 918565 AC2 Blanch, SY was swiftly followed by another train journey, this time to the unfamiliar north, to Warrington Bank Quay station and to the open-backed lorry waiting to whisk recruits to RAF Padgate. In a strange place, he was in fact now unwit-tingly resident in the diocese of which he would one day be Bishop, and in a parish whose church and clergy he would later know so well.

He seems to have settled down quickly. Rather surprisingly, he found himself drafted into the RAF police, soon ranking as corporal. Perhaps it was his evident way with people and obvious inner discipline that led to him being drawn along this path before he began training for aircrew duties. More surprisingly, perhaps, it was service life itself that was to provide the sphere in which a recently agnostic frame of mind and a semi-detached asso-ciation with the Church would become both faith in God and commitment to Christ.

There were several reasons for this. Writing in his journal towards the end of 1942, he referred to what he called his 'intellectual conversion' of 'three years ago'. This seems to have owed much to Eric Atkins, the curate of Holy Trinity, Tulse Hill, soon himself to become an RAF chaplain. Eric had been a scientist by profession before ordination and it seems that Stuart found in him a mind as well as a heart to match his own. Stuart's 'intellectual conversion' seems to have been a rational conclusion that faith in God was as well founded intellectually as any conceivable alternatives and provided the best path to follow. On the night before Stuart left home, Eric had given him a present which, together with his Bible, he took with him into the RAF. It was H. E. Fosdick's *The Meaning of Faith*, a three-month set of daily Bible readings and comments. He subsequently acquired three other volumes by Fosdick that were organized in the same way, and they became part of his life over his first year in the forces. For someone who recalled 'dissenting fiercely from most of what the curate stood for', his new habit of reading the Bible makes it clear that his quarrel was not with the Bible. Almost certainly, the quarrel would have been with organized religion in general. Forty-three years later, when he sent Eric Atkins a copy of his latest book, *Living by Faith*, he inscribed it with the words 'To Eric, with love from Stuart, and in deep gratitude to the one who more than any other helped me to begin "Living by Faith"'.

Following basic training and drafting to police work, Stuart was posted to Croydon while the Battle of Britain was being fought overhead to be followed by the London blitz. Throughout it all there was the tedium of routine duties to fulfil, rotas to compile and administer, difficult colleagues to endure, and occasional dangers to confront. On one occasion he had to deal with a group of servicemen struggling around a loaded pistol that was lying on the floor. His diary doesn't record what he did, only what his feelings were at having to take swift and effective action. On another occasion he humorously records the decision he and a colleague made to carry arms on a trip to London in order to arrest someone absent without leave. They tracked their quarry to a crowded restaurant and felt all eyes on them as they approached him with their guns prominently attached to their bodies. The man concerned gave himself up without struggle. Stuart found it a strange role to act out in public.

With off-duty hours no longer claimed by London commuting, domestic duties, and social pleasures, his mind clamoured for activity. He read voraciously. He engaged in discussions organized by the chaplains. He started to write. Uncongenial though it was, this loss of civilian freedoms brought more space for thought. Together with the routine discipline of service life, this discovery lay behind the theme of one of his books, *The Trumpet in the Morning* (1979), in which he explored the ways in which law is necessary for the enjoyment of freedom. So it came about that the basic fashioning of his discipleship and the making of his ministry was very largely achieved in wartime service. In fact, the RAF became a sort of secular seminary which left its mark upon him through all the vivid growth and development of his later years.

SPIRITUAL QUEST

By the end of 1940 he was already launched upon a spiritual quest that he began to record by pencil in a series of pocket notebooks, small enough to fit snugly into battledress breast-pockets. He began on 31 December. Writing in RAF Heaton Park, Manchester, on New Year's Eve 1940, he noted: 'The end of what might have been the worst year of my life but has proved the best – the beginning of a new life. Before me these standards: absolute honesty, absolute purity, absolute unselfishness, absolute love.'

Over the years, Stuart frequently spoke of one particular Christmas when his home leave was cancelled and he was put in charge of the camp guard. The story is told in many publications of how, with nothing else to do, he opened his Bible, read the Gospels, and suddenly found faith in Christ. This first notebook account of New Year's Eve 1940 might lead one to suppose it related to that particular event. Not so. That momentous day was still two years distant. The earnest resolution of New Year's Eve 1940 was only a step along the way, and the way was long. His enlightenment and commitment at Christmas 1942 may have been swiftly accomplished when it occurred, but the road leading up to it was long, painstaking, hard, and thoughtful.

There seem, in fact, to have been three major stages in his conversion experience. If his intellectual conversion had been the first stage, then New Year's Eve 1940 seems to have marked the beginning of the second. It records the sort of step taken by many people of faith who understand Christianity principally as a call to moral perfection: 'Before me these standards: absolute honesty, absolute purity, absolute unselfishness, absolute love.' The following months led him to discover that those who pursue such an ideal are destined to find its practice unattainable, even when the arduous lifestyle it calls for is willingly embraced. How hard he tried, how difficult he found it, and something of where it led him is indicated by the pencilled notes of his pocket notebook journals – Sunday, 12 January 1941: 'My communion is not as regular or as deep as it should be. The fault is in myself largely, and also, I think, in the manner in which the Padgate service is conducted. . . . "That I may be ready for thy perfect service hereafter" . . . why do I always hesitate before that one?' 14 January: '6 p.m. How am I living up to the four absolutes?' Thursday, 16 January: 'A lad has just come into the room and asked to my astonishment whether I am studying for the church. There is still a widespread belief that an interest in religion must commit a man to professional work.'

In wondering what to do with the rest of his life after the war, early thoughts of ordination were already fading against the possibility of some other participation in public affairs – possibly politics. A long evening's conversation with an acquaintance during some days on leave is noted in this way – 19 January 1941: 'We had a grand evening together and talked ourselves into something like coherence. Our discussion, which like any discussion which involves an ideal and a world order, invariably falls back on Christ. He crystallised in a single life all that was fine and noble in humanity and added something else which no man has ever done. We have both tried to evade that truth and give Christianity another name. The more intimately I see parish life the more convinced I am that I can play a better role in public affairs. There we are needed. The threat of invasion looms nearer and despite its inevitability nobody seems very concerned. I pray that our leaders do not show the indifference of their people'; 23 January: 'Read "Christianity and the Social Order" (Temple), but its writer is obviously putting too much faith in present machinery and a discredited church. Every day I grow more conscious of a mission and especially yesterday of my inadequacy too.'

On 10 February he wrote about his inner life as 'struggling within the ruins of a deep-rooted egotism', and goes on to describe feelings that probably had their tap root in childhood trauma: 'An infant crying in the night, an infant crying for the light and knowing no language but a cry, so I must remain until weaning.' And on 25 February: 'Helpless and alone I pray for life. No man hath quickened his own soul'; Sunday, 28 February, 8 p.m.: 'A day which has not quite fulfilled itself and I feel battered in spirit after long contact with the padre's vehemence. But thank God he's young and real and there is no pride in him. I shall be returning to the chapel in a few moments, when the discussion group is over, where I hope to spend two hours or so with Christ.'

The spiritual dilemma of one who would be perfect but finds he cannot be so is specifically addressed by the gospel of Christ. In the spirituality of world religions its solution is one of Christianity's most distinctive features and is the open secret that can remain strangely closed for mysterious lengths of time to men and women of moral excellence. It seems to have been closed to Stuart even while enthusiasm for Christ and the will to serve God prompted a chat with a service chaplain about the possibility of ordination.

Nevertheless, although a crucial development in his inner life was two years in coming, those years of spiritual endeavour were far from fruitless. His inner struggle, prayer, serious reading, regular church attendance, practical concern for others, and high standards in work and relationships all entailed a deal of learning about, and considerable insight into, the religious life. Together with the illumination that followed it, this underlay much of Stuart's later thought. It may also have fostered the interest that he later developed in the varied spiritualities of people who practise the same religion from different starting points. In the meantime he was soon to have a soul friend with whom he could share his search.

The posting to Croydon made possible some occasional visits to London. One day in 1941 when on leave he was invited to a family party at which he renewed acquaintance with a friend from childhood days called Brenda Coyte. They had first met at a fireworks party at around about the age of 12, and at family parties over the intervening years. Unsettled by the call-up of so many of her generation, Brenda had recently exchanged university study for wartime work with the YWCA in London. On this latest meeting there was an instant mutual attraction between Stuart and Brenda. 'That first occasion when Stuart came to tea with us, we fell in love! It was a very powerful attraction, and it lasted. It was as if God had banged us together for his own purpose,' said Brenda. It certainly prompted the following letter from Stuart: '24 September 1941; Station Headquarters RAF Croydon: Dear Brenda, I am expecting to go into London one day next week. Would you like to spend the evening with me? My apologies, Brenda, for what must seem to you an abrupt and unaccountable letter. But I do hope you will come.' The meeting took place. On 1 October Brenda wrote to Stuart, enclosing a copy of Helen Waddell's *Lyrics from the Chinese*: 'I thought you might like something to read. . . . Do you know that poem in Chinese Lyrics:

> White clouds are in the sky.
> Great shoulders of the hills
> Between us two must lie.
> The road is rough and far.
> Deep fords between us are.
> I pray you not to die.'

It was the beginning of a correspondence that lasted for five years, and in it each explored and discussed their own and each other's life and faith.

AIRCREW VOLUNTEER

Towards the end of 1941 Stuart volunteered for aircrew duty. All aircrew had to be volunteers and it is clear that he did not take the step lightly, well aware of its implications for Brenda and for his anxious mother. But having shared RAF life during the Battle of Britain and during the blitz, he was ready to help fill the high-risk ranks of aircrew members. The bombing of Pearl Harbor on 7 December 1941 brought Japan into the war and flagged up the theatre of operations into which his remustering would take him. En route for aircrew training, Stuart and fellow airmen lived in tents and worked on a local farm near Ludlow. Brenda, meanwhile, had joined the Land Army and was herself working on a farm at Ockley Court in Surrey. Their respective agricultural endeavours provoked mutual salutations and commentary in their letters:

Brenda (27 April 1942): 'I agree with you that the spirit is in some way aloof from the body and the mind, but nevertheless it is through the body and the mind that we apprehend the things of the spirit. The grace of God comes to us mostly through the ordinary things of the world, through ordinary people. Is not the sacrament ordinary bread and wine transformed?'

Stuart (5 July 1942): 'I do pray that the quietness of the country, the slow faithfulness, will enter into you, for that is something you need above all. "O'er moor and fen, O'er crag and torrent still, Lead thou me on". I never hear that hymn without a strange tug at the throat, and I have heard it tonight in Ludlow Parish Church. Strangely it has given me a new resolve – to soak myself in the music of the psalms, to read them with the first eyes. Will you try them, too – the mammoth wisdom of the ages which make our small philosophies look small?'

Brenda (21 July 1942) [who would have had no thoughts of a Bishop's Lodge or a Bishopthorpe Palace, hidden in the future]: 'There is a lot to be said for living in a large house with years of history behind it: one has a delicious sense of space and freedom and it is possible to live with other people without falling over them all the time.'

A few days later Stuart joined Number 12 Initial Training Wing at St Andrews in Scotland:

Stuart (26 July 1942): 'From a line of tents at the foot of the Welsh hills to the finest hotel in St Andrews. . . . Don't distrust simple happiness, as occasionally I do, make it a part of you for ever. This is a formidable device: I am talking to myself as well as to you'; (2 August): 'The officer who met us at the station was junior housemaster in my house at Alleyn's, director of house concerts and lecturer in current affairs.'

The chaplain at RAF St Andrews was the Revd Desmond K. Dean, a clearly spoken and convinced evangelical. In his first talk to the newly arrived trainees, Desmond Dean told them why he was a clergyman, and why he was there. This involved describing his experience of being 'born again' on a certain day in a certain year. The talk included clear parameters for Christian faith and life delivered with all the brisk urgency of a godly man concerned for young men facing the all too vivid prospect of death in aerial warfare.

It was at one of the Padre's sessions that Stuart met someone who was to become a life-long friend. Canon John Morris writes:

I found myself sitting next to him one evening at the Padre's house. Desmond Dean would trail his coat provocatively at what was called the 'Padre's Hour'.

After a short evangelical address he would invite questions and comments. The chaps would oblige with a mixture of ridicule and (mostly) hostile questions. I was impressed by the way the Padre stood his ground, kept his cool, and commended his Christian belief to us warmly and sincerely. During those controversial sessions I began asking myself whose side I was on and in subsequent talks with the Padre enrolled myself as a trainee believer.

The Padre and his wife had open house one evening a week. There was some discussion, the Padre would lead some vigorous hymn singing from the piano, and, last but far from least, there was supper which we hungry airmen would attack with evangelical fervour. Stuart had a corporal's stripes on his uniform. . . . Being a mere AC2 I was conscious of the difference in rank but Stuart's friendly manner bridged any uneasiness I felt at being very new in the service of King George VI and even newer in the service of the Lord. And so it was to be throughout our subsequent relationship, for while I recognised in him a superiority of intellect along with a deeper, surer grasp of what it meant to be a Christian, his manner to me, as it was to everyone, was of outgoing brotherly affection, not embarrassingly hearty, but evenly good humoured, gentle and considerate. He had authority without being authoritarian or in the slightest degree puffed up.

At this stage Stuart felt the need to make enquiries about ordination. On one of his days off he went into town to see a film only to discover that it finished too late for getting back to camp. Acting on impulse he knocked on the door of the Bishop of St Andrews. In later life he often recalled the occasion with special affection for the Bishop who, happening to be at home, provided a kindly and spontaneous response long lasting in its influence.

SOUL FRIEND

The application Stuart brought to bear on exploring faith and its practice raised problems for the way he thought through his relationship with Brenda. Keen evangelicals were left in no doubt about the need for any potential partner to be of the same mind and have the same commitment. For those contemplating ordination, this requirement was absolute. The partner had to be one whose first devotion was to God in order for that common devotion to be the basis of the relationship. So it was that Stuart brought to bear upon his friendship with Brenda the sort of scrutiny to which he subjected himself.

It was a difficult time for them both, and perhaps specially so for Brenda who did not have the same kind of fellowship as Stuart in which to raise her questions, air her doubts, or discuss her faith, nor had she the range of exciting occupations that were coming his way. Their correspondence reflects these concerns. They recommended to one another books they found helpful to faith and shared their experiences of reading the Bible, and of prayer and worship, and gradually it became clear to both that their respective journeys of faith could be shared:

Stuart (16 August 1942 – after a trip to the dentist): 'Behold an engineer, an astronomer, an armourer, a signaller, a lawyer, a doctor, a meteorologist, and, by the power of heaven, a navigator. All this without a single wisdom tooth.'

Brenda (19 August 1942): 'It seems by the end of this course you will be jack of all trades and would-be master of piloting. What an impressive list of qualifications, by far the most necessary of which is golf! And all acquired in three weeks. The RAF does indeed work fast. The Land Army is "comme la tortoise". I have been learning the arts of thatching but have been told that it takes 50 years to become an expert thatcher. I want to learn to milk but it takes five years to become a good milker. As for breeding cattle – well a lifetime is not long enough to build up a herd'; (8 September): 'I can't imagine you as a pilot. You'll be thinking about the philosophy behind cloud formation when you should be watching for a good landing place.'

The RAF, however, did not work quite so fast. Training commissioned aircrew was a long and costly process which was to go on for the best part of a year. After St Andrews came RAF Heaton Park in Manchester, with officer training at Cranwell scheduled for after Christmas.

Stuart and Brenda both ranged widely in their reading, their letters exploring faith and discipleship. After tackling Baron von Hugel's great analysis of the spiritual life, Brenda came across a book called *Midnight Hour* by 'Nicodemus', the pen name of Melville Channing Pearce whom they got to know years later. *Midnight Hour* made devastating comparisons between New Testament Christianity and much church life of the day and made a lasting impression on them both. The autumn months were laden with significance and Stuart enquired once more about ordination, writing to Desmond Dean to see if he would be one of his referees:

Stuart (13 September 1942): '"I fled him down the nights and down the days" . . . the only difference between belief and unbelief is that one [belief] accepts the inevitable and learns to rejoice in it, the other flees and fears forever. . . . My prayers have been for strength – to face that from which the whole of this old self would recoil, the demands of swift, incisive, instinctive action with the bottomless pit below. But inherent in that petition is that for which I came into the world – to be as steel that is tempered in the fire, yet to be as clay in the hands of the potter, to learn the power that proceeds from obedience. . . . [People fail] yet there is room in this world for St Francis and for Cromwell. [The Lord] will change men who can be ruthless in the name of God and tolerant in the name of humanity. . . . Ruthlessness and intolerance have the same source and that source is love; kindliness, affection should be the symptoms of that love, but they may be only indicative of a sentiment which has shirked the final demands of God, which is the substitute for that . . . intolerable urgency which is the driving force of man. I dread to write like this. Do, darling, apply the correction of your sense to that which appears abominably cruel; the rose is lovelier than the root.'

Brenda (16 September 1942): 'Do not dread to write what you really feel; only so can we ever get to know and help one another. You too must go further. It is the quality of loving mercy that I pray may be developed in you. God has given you great powers and shown you a great light, but without that quality I do not think you will be able to bring men to Him. Men are human and weak. When they have been burned out by the flame of conversion they need patient, loving understanding that will encourage them and help them through that difficult period of reconstruction.'

Stuart (20 September 1942): 'I am aware of a tremendous weakness which you are right to emphasise, and it is a weakness of feeling. Two and a half years of attempted Christianity in the service has won a certain amount of unwilling respect, it has caused self-questioning, it has thrown many a normal way of living into confusion. But it has never, so far as I know, won Christ a single disciple. The springs of my own belief are too personal and too obscure to be of practicable value to anybody else.' (He apologized for taking the risk of sending letters which could not quite say what he meant.)

Brenda (23 September 1942): 'Your letter was a great relief to me, for like you, I wrote under compulsion and had to take the risk that you would not understand it in the way I meant it. But without taking risks we should not get anywhere and I do believe that though many frills may be omitted the core of the matter expressed in heat is usually true'; (28 October): 'It will be difficult for you to acquire the grace of humility and a sense of the great mercy of God. You have too many gifts and have not failed sufficiently in life.'

A longer than usual spell of leave brought them closer together than ever. Brenda was able to stay with Stuart and his mother at their home in Worthing, and there Stuart's mother, who was within 18 months of her own death, was able for the first time to talk with him about her own obvious but undisclosed unhappiness. It seemed to be a healing experience, and she obviously took to Brenda. Before leaving home again for Heaton Park, Stuart made the following entry in his journal:

> Monday 30 November: The interpretation of the spiritual content of these past few weeks is beyond my capacity. I can only acknowledge with gratitude contact with the Spirit and pray for its indwelling, can only acknowledge a warmth of feeling and pray for its establishment. . . . There was also a cold clear light about us as we walked together on Saturday evening. What started as the ramblings of a man determined to bring reason to bear upon emotion ended in the revelation of God for the first time to ourselves as a unity and not as individuals aspiring to unity. . . . The intellectual conversion of three years ago did not excise from my heart that expectation of emotional bliss and emotional adventure divorced from effort. . . . In that conception there was no need for the surrender of that precious self which I have struggled to preserve, lonely and unshared. 'You hate to be invaded'. I wonder if many of Brenda's assertions will later find acceptance as this one has found? When I hesitated to invite Brenda here for the week I hesitated not for Mother's sake but because the last thing I wanted was to share myself, to surrender the keys and endure the scrutiny.

Writing to him on 4 December 1942, Brenda said:

'I've just been reading *Midnight Hour* again. [Quote:] "I can only find religious reality not on the plain of piety but upon that of mysticism, not on the level of conduct but in the abyss of being from which conduct comes". [After referring to matters of self-denial and celibacy . . .]: The hardest way is to live the ordinary married life of man and woman and yet to live a completely surrendered life, "caring not for one's own life", for in marriage there are two people who must both be constantly surrendered. Am I wrong?'

Stuart (10 December 1942): 'Mysticism is not itself a virtue, certainly not the prerogative or even the mark of the great man or woman. It is difficult to understand, more difficult to convey the meaning which is implied in the word "mystery", true religion and superstition are its well begotten and misbegotten offspring. . . . The mystic may be able to find the answer in the depth of his own being and may, if he be a poet too, be able to express it. [Mysticism] cannot yield its substance to logical and probably not to artistic interpretation; . . . Christ was not a mystic, nor for that matter was he an artist, scientist or philosopher. He was the son of God. He was the light, these are the colours of the spectrum which compose the light, and without them we cannot plumb the depths of his being.'

Brenda (13 December 1942): 'You are like a steady river ever flowing on towards the ocean; I'm a turbulent mountain stream at the moment'; (14 December): 'I've just re-read Von Hugel's *Life of Prayer*, and for the first time have understood it, or most of it! And I have possessed that book for five years!'

Stuart (16 December 1942): (Quoting the second stanza of a poem called 'The Dancers'):

> 'So when I saw you stand the other night
> Like a child, waiting in the wings of life,
> And from the crowded stage a shaft of light
> Glanced on your face, alone in its own sky,
> The scene was cut with tears, quick as a knife.
> There were no dancers, only you and I.'

As Christmas approached, so too did anticipation of home leave. Brenda wrote with delight to say that she had been released from duty not only for Christmas Day and Boxing Day, but also for Sunday, 27 December. Expectations ran high. But then on 21 December Stuart's name appeared on Station Routine Orders as i.c., the camp guard for the holiday period. The blow fell as he was digesting a letter he had received from Desmond Dean:

My dear Stuart, This is not going to be an easy letter to write, . . . for I know of no one more fitted in natural gifts for this greatest of all callings than you are. . . . When all this has been said, however, I think you have known me long enough to realise that I have left something out. It is this something which more than once I sought opportunity to chat over with you – and somehow it didn't come. . . . You will, I expect, remember the remark I made in my initial talk with your flight. It was to the effect that the only reason for my being in the Ministry today (and a chaplain in the RAF) is that I have had a very real and personal experience of Christ as my Saviour – an experience dating back nearly 20 years. My 'birth from above' (John 3. 3 A & RVM) . . . not wrought by any of my own doing (that Titus 3. 5ff I wrote in your NT, Eph. 2. 8–10, etc.) but by the grace of God in reply to an act of faith. . . . Quite frankly, I should have no message for the lost world if it were not for such an experience as that. . . . On the basis of this initial step, I believe all Christians, and especially all who are called to be the spiritual pastors of Christians, are called upon to be utterly separate from the world . . . and wholly given up to God, finding in the infilling of the Holy Spirit victory over all known sin and in every time of temptation.

All this is infinitely more than a mere matter of outlook. I know it has been set aside as 'the contribution which the evangelical school has to make to the church'. I cannot regard it like that, and I cannot think that the NT supports such a view. I believe it to be absolutely vital to every soul, and to every fruitful ministry. And so I write to ask you, humbly conscious of my own failures, that you will prayerfully examine your own heart and life afresh, in the light of the Scriptures, and see what God would say to you concerning these things. . . . Yours most sincerely, Desmond K. Dean.

With these words echoing somewhere in his mind, Stuart contemplated an empty barrack block and minimal duties in an almost empty camp. But there was another letter from Brenda in which she quoted from another book she had just read. It was *The Jesus of History* by T. R. Glover:

Glover makes lots of the Parables come to life for me. And strangely enough after discussing the stories of the man who found buried treasure, and the Pearl Merchant who found the rare pearl, he says that 'in passing we may notice that these stories suggest that this experience (i.e. the finding of the realm of God) may be reached in different ways. In the parable of the seed and the leaven, he indicates a natural, quiet unconscious growth, a story without crisis, though full of change. To the Treasure Finder the discovery is a surprise – how came Jesus so far into the minds of men as to know what a surprise God can be, and how joyful a surprise? The Pearl Merchant, on the other hand, has lived in the region where he makes his discovery. He is the type that lives and moves in the atmosphere of high and true thought, that knows whatsoever things are pure and lovely and of good report, of help and use; he is no stranger to great and inspiring ideas. And one day, in no strange way, by no accident, but in the ordinary round of life, he comes on something that transcends all he has been seeking, all he has known – the one thing worth all. There is little surprise about it, no wild elation, but nothing is allowed to stand in the way of an instant entrance into the great experience – and the great experience is, says Jesus, God.'

And so Stuart watched thousands of men stream out of the camp for their Christmas leave leaving behind the station duty officer, the station orderly officer, a few cooks, and the camp guard, with himself in charge of the latter.

MIDNIGHT HOUR

Before thinking about what happened in the next momentous days it is important to know something of *Midnight Hour* by 'Nicodemus'. Its title alluded to the Jewish scholar's night-time visit to Jesus recorded in chapter 3 of John's Gospel. Published in March 1942, it was an unusual book with a rare power to show the inner turmoil brought by war into a man of orthodox Christian faith. The overpowering sense of evil let loose in the world was something he felt within himself. It radically challenged a faith painfully rebuilt by the author after the First World War and now found desperately wanting. Moreover, the Church as he knew it – for all its historic devotion and beauty – seemed irrelevant to the forces of human nature laid bare by war.

Looking to Christian literature for help, 'Nicodemus' found two kinds, one powerful, one weak:

Yet the terminology, and, apparently, the doctrine are identical. . . . What is the difference which leaves the one tasting of reality, the other of milk and water? Is it that the one is Christianity really reborn from a real death, the other only 'shamming dead'? The one really 'a new creature', the other only a corpse? [pp. 55, 56].

I have recognised 'religion of the spirit' (apart from Paul and the Gospels and epistles) in Barth, in Kierkegaard, in that little book which has always haunted me since I first read it, *Letters of a Modern Mystic*, in the greater mystics, in much of the work of Evelyn Underhill, in Oswald Chambers' realistic book *My Utmost for His Highest*. I have seen it in rare men, in the Carmelite monk who preached this Christianity of the Spirit so silently to me in Iraq, in Charlie Andrews, in Bishop Gore. . . . It is the mystery which was kept secret since the world began and remains secret to all, however learned in theology or good in life, who have not found that 'Open Sesame' of full surrender and rebirth . . .

Over against it, but for ever being substituted for it, masquerading in its 'seamless robe', is this other Christianity – a Christianity 'of the flesh', of fertility-faith, of the 'status quo' and the 'vested interests', of 'decency and good form', where the 'sword of the Spirit' becomes a sewing machine, where grace becomes virtue, and the wind of the Spirit the bellows-blast of 'uplift'. And that is what, in the main, so it seems to me, Anglican Christianity has become – a

Christianity not separate from the world but come to terms with it, not 'led by the Spirit', but guided mainly by morality and 'good form'. It is Christianity tamed and domesticated; for the rage and splendour of Spirit-possessed men we find 'decency', mild manners, kindliness, for the flame of Christ's love, amiability, for the passion of Paul's 'charity', 'charities' [pp. 62, 63].

Our Christianity is sterile because it is shallow; a regenerated Christianity must have descended to the depths; in the words of Baruch we have 'forsaken the fountain of wisdom'. But mere mysticism is not enough; we must seek the fountain of that wisdom. Again, what mystical theology is to the mind, contemplation is to the spirit (in contrast to that meditation which most of our modern theology is) and the practice of the presence of God is for Christian living. For he who meditates (as the derivation of the word implies) takes thought, takes care, but he who contemplates is beyond care and the taking of thought. When we meditate we are men, when we contemplate we are children of God. . . . The Church today seems, as a whole, to be as bankrupt in the science and art of the spiritual life as it is, in the main, barren of true contemplation or real wisdom drawn 'de profundis' from the fountain of wisdom . . .

LOVE CAME DOWN AT CHRISTMAS

For all their exciting developments in faith and relationships the preceding months had lacked one important thing, and it was something that Stuart prized more than most: a private place in which to pray, think, and read. The best place he could find for this was a cold, stone wash-house and he would go there in the early hours of the day. Although Stuart wryly accepted the discipline of deprivation, it gave him little opportunity for the sort of study, thought, and prayer for which he craved. Now, suddenly, and in the most unexpected way, everything had changed. Practically the whole camp was available to him! It must have seemed that confronted with his two prayers – one for Christmas leave and the other for space and time for prayer – God had chosen to answer the more important one. For one who had lacked such a place, the familiar but now deserted hut in an all but empty camp become what in six days' time he would call 'the Father's house'. Here he confronted the radical question posed by Desmond Dean. Here he pondered the parables of the pearl of great price and the treasure hid in a field. Here he lived with the inner crisis of 'Nicodemus', as described in *Midnight Hour*. Here he came to terms with its drastic requirement of death to self.

This is the point at which the pilgrim pauses. How can such concerns be free of fanaticism? What is it to 'die to self'? How can consent to this kind of 'death' be the act of a healthy mind? To be born, loved, nurtured, and grow is all a gift of God. In what sense can God wish the return of that gift? What does this kind of death mean? Clearly it does not mean extinction. It is as far removed from suicide as it is possible to be. Whatever it is, the body survives. So does the mind. So do basic instincts. So does personal identity. So do the interrelated deposits of memory and sense impressions. How then are they to be employed thereafter? What is the difference between that which has been and that which is to come?

A healthy mind and spirit will only come to such a watershed if its concern is not for death, but for a larger life freed from the sin that hinders, harms, and restricts it. But it is in the nature of sin to appear as being nothing other than life itself – not just part of life, but the whole of it. To surrender the kind of self-love that the Bible names as pride is a real kind of death. To peer beyond it is to peer into mystery. And it is that which creates the inner drama of a spirit at its turning point.

Thus far, surely, Stuart had got. But how was he to take the fateful step, and what would lie beyond it? To contemplate such things puts the study of the Gospels on to a different level. It is the level on which they are meant to be read. It was the level on which Stuart read them now. And over the next few days in that quiet and empty hut he did so – over and over again. The content of the gospel story, the character of Jesus, the nature of his being and his ways, the underlying perspectives of his roots in Jewish history, the world-wide reach and relevance of his concerns, all combined to present a vision of life far removed from fanaticism, secure in the structures of sanity, compelling in its attraction, and warm with the presence of a loving Creator.

Jesus' death and resurrection formed the threshold of the new life. To embrace the life that lies beyond 'death to self' was not to embrace a void, but to embrace one who is the resurrection and the life. In this fresh encounter with the living core of the gospel narrative, Stuart had found the companion who promised the substance of an otherwise unguessable future, the Lord of life in whom he would live after he had 'died to self'.

His notebook entries for those crucial days do not refer to this experience of reading the Gospels; this is something he repeatedly talked and wrote about later. But his many accounts of it are the context of what may be gleaned from the entries in his journal for that week. Better than anything they suggest the interior life of a tall NCO, crisply turned out, erect, and full of genial authority, mustering the guard for their morning and evening parades to raise and lower the flag, to be inspected by the orderly officer, to keep an eye on the gates, and to pass the rest of their time as best they could:

Monday, 21 December 1942, 7.30 p.m.: That there has been something seriously amiss in my living and praying during this past week or so I could not deny. And the reason? Indifferent health, irregularity of hours, lack of a place [to pray], the uncertainties of leave – yes, all these are rather the product than the cause of the disorder which is radical. Plans have been constantly frustrated, energy has been fruitlessly expended on a variety of worthless causes, my attitude towards Fred has been ludicrously wrong.

And now a letter on much the lines that I had expected from the padre – expected because I am conscious of a paramount need without which my faith is the faith of the Israelites, stern, just, but lacking Christ. The language of salvation does so easily repel me from the acceptance of that which is greater and deeper, thank God, than the language which expresses it. I remember with what surprise I heard the padre or his wife speak of one who 'was converted last night'. Is it a denial of the issues, a basic fear of utter surrender that makes that ingenuous assertion sound unreal? Whatever happens I must follow the padre's advice, search the reins of my heart with an eye watchful of prejudice, must not make it a bone of theological contention – so easy to blind yourself to a palpable need by losing the perception of it in controversy.

A week in camp. It will not be in vain if it enables me to read *Midnight Hour* before I see Brenda again, if it enables me to serve honestly. And it should not be too bad for Mother if there is a possibility of my coming home after Christmas. But how I hate these telegrams, these grisly messengers of disappointment. I long for them – Brenda and Mother.

Tuesday, 22 December 1942, 10 a.m.: I have looked out across the lake ruffled with the wind, dark with reflected cloud and have found a new and sterner mood. Progress now waits upon my own readiness and the depth of preparation for that final act of surrender – the loss of self and the acceptance of Christ. Suddenly, along the pattern set by others, or gradual in the manner of my own development – I cannot tell which it will be, but that it must happen I no longer doubt. Not to vain regret is this week dedicated but to grim, costly preparation. Further I cannot look.

Wednesday, 23 December 1942: The critical eye has no place here. These have been hours of longing, the hours of loneliness. Christ cannot live in me until the decision is made by me – many are called, few are chosen. Oh God, I cannot fail now and live, the past is dead and all the glory thereof, there is no life for me save in the Cross. Two nights now I have heard that insistent urgent call – 'come', 'come'. 'Unless ye become as little children. Come unto me – for my yoke is easy and my burden is light.' God show me the way, Christ accept my surrender. Indeed I am conscious of him, watching, drawing, guiding this hand, tearing this heart.

Thursday, 24 December 1942: I can only write of the deepening, terrifying awareness of what surrender to Christ can and must mean – a prisoner for life, never able to accept the standards of the world. It has indeed meant separation and separation cannot be achieved except in the new birth, a new creature, the death of Stuart Blanch, the drowning of this feeble creature in the ocean, the plunge, the terror, the emergence of a new song.

A day of reading and prayer, timeless, but the interruptions of men and planes passing – a symphony, transient across the still deep music of God. So will it always be now until I have learnt to accept Christ and to live in him in the world in my stead – an unbearable, ghostly shadow-play without form or meaning, remote, seen as from the grave, dwarfed by the final fact of death. I am dead now, waiting for the shudder of a new life, deep in the womb, await-ing birth. I have knocked and await now the drawing back of the bolt, the silent opening, the step into the darkness, the blinding of the light, then, pray God, the warmth of a family, children's laughter. But before that, the Master and life with him in the storm, head down, driven, blinded with the glimmer of a great light and the chasm between. 'In my Father's house are many mansions, if it were not so I would have told you'.

Christmas Day 1942, 8.30 p.m.: O Christ, can I tell them that you have accepted this surrender? Or will the days roll over me and leave me bewildered, crushed, but not reborn? 'But if he will not give him because he is a friend, yet for his importunity he will rise and give him as many as he shall need.' This day love came into the world, that which prophets and kings desired but sought in vain, and artists and philosophers and scientists, and it was revealed to the pure in heart.

Saturday, 26 December 1942, 10.30 p.m.: So the week is past and there is the sadness of leaving the warmth and security of the Father's house for the world that will test the Father's disciple. In praise, and worship and thankfulness, in prayer, in remembrance of a dark hut set in the stillness, of a bird's voice recall-ing the beauty and the majesty of nature, recalling the vows of youth half made and long forgotten, recalling the spring, and the burgeoning of God in man, recalling more beside that proceeds out of the depth and can only be captured in the depths – the voice of a bird. To be a prisoner of Christ for ever as long as

I shall stand this side of death, to carry his Cross, to share his intolerable loneliness, to be separate from the world, to be born again.

Sunday, 27 December 1942: Returned to the business of ordinary living with a rare conflict of feeling and will, of hope and fear, of praise and prayer. Waiting for the morrow now and whatever it will hold.

Among his many references to this particular Christmas in the years to come, the allusion that seems to get closest to expressing the experience of these days appears in his book *Living by Faith*:

The reading of them [the Gospels] filled me with a sense of awe and invested that particular Christmas with a glowing warmth that I had not expected . . . 'If this is not true', I said to myself, 'then nothing is true' [p. 18] . . . What I experienced . . . was not a happy resolution to all my intellectual problems, but a sense of the overwhelming power of God present in the life, death and resurrection of Jesus of Nazareth. . . . Christian life, i.e. the will to sacrifice . . . is the 'ground plan' of the universe and we who have by the grace of God been made at home in it must then learn the rules of that house. And there is only one rule 'for God is love and he that loveth abideth in God and God in him'. But that is no longer a rule imposed from outside but the outworking of the divine aspect from within. We cease to strain after an external standard of life to that which is truly inaccessible but we live out in the freedom of the Spirit that which only our human aspirations and desires thought.

NEW LIFE, NEW PARTNER

As the camp filled up with returning men, Stuart eventually got his Christmas leave. It began, as Brenda's ended, on 28 December. It was a time for absorbing his recent experience. On 30 December 1942 he wrote in his journal: 'The days of fierce petitionary prayers are over, for these were the days when I tried to speak to God as though Christ had never bridged the gap.' On 31 December he wrote: 'These days are yielded over, as they must be, to the steady, often unconscious effort to capture in the heart what the intellect accepts and endorses, to dig beyond appearances to the root, beyond the word to the meaning. "Ye must be born again" – the profoundest complex of rejection and acceptance that any man can face.'

On that same New Year's Eve Brenda was writing to him as follows:

Here are some of the things I appreciate in you: (a) the fact that once you have put your hand to the plough you never take it off again. A quality of steadfastness that enables one to rely on you: (b) your intelligence – ability to think clearly, and so – freedom from 'littleness' of mind and a concern with the 'care' of life; (c) your sense of humour; (d) your honesty with yourself and humility, which makes for growth; (e) your capacity for love – latent but strong. But above all it is what you are which is your greatest gift to me, for being with you and coming to know you, the seed of the Spirit which had already been sown in me was enabled to grow.

It is at this point in their correspondence that the possibility of marriage is mooted. It is clear that they loved one another, but far from accepting this as a sign that they should marry, Stuart found that it presented a major spiritual challenge. He had to be sure that Brenda was not competing with God for first place in his heart, nor he with God in hers. Once sure about that, he had also to be sure that marriage would support and enhance his sense of vocation, and not block, divert, or weaken it. He also had to cope with the evidence he had encountered of failed or unhappy marriages in the lives of other people. Finally, he was apprehensive of the special pains and pattern of wartime marriages, with their long separations, passionate reunions, and anguished partings.

Brenda's letter of 12 January 1943 indicates the rate at which their relationship was now developing:

Brenda (12 January 1943): 'I am fast coming to the conclusion that love is an active state of being, not a passive one, and therefore can only be defined in action. You cannot "love" unless there is something to be loved. The action of loving requires two units and we only know love insofar as we give up our whole selves to the other unit. That does not mean, necessarily, that we do in actual fact make plain to the other unit all that is in us, but that we must be prepared to do so. There must be no door that we are not prepared to open if necessary. That to me explains the meaning of "perfect love casteth out fear"'; (27 January): 'Your first overwhelming joy may not endure, for we must be tested by lack of joy. I came across the following passage in Strachan's book which struck me forcibly. . . . "Many who think they cannot believe today have never really had Jesus, as He really is, presented to them. They try to think of Him through a mist of abstract theological doctrine, or ecclesiastical prejudice, or outworn theories of the inspiration of the Bible, or the musty atmosphere of a lifeless church."'

Stuart (1 February 1943): 'These have been strange weeks. Parallel with the collapse of pride seems to go the dissolution of mind and as I have lived in the past for thought . . . I am content for the first time in my life to let impression flow in without attempting to integrate it. . . . I have seen the glory of a naked tree and heard the thrush singing at its work and have been glad for them.'

On 25 February Stuart was posted to No 1 Radio School at Cranwell. A fellow trainee, Brian Dagnall, who had known him at Heaton Park, found himself assigned to the next bed to him in the barrack block; he said of Stuart:

> That evening, before getting into bed, he fell on his knees and said his prayers. To do that in front of a room full of airmen needs a lot of courage. Next morning he was up before the rest of us and spent half an hour or so studying the Bible. This pattern of quietly reading the Bible or other relevant books – in the open air when the weather was suitable – continued for the rest of the course. He also, of course, helped with the services run by the chaplain, Richard Amphlett. He and I had one rather satisfactory arrangement. Having been in the RAF police he was a specialist in polishing his boots, an activity I was not good at, so we agreed that he would polish my boots and I would polish the lino around his bed space. This continued for the rest of the course.

Stuart was obviously glad to be in a structured training regime, saying on 27 February, 'Cranwell imposes its merciful routine.' Here he also met up again with John Morris, whom he had first met at St Andrews, who writes:

> We saw one another regularly at the Station church. Here the Anglican chaplain was Richard Amphlett, aristocratic, slightly eccentric in manner, enthusiastic and infectious in his love for God, and his devotion to the Church of England. He was a great talker and some of our discussions while I was being prepared for confirmation would go on into the early hours of the morning. Richard Amphlett took a continuing personal interest in those of us who attended his Sunday sessions and kept in touch with us for years afterwards. I know he had a special admiration for Stuart because he told me so and I recall him confiding in me on one occasion that Stuart was a man of prayer. He had noticed that Stuart was not only a regular at the usual services but would spend off-duty time quietly in the Station church when no one else was around.
>
> Richard Amphlett encouraged us to read widely and introduced me to writers like William Temple, Jacques Maritain and Evelyn Underhill. He had a standing order with Thornton's of Oxford for second-hand commentaries of

the Gore, Goudge and Guillaume *New Commentary on Holy Scripture* with which he would equip those of us willing to have a stab at some serious Bible study. Such volumes were quite heavy in an airman's kitbag yet were faithfully toted from posting to posting. RAF chaplains in Canada and elsewhere were intrigued by this succession of air cadets with their *New Commentaries on Holy Scripture*. Several of us subsequently offered ourselves for ordination and were accepted for training.

Meanwhile, the letters between Stuart and Brenda continued:

Brenda (28 February 1943): 'Always you put me back on the straight and narrow way when I am beginning to wander off on my own'; (1 March): 'Your chief difficulty is – I believe – an inability to, and dislike of, sharing yourself and all that you hold dear with others. Yet if you are to be a priest it is essential that you should be able to do that . . . out of that merging can come something far greater than either personality separately.'

Stuart (19 March 1943): 'I believe that we are called to live and work together in Christ, together to bear his cross unto death. Will you come with me?' (20 March): 'Perhaps even you could not have known how deep rooted was my prejudice against marriage. You attribute it rightly to an almost passionate love of spiritual and mental privacy and to the not unjust observation of so many marriages I have witnessed which have spelt not the beginning but the end of aspiration.'

The wedding was arranged for 10.15 a.m. on Saturday, 12 July, at St Barnabas, Epsom.

Stuart (12 May 1943 – referring to Brenda's wedding corsage): 'I have no objection to sweet peas but somehow I do object to the vegetarian name they carry, so let it be carnations . . . '; (20 May): 'It is remarkable that the emphasis upon the emotional tyranny of romantic love has grown with the decline of the love and knowledge of God.'

Brenda (26 May 1943): '. . . the main difference between a man's faith and woman's faith [is] men are too easily led away by their minds into impersonal discussion and reasoning, whereas women being subjective and practical immediately apply what they hear to their lives and neglect to think of the broader outlook.'

On 12 June, Brenda, having mentioned the church's wedding and organ fees, which totalled £2 9s 0d, wrote: 'I have been romping through the Acts of the Apostles during the past week. . . . It is amazing how one can "hear and hear and not understand, and see and see and not perceive" and then quite suddenly the light shines upon it and all is intelligible. Do you find that too?' On 10 July, referring to thoughts of missionary work abroad, she wrote:

> Work in one's own country is far less attractive; no newness, no strangeness of thought, in England a constant battle against half assimilated thought and the overlay that centuries of dusty Christianity have placed upon the Gospel message; much to be broken down before one can begin preaching the Gospel. England is in the grip of an evil far more deadly than heathen practices, more deadly because more subtle, rarely blatant, needing to be dug out before it can be brought to the light. . . . Where our task will lie I don't know; I'm prepared to go anywhere. But I feel that the need of our country is very great.

Amid such exchanges the great day dawned. The wedding at St Barnabas, Epsom, embodied catholic and evangelical emphases. It was a nuptial mass at which the vicar, Father Anderson, presided, and Eric Atkins preached. Stuart and Brenda carefully preserved among their souvenirs of the day the carefully and neatly typed script from which he spoke:

> This is 'Holy Matrimony'. . . not so much a legal ceremony as a spiritual milestone. Not the settling down into a rut but the blazing of a new trail. And together Stuart and Brenda will be able to achieve more for God and His Kingdom than both of them could alone. . . . Unfortunately they will soon be separated again. The future is full of uncertainty. But as we look down the years that are to be, neither we nor they need have any fears for that future. . . . One of the greatest needs of today is not peace treaties or blue-prints of a new order, but Christian homes; homes where people can become more sure of the reality and power of God. And the home of Stuart and Brenda will be a home like that. It will be a place of refreshment for many who are worn and weary with the battle of life.

CANADA AND INDIA

Shortly after their four-day honeymoon in the Cotswold village of Bibury, Stuart was back on the parade ground – 'hours and hours hopping patiently from one foot to the other, leaning forward to relieve the weight, dressing by the right and standing at ease . . . ' But then the door of the world swung open and he was sea-borne, watching the broad wake of the ship pushing crowded and embattled Britain farther and farther behind as they headed for the vast-ness of Canada. His ship, requisitioned for wartime service as a trooper, was the great *Queen Elizabeth*.

From the ample embrace of Halifax harbour he went via Moncton, New Brunswick, to Port Albert in Ontario. Carried with him was a sealed note from his former chaplain Richard Amphlett addressed to the chaplaincy staff he was to meet in Canada; this note was later returned to Stuart. It said that Stuart was 'an extraordinarily fine Christian with a wonderfully developed spiritual life: a real "man of prayer" in the fullest sense. . . I know you will like him. He has become quite one of my best friends.' Life in Canada brought new friendships with chaplains there, among them Wing Commander Gerald (Gerry) Gregson whom Stuart took to in a big way ('a glorious man', he noted in a letter home).

At Port Albert Stuart got used to the teamwork of flight. Night flying gave him experiences of detachment, almost of the suspension of life, within a roaring machine seemingly suspended in a void but needing his calculations and directions, together with that most chilling of all decisions: saying when considerations of fuel and distance meant turning back from a specific mission. The added edge of learning how to make life-and-death decisions for others as well as himself weighed heavily on him – indeed, he carried the thought of it for the rest of his life. Here he also acquired what was to be a life-long inter-est in observing the weather. Right through to retirement days, one of his hobbies would be noting atmospheric pressures, cloud cover, wind force and direction, visibility, and rainfall. These seem to have been natural develop-ments of a childhood shared in the friendly company of weather-wise people.

It was with Canadian counterparts of such people – Ontario farmers – that he soon found warmth, hospitality, and friendship. Walks in the country brought him one day to a locked church. A friendly farmer who kept an eye on it unlocked it for him and then invited him to his farmhouse where he became a welcome friend of the family. The farmer had a son serving with the Canadian Air Force in England and letters soon crossed the Atlantic arranging for the son to be welcomed in England by Brenda and Stuart's mother. Although enjoying study groups and worship at the camp, Stuart also entered into local church life, enjoying it Canadian-style. And by the time he made the long train journey back to Montreal, he had absorbed a deep sense of a wider Church and a wider world. Once more the great troop ship – this time the *Ile de France* – successfully ran the U-boat gauntlet and Stuart was back in Britain with altered perspectives.

Following a short period of leave with Brenda, he was posted to India and the air campaign in South East Asia where, in the war with Japan, the role of the allied air forces was proving to be a critical factor. On board ship for India, Stuart and his colleagues would have been well aware of the kind of men they were joining. They would have known about the famous 'Hump Run' over the Himalayas in which, from the summer of 1942 to December 1943, heavily laden Dakotas carried supplies into China, crossing largely unmapped mountain ranges in which 20,000-foot peaks separated jungle-choked valleys. It was an oft-repeated journey, dauntingly characterized by vicious down-currents and tremendous side winds with no possible emergency landing places if disaster struck.

The date of 7 March 1944 had brought the Japanese invasion of the Indian state of Manipur which in turn called for air supplies to be flown into the area under attack. This was the same month in which 9,000 men and 1,000 pack animals were flown in behind Japanese positions in order to cut off lines of communication and supply. Joining these veteran flyers, Stuart would spend the next 18 months in Douglas DC3s – the fabled Dakotas – which were prominent among the 90 RAF and USAF Squadrons deployed in South East Asia.

For the men, crowded together for four weeks in ever-increasing heat, unable to receive mail from home and thrown upon their own resources, the journey had a character of its own. In his daily reading Stuart was using Bible Reading Fellowship notes on the 'Gospel According to St Paul', and one of the chaplains, Padre Brook, approached him about the possibility of starting a fellowship meeting. Finding a place to meet in was a problem, but three times a week a good number of men managed to gather somewhere – on deck, in the hold, in a passage, or in a dining saloon. The gatherings proved to be a great success with the first meetings being built around readings from Dorothy L. Sayers's drama, *The Man Born to Be King*.

DIFFERENT PATHS, ONE WAY

As Stuart disembarked in Bombay, Brenda sought ways of fulfilling her own vocation, becoming for a while part-time secretary to the local vicar, and busy in the Sunday school and youth club. The parish church, however, provided little fellowship of kindred spirits or helpful teaching in the faith, and she also found the services dull. Following introductions, she struck up a friendship with both the young minister of a local Free Church and his wife. The Revd Harold Fife's Bible teaching and evangelistic ministry partnered a warm and welcoming church fellowship, and the combination gave her a spiritual life-line that she firmly grasped.

Stuart's and Brenda's respective spiritual journeys then took different paths, provided varied experiences, and disclosed different perceptions as, half a world apart, they sought to grow together as husband and wife. The story of those interlinked paths is best told by quotations from the many letters faithfully sent and carefully kept by each. In the correspondence there is little reference by Stuart to his very full flying schedule, which was the daily background to all he wrote. Their concern was to grow together rather than grow apart:

Brenda (4 September 1944): 'It is a pity the fellowship of the Nonconformists and the sense of worship that the C of E has cannot be combined, isn't it? Neither is complete and satisfying without the other'; (6 September): 'That fellowship which we know with "Nicodemus", O. Chambers, Thomas à Kempis, Gerald – and many others of whom we do not yet know – I have found again, this time Amy Carmichael. She founded the Dohnavur Fellowship in India.'

Stuart (5 October 1944): 'Strange to be in a country where there is no British working class, and I begin to understand why some of our countrymen are not eager to leave . . . '; (8 October – referring to learning the local language): 'My efforts were well appreciated and quite a few of the Indians gathered to give advice and encouragement. We begin to look like those other odd little groups that gather and talk so furtively; near the club an old man with black tangled hair and scanty clothes sits beneath a great tree and holds a daily audience. Socrates in an Indian village.'

Brenda (12 October 1944): 'I am starting a small library for my Sunday school class – missionary and religious books only – as they seem to want something to read.'

Stuart (22 October 1944): '. . . am in touch with Command Chaplain over here and am enquiring, amongst other things, about library facilities. He has sent me a few forms to fill up as a provisional ordinand. . . . Usual variety with five lines to say "yes" in, and half a line to explain what caused you to decide "to study for ordination".'

Brenda (28 October 1944): 'I . . . have wondered what was going on in "your deeps". But as I am aware that these are days of preparation for new ideas, new leaps, new plunges, or new revealing, it has not troubled me unduly . . . [The Dohnavur books] are meat and drink to me and will be to you – because they make clear those eternal truths that we had begun to stumble upon, had felt to be true but found little confirmation among much that we read or saw. . . . The Downs were heavenly – brown patches of ploughed earth, delicate brown bare trees, topped with gold of dried oak leaves. Green Downs, rolling hills, puff white clouds – a blue sky and a blue sea. And peace.'

Stuart (30 October 1944): 'Lovely evenings they have been when the sky bears upon it the great red flails of the dying sun, when the air cools and the crickets begin their nightly chorus. A tremendous thunderstorm on Saturday night with the whole canopy echoing and the lightning flickering across the verandah rails. But the sun is back and the ground is thirsty again'; (6 November – after a 1,200-mile train journey to Calcutta): 'On Sunday morning I got up early and went to Communion just after dawn . . . a hymn of praise at least half a mile long when the whole of nature awakes and proclaims "God is love", and the bells chime in and punctuates its verse. Not very long ago I should have been highly displeased at the conduct of the service – some of it inaudible, most of it quite unintelligible on any level to one outside the flock – and yet the worship was real, the priest cooperating in the well-known celebration, not leading it, or taking anything to himself nor abrogating anything that is God's; quiet, inconspicuous, a real priest . . . [later] I went to evensong and there heard this same priest speaking of the church, the church as the body of Christ, ineffably, sublimely bigger than the mean, sinful Christian men who help to compose it. "May God's saints pray for you, God's angels guard you, God's blessing be upon you now and always". – A glorious blessing and afterwards we went to his billet and I found out that he was (i) a brother of the Community of the Resurrection, (ii) Chief Chaplain (Colonel) of the East Asia Command.' (This was Cecil de Vall, a former First World War pilot with whom Stuart was to form a landmark friendship.)

Brenda, meanwhile, had been making her own spiritual discoveries in St James's church where the preaching of the Revd Harold Fife and the fellowship of a lively congregation were having their impact. She wrote that after the service she had 'come away feeling my spirit has found something to bite on'.

Stuart (13 November 1944): 'What little Urdu I have has proved very useful and it is amazing how far you can get with the words for "God" and "Father".'

Brenda (1 December 1944): 'The service reminded me of my childhood. They seem to be interdenominational at St James! More and more God seems to be training me to see the futility of all these divisions in the church, that in Christ we are not divided. I often feel that I should be a lot happier in a remote mission field where services were simple praise, etc. I'm so tired of complicated liturgy, convention, unreality.'

Now attending prayer meetings, Brenda was entering a rich stream of spiritual experience very different in its outward trappings from Stuart's discoveries in Anglo-Catholicism. And the variety of their experience was something Stuart took to heart:

Stuart (6 December 1944 – in filling out a form related to ordination he had been wondering about his churchmanship): 'One minute the priest swallowed up in the service of the church, next the evangelical desiring nothing save the salvation of another soul. Somewhere between the two extremes lies the narrow way; the church cannot be just regarded as the confluence of individual believers . . . but the Bride of Christ, greater than the individuals who comprise it.' [In response to Brenda writing to him that she has been introduced to the true type of evangelicalism]: (17 December): 'Somewhere between the non-conformist freedom of worship and the liturgy of the church lies the way; the one is too dependent upon the person, the other too often provides a refuge for the uncommitted . . . the church should be pastoral, but should be, too, a witnessing, seeking church'; (21 December – writing of Christmas): 'Adoration is wonder grown up'; (24 December): 'Midnight Communion this evening and we, the angel voices, are singing Merbecke.' (Assistant chaplain general and pastor for provisional ordinands was Canon Reginald Diggle, who now harnessed Stuart's skills to matters farther afield. This included flying together to the consecration of a new church.)

Brenda (12 January 1945): 'Every now and again you let fall a sentence which makes me realise that there has been a revolutionary change in you, though there has been no hint of it in your letter.'

Stuart (19 January 1945): 'Yes, the change that has been wrought in me is that my faith has been shaken rotten – not by adversity or darkness but by blessing and light!. . . . Make no mistake, the Truth is a terrible thing'; (21 January): 'The nearest RAF padre has asked me to help with some of his Sunday services on other units, but that would mean deserting our fellowship here; and, however small, I think that is more worthwhile – Canon Diggle has suggested that I should be chaplain's assistant to our own unit and that may entail being licensed as an RAF lay reader. . . . Much of the pleasure of this morning's walk I owe to the fact that you would have enjoyed it'; (23 January – on the subject of Bible reading): 'The great danger of having a time-limit is that it will hasten over the profound and ponder over the insignificant. Have you tried reading over one particular incident in one or all of the Gospels every morning for perhaps a week or a month or three months – the transfiguration, the crucifixion, the temptation, the last supper. These are the consummation of all Bible teaching, and, as you follow, you will be led back into the Old Testament to the roots, forward through the New to the fruit which is – truth. And each day let your mind and spirit rest, as he calls you, perhaps on one verse, perhaps on two words; chase every thought, every echo, the length and breadth of the concordance and then with mind refreshed and directed, rest again on that which the Holy Spirit has illumined.'

At this time Stuart became a frequent visitor to the home of the garrison chaplain, Cecil de Vall, where late evening coffee and conversation would sometimes carry on into the next day. While the learning process involved was almost certainly mutual, it is clear that Cecil de Vall's spirituality made its mark on Stuart's.

Stuart (Ash Wednesday 1945): 'If you want to know what free prayer can mean listen to one who has been reared on a liturgy, whose heart and mind have been interpenetrated with a truth that is both beautiful and eternal.'

Brenda (16 February 1945 – having encountered and been impressed by the inter-denominational life of the China Inland Mission): 'I don't think you will ever get me to work happily in anything restricted to one denomination, darling! Shall have to hope that you feel the same way.'

Stuart (19 March 1945): 'You are a member of the Holy Catholic Church, not of a deployed confluence of believers who meet for edification but the Bride of Christ.'

Brenda (3 April 1945): '[Yes, but . . .] it is not belief in a doctrine that changes a man's being, it is knowing and loving Christ. Personally I think it is because the C of E tends to put the Church before Christ or the Holy Spirit that it has no power and is so dead.'

Stuart, busy in his spare time writing essays for Canon Diggle, had arranged to spend his leave at Dohnavur where he would be able to meet Amy Carmichael, and it was here that he heard news of the end of the war in Europe:

Stuart (Dohnavur, 8 May 1945): '. . . a service [celebrating the end of the war in Europe] was held in the house of prayer, and the children sang and waved their flags and looked jealously for a smile from Godfrey Webb-Peploe who presided over the rejoicings. Norman Burns has been commissioned to sit up until 1.30 tomorrow morning to take a record of the King's speech'; (12 May): 'If love be the crown of the Christian life, then Dohnavur is the way. Not able to understand a word of the language [it was not the one he had been learning] I can yet feel the tenderness that is bestowed upon the poor, crippled leprous men and women that look for healing in the hospital and their gratitude is patent. In all but thought these have been quiet days. . . . "Spreading a few beams of reality" – this minimum service begins to look like a distant maximum'; (14 May): 'With Bertie the padre to project slides in the open air in nearby village. Meanwhile I am pushing on through the Old Testament, attempting to write a summary of its history, and dispel that uncomfortable sense of confusion which obscures the mighty fact of the power and revelation of God – the same yesterday, today and forever. I have been reading too from Bishop Moule – recommended for our united consideration, for he was an evangelist – and Bishop!' (21 May – having given a lecture in Hindustani about the RAF to members of the community): 'Glad for a wife who does not always mount on eagle's wings – for the eagle is a lonely bird'; (23 May – after a personal visit to Amy Carmichael): 'I spent about half an hour with her on Monday evening . . . the lovely selfless woman whose spirit breathes through the pages of her books . . . our names are written together at the end of her New Testament'; (6 June – having been reading the biography of Frank Weston, Bishop of Zanzibar, lent to him by Cecil de Vall): 'Not for nothing have we been introduced to the extremes.'

Brenda (8 June 1945 – referring to the Church of England): 'In theory, all its doctrines are admirable, but it rarely seems to put them into practice; its emphasis is mostly on organisation, not on the Spirit, on Church worship not on evangelisation. . . . God is quite clearly calling me out of the C of E. I cannot leave it without you. And I know what such a move would cost you – at the moment. But I know also that . . . when once the Spirit can overcome in you the power of the mind and set you free, you will understand.'

Stuart (June 1945 – referring to the disestablishment of the Church of England): 'Perhaps we shall have to admit that, through lack of individual conviction, we cannot sustain that position [of being the established Church] but let nobody deceive themselves that that in itself will be a forward step; we shall have loosed our hold on the national conscience, we shall have admitted that the ideal of Christian government, the marriage of Church and state, a theocracy in fact, is an impossible ideal. Disestablishment may be the will of God for us but it will be God's merciful concession to our weakness, not the spread of our wisdom . . . '; (24 June): 'How unimportant the apparent issues between Church and nonconformity are. Apart from the initial cause of dissent they are, I believe, the product of half-understanding, of immature emphasis. On the whole nonconformity teaches the glorious spontaneity of our fellowship with Jesus, and indeed, if that is missing the spirit fades and dies. Yet if we are precious souls, called to be holy and perfect, it is only natural to practise the exercises of the spiritual life as painstakingly as we practise our scales at music. You and I are called to be one flesh to represent as it were in one body the balance between apparently opposite revelations; once we seek to exalt one opinion above the vital witness of true unity we shall be in serious trouble.'

Brenda (26 June 1945): 'God doesn't always give us reasons with His commands. He can't, and I don't think He will. . . . That faith has to act without reason, very often. Think of Abraham and Sarah . . . God is GOD, the unexplainable.'

Stuart (19 July 1945 – after a spell of putting boot polish on Bible and prayer book covers to retard the damp . . .): 'Went to [Calcutta] Cathedral yesterday evening and had the temerity to cross swords with G. B. Elliott in discussion – fools rush in. It was a good meeting and he is a grand man'; (29 July): 'I woke early this morning and tottered down to the Cathedral for the 6.30 a.m. Holy Communion; the shopkeepers were still asleep on the pavement close to their work, the commerce in food stuff was beginning and in front of me trotted a carrier with a basket full of live chickens on his head – a strange head dress of squawking, fluttering feathers whose possibilities only a Parisian designer could realise. It was cool. Communion was held in a plain, beautiful little chapel with large French windows opening onto the Cathedral lawns; a lake gleaming under a cloudy sky, ruffled with the breeze, the trees rustling. The service was taken slowly, lovingly and G. B. Elliott spoke for a few minutes on the Gospel, and once in a way I could wait afterwards, quietly considering what had happened and remembering the price that had been paid . . .'

Brenda (18 August 1945): 'Your religion is in danger of becoming an introspective faith. I can't put my finger on the trouble, and yet I can feel that there is something astray in your letters, a wrong emphasis.' (Here she mentions inspiring fellowship with two new friends, Miss Settle and Miss Hankinson of the Egypt General Mission.)

Stuart (20 August 1945): 'The service of induction as a lay-reader was held the Sunday before last [12 August] and I pronounced rather falteringly those tremendous words "I will" . . . the deep satisfaction which, with all the caution in the world, I could not resist.'

On 26 August Stuart moved from Calcutta to Burma.

Brenda (31 August 1945): 'We have been controversial of late. Please God, that He may overcome our obstinate natures and unite us in Christ, for in Him God hath blessed us with every spiritual blessing.'

Stuart (4 September 1945): 'We must make an effort, not necessarily to change our opinions, but to acknowledge with loving and generous hearts a double contribution to a single, wedded life'; (6 September): 'Long ago I used to fear happiness as the herald of darkness deepened by the light that preceded it.'

On 27 September Stuart mentioned that he had for the first time added the possibility of university to his post-Air Force options. While these included a return to insurance, he no longer mentioned journalism, although he did include among the options work on the mission field. 'My mind is open,' he said. On 30 September he conducted a service in the new chapel for the first time – the chaplains doing duty three Sundays each month and he on the fourth. His text for the first occasion was: 'Ye must be born again.'

Brenda (30 September 1945): 'I'm not at all sure in my own heart that God is calling you to the Ministry. Are you absolutely dead certain about it? Has He given you any gift for preaching? Has He shown by the results of your ministry among the men that He particularly wants you for that? . . . Beware of being urged on by the others however greatly you respect them. Don't undertake it unless you are sure without any shadow of doubt that "to this end you were born".'

Stuart (5 October 1945): '"Love all things for Jesus and love Jesus for Himself" – I need a dose of Thomas à Kempis'; (8 October – from Cawnpore): ' . . . very hot still, so hot that it sends the occasional shiver down your back, but strangely invigorating. The services yesterday were a delight. Morning Prayer was something like I imagine an early Christian meeting to be – a small company, well known to one another, amidst a suspicious and indifferent world; I have never heard psalms and hymns sung so vigorously (or accurately) by a small congregation and Jack (the organist) pointed the psalms as if he had been doing it all his life. More and more we look to the few – a priesthood to the world; I don't think Jesus ever envisaged the church as anything else – the leaven in the lump, working secretly, upholding those who know it not, and would probably resent it if they did, with prayer and intercession; something here which was inherent in the OT sacrificial system – and Jesus came not to destroy but to fulfil'; (15 October – back in Burma): 'Our clergymen talk too much and pray too little'; (21 October): 'Cecil de Vall and I talked from 9 p.m. to 2 a.m. . . . I am sure that the joint call to us as man and wife is rare; not many men and women who step into the ditch together step out together.'

Brenda (24 October 1945): 'We're apt to have such high-falutin ideas of our future, whereas possibly His plan for us is an extremely ordinary, dull one – to our view. . . . We're having 70 m.p.h. gales, torrential rain, raging seas that even come over the front, and lots of mines being washed ashore.'

Stuart (31 October 1945): 'The chapel looks delightful now, with fresh flowers and clean white altar cloth, with its straw mats and low green forms. . . . If only we could persuade the corporation employees to stop the pump next door, and the washerman to desist from slapping his clothes during Holy Communion it would be a sanctuary indeed.' (With demobilization approaching, Stuart noted that 200,000 dockers were on strike.)

Brenda (October 1945): 'God knows what's best for us for His plan and when the time is come He will show us the why and wherefore of these years. . . . Just as Betty and Cecil [de Vall] and Mary and their home have helped you, so the Fifes and their home have helped me.' (One day in October 1945 Brenda made the important decision to apply for membership of Harold Fife's church. Her decision to do so without consultation and agreement greatly upset Stuart and brought to a head their long-running debate about denominational differences.)

Stuart (31 October 1945): 'If there were one thing in marriage which I dreaded, it was the sense of inevitable restraint, a loss of personal identity. Nevertheless, we are married and we have to recognise that we are not allowed an unrestricted freedom of choice; we cannot take decisions as if we were single. Now for you, and no less for me. That is likely to prove, at times, irksome, a drag on spiritual advance, an incitement to impatience. If we are given a conviction, we can assume that it represents a call or challenge to us both: and not, and I pray never, a ground for separation or estrangement; we have just got to have faith to believe that God's will can prevail through the instrument which he has created – our marriage. Independent action by either of us, even with the strongest reasons, can only weaken our unity, tarnish our love and hinder our effective witness'; (16 November): ' . . . regretting with real sorrow the harsh inexcusable things I have written. . . . You will gather from my violent reaction to any infringement of it the supreme value I am coming to attach to our marriage, because in it lies the possibility of a blending which could not but be denied to the confines of a single personality. You have compassed something at St James' which is perhaps foreign to me, a simplicity of approach to the unconverted to which my training ill fits me. Here, in India, I have been trying to hold on to two Christian essentials, save in the highest reaches apparently incompatible but yet in the providence of God harmonious and beautiful. (1) The importance of the individual; (2) the importance of the Body of Christ. You have come down heavily on the first, I almost as heavily on the second. The apparent result – divergence of opinion; the real result a deeper, lovelier symphony.' [On 13 November Brenda wrote of the grief she felt at the seeming implications of her unilateral move. Stuart replied as follows] (16 November): 'Being angry with my wife is like being angry with God – almost unforgivable, at least, so much I have gathered from the past week or so's disorders. If I can't live the spiritual life with you I can scarcely live it at all.'

Brenda (21 November 1945): 'We shall find that the two emphases you mention are in reality complementary'; (23 November – quoting from a book she was reading but did not name): '"our lives, my life, is the answer to someone's prayer, prayed perhaps centuries ago"'.

In late November Stuart attended a selection conference for potential ordination candidates which was held at the Bishop's House in Calcutta:

Stuart (28 November 1945): 'Broadly I have told the interviewers that I am not sure of the specific call to ministry in the Anglican church, that I am sure that the call, whatever it may be, is to us both. . . . Canon Diggle is astute enough and loving enough to understand that burning need, and the Bishop has been a real tower of strength and comfort; I confess that I felt an infant-in-arms in his presence, for he is tall and spare with white hair and a crisp deep voice and a face that reveals'; (3 December – having received Brenda's response to his letter of

31 October): 'I know how difficult it is, as it were, to stand aside from conviction and enthusiasm, and weigh quietly their final implications. . . . It was a happy week we spent in Calcutta – much better than I had expected – and we were in touch with the cosmopolitan travellers who stay in the Bishop's House en route for new stations or on leave. I wish our English bishops were as approachable, and shared common table and common room with any who liked to join them; the services people really do appreciate it.'

Brenda (12 December 1945): 'Shopping is ghastly this Christmas – there isn't anything in the shops except at a fabulous and entirely-beyond-the-value price. . . . The shoe shops open for about a quarter hour each day and sell their quota. The housing situation is hopeless; the coal is all stones. Even next winter we are promised only two and a half pints of milk a week.'

Stuart (Sunday, 16 December 1945 – back in Bombay en route for a ship home): 'Back where we started about fifteen months ago; we left Calcutta yesterday morning . . . and arrived here in Bombay just after lunch. The CO did his last landing and I did what I hope will be my last spot of air navigation. . . . I spent five days with Cecil [de Vall] – two o'clock or so every night and up the following morning for prayer and Communion, it was a bit tiring but we thrashed our way the length and breadth of Christian doctrine and practice'; (21 December): 'I am attempting in my spare time to trace the chronological development of St Paul's teaching; it is a fascinating study but involves hours of patient reference hunting, and there are times when the armchair claims me for its own, and Thessalonica tends to fade into Ewell, and Corinth into Worthing, and a certain Mrs Paul rises up and dominates the scene'; (19 January 1946): 'Well there is a very fine looking boat with battleship stern and greyhound lines lying at the dockside [the *Capetown Castle*] – we are due to embark this afternoon after lunch. . . . The sea and all that is within it thunders His praise.'

THE 'LONGEST JOURNEY' ENDS

Stuart's ship docked at Southampton on 6 February 1946. His 'longest journey', begun on the train to Uxbridge on 15 March 1940, had finally ended. But now he saw England with fresh eyes, and Stuart's and Brenda's joyful reunion was set against a sombre background in which the cost of global warfare was having to be paid for by every home and family. The infrastructures of too many countries had been ravaged, Germany's food production system had been destroyed and, even as Goering and Ribbentrop went on trial at Nuremberg, food had to be found for millions of Germans; and the day after Stuart stepped ashore there were speeches in Parliament about tighter rationing. Meanwhile, not all wartime weddings had survived and special measures were needed to process a backlog of 55,000 applications for divorce.

The six-month-old Labour government was tackling its work under a 'Let's Face the Future' slogan and not everyone was facing it in the same way. Massive rethinking was needed, one sign of which was the meeting in March 1946 when the British Medical Association launched a fighting fund to oppose the introduction of the National Health Service. However, in May, the month in which bread rationing was introduced, the Ministry of Education announced grants – with effect from the following October – for students otherwise lacking the means to take up university places, a measure of immediate relevance to Stuart's plans.

As church people pondered their faith and worked out ways of applying it to this strange new world, two currents of life, which had been running side by side since 1918, were making themselves felt. There were the beginnings of a revival in biblical Christianity, with writers like C. S. Lewis and Dorothy L. Sayers being widely read, and Christianity being taken seriously in intellectual circles. At the same time there were the effects of the kind of Christian social thinking that William Temple had been writing about, together with considerations arising from such gatherings as COPEC in 1923. While the faith was, on the one hand, seen more clearly as vividly relevant to the individual, it was also seen as more than a matter of private devotion and subjective experience. The Church was not marginalized by the social revolution in which it was involved, but was a vital partner of government in far-reaching social change. The death of William Temple in 1944 had robbed the nation of a leader who had held these concerns together as one. There were to be plenty of well-meaning people trying to drive a wedge between them in coming years, but they would have the Bible itself to contend with – and intriguingly it was on 8 February 1946, two days after Stuart landed, that the New Testament part of the Revised Standard Version of the Bible was published.

In finding his faith and also his vocation in this new kind of world, Stuart belonged to a special generation of people – one that had grown up between the wars. They knew the years that not only separated the conflicts, but also created them. Stuart's generation was beginning a new life by absorbing the fact that 55 million people had died, and that few of the world's problems had been solved. The world, however, was different again from that of 1918 and would continue to change. Politicians, thinkers, writers, artists, and theologians had as much to do in their own specialized spheres as did the millions of families reassembling their lives.

Together once more, Stuart and Brenda swiftly resolved their long-running debate about denominational differences, and jointly convinced of Stuart's call to ordination took prompt action concerning their future.

~ 3 ~

Leviticus:
Introduction to the Priestly Life

A CIVILIAN IN OXFORD

In choosing a theological college, Stuart was helped by Canon Reginald Diggle, now vicar of St Giles, Oxford. With his advice, Stuart became a member of St Catherine's Society (now St Catherine's College), Oxford, with a place at Wycliffe Hall. As was the custom in the years immediately following the war, newly returned servicemen were assigned to an accelerated two-year degree course. In this way, Stuart gained a first in theology before completing a third year of ordination training.

In the early days Stuart was required to live in at Wycliffe Hall. Fellow student Paul Rimmer recalls him as a specially helpful next-door neighbour:

Stuart's room was next to mine on the third floor. The winter of 1946–7 was extremely severe. Coal was not only in short supply but virtually non-existent. Food was sparse. Electricity cuts were frequent. Shops were often lit by candle-light, when the light failed. The water jugs in our bedroom often were coated with ice. It was during this somewhat depressing period that every morning I was woken by a knock on my bedroom door, and Stuart would place a steaming hot cup of tea on my bedside cupboard. After that one could face anything. The Hall at that time was filled with many ex-servicemen, many of whom had had distinguished careers in the forces. Stuart eventually became President of the Common Room, and his good humour and balanced personality was a stabilizing influence.

The Principal was Canon Julian Thornton-Duesbery, who was, it seems, a trifle wary about the effects upon college life of an influx of married men. At first he ruled that no wives were to live within ten miles of Oxford. Then, wisely adapting to changing times, the Canon relaxed the rule and Stuart and

Brenda were able to look for their own home in Oxford. Another married student in the same circumstances was an old RAF friend, John Morris. He and his Canadian wife Elsie also needed a home for degree studies before John went on to prepare for ordination at Cuddesdon. After a happy reunion between Stuart and John on the steps of Oriel, they agreed that whoever found a house first would share it with the other couple.

Consequently when Stuart and Brenda got a house in Wharton Road, Headington, all four of them moved in. Brenda, within three months of having their first child, Susan, recalls how 'the men had the front room as their study with their typewriters, and Elsie and I had the back room with our two babies, and a small kitchen. And of course we had to share our friends. We used to have a lot of students coming up, of all nationalities. People in the road, if they noticed an African, said "You must be looking for number 62".'

Stuart's tutor at Wycliffe was Canon Douglas Vicary. Their paths were to cross again in later life, but at Wycliffe Canon Vicary recalls the quality of Stuart's work: 'His work came back polished. Beautiful stuff. Tutorial work was a pleasure.'

One direction Stuart's academic interest was to take surfaced in the essay he wrote for his priest's ordination examination. This was produced during his diaconate – the first year of his curacy. It was a substantial piece of work about prayer, and embodied reflections on his own spiritual development. He was concerned that many books being published about prayer were pre-occupied with it as a means of self-perfection. Stuart broadly categorized this as 'mystical prayer', also giving it the name of 'systematic prayer', because of the systems it employed. Noting its virtues, he nevertheless regarded it as essentially self-centred, having as its primary aim that of benefiting the one who prays. This 'systematic prayer' he contrasted with 'prophetic' or 'evangelical' prayer, which he saw as being caught up into the activity of God. This, he argued, is possible when people realize what God has done for humanity in removing the barrier of sin and giving the Holy Spirit, enabling prayer to become praise, thanksgiving, and co-operation with God's will in daily life. Typically, he concluded by suggesting that the full range of prayer's possibilities embraces both kinds. The examiner was Canon V. A. Demant, whose written reply was a model of its kind. He said how much he had enjoyed the essay, adding that a greater emphasis on praise would save mystics from self-preoccupation and deliver evangelicals from activism, and commending the Book of Common Prayer as a model combination of both approaches. Eight years later a development of these ideas was embodied in the theme Stuart proposed for a BD dissertation, but by then his approach had six more years of pastoral and devotional experience built into it.

That experience was to begin with a curacy that, remarkably, did not involve the family in moving house. It was at All Saints, Highfield, in Oxford, with the Revd Cecil Markby, a former CMS missionary in Uganda. Stuart was made deacon on Trinity Sunday 1949 and ordained priest on Trinity Sunday 1950. Unfortunately, any diary notes he may have made about such momentous occasions do not seem to have survived. He did, however, write brief letters to Brenda from the ordination retreat. The first began: 'A note from Adullam's cave – though we are not all discontented or in debt!' He gave the address of his other letter as 'De Profundis', saying 'so far the retreat has been very pleasant and not too arduous. . . . We have had a rehearsal for the service this afternoon; it will be a miracle if we contrive to do everything at the right time.'

A CURATE'S CONCERNS

The Oxford curacy worked well. Brenda reflects:

> I think his time as a curate was very crucial because there he tried out a lot of ideas. One of them was using maps and plans in a sermon. They were all much too elaborate and advanced of course, but then curates don't realise what's the limit of the congregation. One day he tried speaking without using his notes, that's to say without looking down, certainly he never read his sermons. I remember the first time he tried it. He didn't look up enough at the people and it looked as if he were reading. So when we were walking home with Cecil I said to Stuart: 'Well you really need to look up a bit!' And Cecil said: 'Don't get in front of the Holy Spirit.' I could see what he meant. You have to be careful when you make suggestions or criticisms. I learnt my lesson.

One natural gift was his voice. John Morris observed that

> it had instant appeal – his voice never varied in all the years I knew him, and remained consistent whether he was speaking privately or in public. His inflections were always natural and conversational. His tone was always warm. It somehow conveyed smiling fellow-feeling and friendship. When he was sharing feelings of wonder, bewilderment, concern or amusement, there was an engaging conspiratorial note. Even when he was firm and unyielding in voicing a conviction or opposing a view he felt to be unworthy or dangerous, there was

no hint of shrillness or tendency to shout. Surely this says something about the man himself.

Patience Markby, the vicar's wife, remembers those days well:

> Stuart was essentially a family man and devoted to his children. [Susan had now been joined by Hilary, born in 1948, and Angela, born in 1950.] I have early memories of the family arriving for tea with a push-chair, three little girls and the dog. It was always fun having them with us, and to be welcomed into their home. Their house was quite small for a growing family, so Stuart converted the garden shed into a study. A neighbour remembers Stuart cycling down their road with a haversack over his shoulder and waving to friends and neighbours as he passed them. At the weekly staff meeting in the vicarage there would often be gales of laughter audible from the study. Stuart was always quick to see the amusing angle in any situation. Yet he also had a depth of spiritual insight. He was a tower of strength to my husband in the parish. Soon after his arrival in the parish he started a Bible study home group which many people found very helpful. This was in 1950 before such meetings were such an established feature of parish life as they are today.

Stuart was also an assiduous hospital visitor and even managed to conduct confirmation classes on the ward at the Nuffield Orthopaedic Centre. Physiotherapist Mary McMaster remembers a day when she was hard at work:

> I was giving a patient treatment in a small curtained-cubicled ward. On the other side were four or five men waiting for a confirmation class to be taken by the new curate, the Revd Stuart Blanch. When the class began and Mr Blanch began to speak, I realized that this was something very special. Fortunately my patient and I were able to hear exactly what was said as there was only a curtain between us. I became more and more enthralled by what I heard. My patient had a longer treatment than usual that day. He liked being massaged and I think he too became really interested in what was going on close to us, though he did not remark on it.

Although life was generally happy, Stuart was discovering the cost of ministry. Addressing a conference many years later, he recalled that 'after two or three years in the ministry, like many others I felt an acute sense of strain. The doctor said: "You can't go round carrying people's burdens on your own shoulders all day – you must leave them with the Lord."' He learned some lessons then that he practised all his life. To his audience on that occasion, he said: 'Try to avoid the sense of being driven from one thing to the next. Keep an hour for quiet between afternoon and evening. . . . I don't know how you'd keep sane if you don't preserve silence like that, periods when you're not doing anything. Prayer is not just another activity but a ceasing from activity.'

Brenda recalls how in 1952:

> We'd been having lots of difficulties in our spiritual life. We both felt we were failing horribly and not getting anywhere. And on Cecil's mantelpiece we saw a little notice about Lee Abbey, which of course had only started in 1946, and we felt rather attracted to this. So we decided that we'd go there for a holiday with all our children – three of them at this time. We had a good holiday and nobody at Lee Abbey said anything at all to us – it was the days of Geoffrey Rogers, Leslie Sutton, and Jack Winslow. We were much influenced by Jack Winslow's talks. And we used to sit and think these over. Then one day we were sitting quietly after a talk and Leslie Sutton came up and sat beside us. He didn't say anything at first, and then he suddenly said to us: 'God can use you two if you let Him'. So we looked at him rather blankly and he went away and didn't say any more. But anyhow, when we went to bed we decided to ask for the Holy Spirit – we thought that was perhaps where we'd got to. [There came then the shared experience of being filled with the Holy Spirit.] That did make a lot of difference. It really did. It doesn't solve all your problems, but it means that you and the Holy Spirit are working together instead of being at cross purposes. So we came home and we were full of glee. And of course Cecil had to put up with us renewed Christians!

It was the start of a long and fruitful relationship with Lee Abbey, and particularly with Geoffrey Rogers, Jack Winslow, and Leslie and Phyllis Sutton. Characteristically, Stuart needed not only to experience the presence and gifts of God, but also, so far as it is possible, to weigh and assess them intellectually. At one level he now reached a fresh understanding of his experience at Christmas 1942. Pondering the next step in his career, he went on retreat and during this time wrote as follows:

> 'Behold I stand at the door and knock, if any man hear my voice and open the door I will come in and dwell with him'. This surely is the scriptural ancestor of those forms of spiritual experience which speak of 'Christ our Lord', of 'accepting Christ', of 'allowing Christ to enter the heart'. I have treated these terms metaphorically and interpreted them as the conscious obedience to the law in the power of Christ. They should apparently be treated spiritually, which

is a very different thing. The central message of the Christian gospel, as Leslie has so persistently pointed out, is the indwelling of the divine or the Creator spirit in the spirit of a man, i.e. the essential ingrafting of the divine personality with the human so that it can be said 'not I but Christ liveth in me'. The expression 'let Christ enter my heart' is unreal only when we are tied to the picture of the human Jesus and forget that He was the 'eternal word' which 'entering into holy souls makes them friends of God and prophets'. . . . We are begotten of the Father and, as natural children, contain within us inevitably some of the life and spirit of the Father, in different combinations and aspects (for no two children are alike). The spirit of the Son becomes ours (not I but Christ) and we are able to cry Abba Father. We are at home in the spiritual universe, the secret of the Lord is ours, we enter into a life that is deathless. All that we are born with is a lack, a capacity for, a hunger after the divine spirit. We are spiritual in the pre-conversion stage not as the Law would suggest, because we all have the seed of life in our hearts, but because we hunger and thirst after spiritual things. In that stage we remain 'seekers'; as converted men we become 'finders'. . . . This then is the essential simplicity of the gospel, that to which through all the labyrinth of the human mind we should teach others. We start and end there – the rest is explanation.

It was with mind and spirit in step and energized, perhaps as never before, that Stuart and Brenda now looked for their next sphere of service. Among the posts that attracted them was one at a theological college in Ghana. The college, though, did not have accommodation for a family of five, so they had to look elsewhere, at which point Canon Thornton-Duesbery said: 'Take a look at Eynsham' – Thornton-Duesbery being by this time Master of St Peter's Hall (now St Peter's College). The Oxfordshire village sounded an unpromising substitute for West Africa, but it was in the gift of the college and a suggestion by Thornton-Duesbery was not to be taken lightly. With friends looking after the children, Stuart and Brenda caught a bus from Oxford for the short trip westward, mildly wondering about the Canon's parting remark: 'The vicarage is a bit unwelcoming.'

THE VICAR OF EYNSHAM

The fifteenth-century church of St Leonard, with its perpendicular-style tower, was easy to find on one side of Eynsham's village square. Its traditional structure and classically English location made it instantly familiar and seemed to touch something fundamental in them. The church was open and empty and they went in. No one could have been more surprised than them by the sudden conviction that this was the place for them. They prayed there, and then, as the implication of their feelings sank in, set off to look at the vicarage – and assess for themselves Canon Thornton-Duesbery's description of 'a bit unwelcoming'.

At first sight daunting only in its size, the lovely Georgian house loomed behind a high wall and a fringe of ancient trees. Twin gateways accessed a short gravelled crescent skirting the 12 steps they had to mount to reach the front door. Brenda's recollections fill out the picture: 'A garden like a jungle, huge trees at the front, and inside huge black cobwebs everywhere. No electricity, only gas on the ground floor, the kitchen was in the basement. It was so rotten with woodworm that when you touched something it fell apart.' John Pym, the local contractor due to tackle the repair work, adds: 'Nothing had been done to any of the rooms for about fifty years, most of the window sills were rotten, and in the rooms not used by the last vicar, who was a bachelor, cobwebs hung from the ceilings in great swathes – you could almost swing on them. The spiders also were monsters – a kick from one of them could have given you a fractured fibula!'

'It was terrible,' said Brenda, 'so we thought, "Golly, how can we live here with three small children?" However, we went back and told Julian that we felt we were meant to go but that we didn't know how we were going to live in the vicarage and couldn't go unless there was electricity. With three small children it would be hopeless. We didn't hear anything – actually Julian was away but we didn't know that – and after about a fortnight we said to one another, "we've got to accept that place wholeheartedly" – without any reservations at all. So we wrote again and said, "Right. We'll go, whatever!"'

Stuart accepted the living, work started on the house, and they moved in on a rainy day in October when two bedrooms and the living room had been made ready. There was, however, no bathroom and the old basement kitchen was still in its original terrible condition. Although the house had been wired, the electricity supply had not been switched on. Bedtime for the children was difficult for everyone. The big house, the darkness without electricity, awareness of the huge overgrown garden, the steady rain, made it all rather frightening for the children. To cap it all – as peace began to descend – there came the ear-splitting wail of the village fire-siren, situated as they only then discovered, on a high post just outside their front door. Bedtime, though, was always story-time and usually Stuart was the story-teller. Story-telling was no short-term stratagem for lulling little ones to sleep, either. Tim Blanch, who was born in 1953 while the family was still at Eynsham, remembers enjoying his father's bedtime stories until he was about ten.

The Induction was set for 3 p.m. on Saturday, 8 November, and November brought snow.

Despite all the dark accompaniments of the new vicar's arrival, the time is remembered by the parishioners as one of light. Brenda Miles recalls her first ever experience of laughter in church during Stuart's first sermon in which he described the fire-siren's welcome. Local schoolmaster Stanley Green remembers: 'My first meeting with him was in the Infants' School on a dark winter's night and a body of very old people gathered under a flickering gaslight in this cavernous room. . . . And from that time Eynsham Church changed in all sorts of ways. He didn't stand up and say "I'm going to do this". It was done – in a sense – very casually. You walked into all these decisions he made. You couldn't help but agree with him.'

Their courage in taking on the vicarage, the way they tackled its problems, and their willingness to receive help, quickly embedded them in local affections. Elsie Floyd – a neighbour who came to help at the vicarage – said: 'When I first went to them they said, "Oh come downstairs" – where they were having breakfast. And Stuart said, "Look at the company we've got!" The rats were running around the rafters.' Another special feature of life during their first nine months in Eynsham was their need to take their baths in the homes of parishioners, a practice involving the happy co-operation of several homes.

The handicap imposed by the vicarage was turned to ecumenical advantage by transforming a section of it into a flat for the local Baptist minister, Richard Hamper, and his wife – with whom they became life-long friends. The Roman Catholic parish priest, Father John Lopes, lived in a white house across the street, and is well remembered locally. He and Stuart soon struck up a deep friendship and the becassocked priest was soon to be seen walking across the road to the vicarage with a copy of *The Tablet* in his hand en route for lively theological debate. John Pym said that these clergy homes were known locally as 'the Holy Triangle'. There was also a Methodist church, and happy relations were swiftly established between the clergy of all four churches.

Work began on cleaning up the church. Brenda took on the task of running a rota of church cleaners which became a Sanctuary Guild, and one parishioner, finding Stuart learning to look after the coal-fired furnace in the church cellar, was impressed to find overalls as a natural partner of cassock and surplice.

There were many old people in the parish, and Stuart came to be admired for the consistency with which he would arrive with a birthday card at the right home on the right day. But he also made a strong approach to young people, which was to create a new generation of disciples. Sunday night in the basement of the vicarage became a focal point of new life for youngsters at St Leonard's. Yvonne Townsend recalls how 14- and 15-year-olds were required to take turns in leading the meetings. Josie Smith was startled to find herself elected chairman of the Youth Fellowship and felt the task beyond her. 'Josie,' said Stuart, 'a good chairman always delegates!' 'Oh, I can do that!' she replied. Sometimes they would go as a group into Oxford and visit the Youth Fellowship in Stuart's former parish. Often they would have students from Wycliffe Hall sharing in their services and meetings. Meanwhile, Stuart and Richard Hamper worked together to create a joint branch of the Boys' Brigade.

Confirmation classes lasted for nine months and included homework – candidates having to write their own life of Christ. Each candidate had two personal interviews, and parents were interviewed also, and before the confirmation service there would be a day retreat in a neighbouring parish. A choir was formed, and learned to sing Merbecke's setting of the Holy Communion, having first been introduced to the mysterious discipline of a metronome. Drama was also used in worship. The service on Good Friday 1953 included a short passion play in which the youngsters had to scream and shout at critical moments. Sermons involved a range of visual aids, including at times a blackboard and pointer. Stewardship was taught and practised. Bible reading was strongly encouraged and a branch of the Bible Reading Fellowship was established. Everybody was encouraged to read widely and a lending library was established in the church. This occupied a revolving bookcase and the act of donating suitable books to the library became known as 'loading the revolver'. Religious books were also taken out into the community for sale at parish events. A horse-drawn type of baker's van became a mobile library and, to the great amusement of the villagers, Stuart and Richard Hamper got in the shafts to draw it through the streets to the local carnival and to sell books there. Wedding preparation was also introduced with the couples concerned being ushered into Stuart's study to be settled down, set at ease, and then asked the all important question: 'Why do you want to be married?' Not surprisingly, the congregation grew rapidly.

Ecumenical life prospered to the point where over fifty people attended a shared weekend house-party in Hertfordshire. In time it became a feature of local life for one congregation to walk in procession from their own church to their neighbour's to share in a service, and in the case of St Leonard's the congregation would be led by the robed choir in the most public way imaginable.

In addition to Eynsham's host community of families who had lived there for generations, there was a more transient population of academic and professional people, many of whom became involved in church life and so more closely integrated into local society. Some, like Elizabeth Tow, came with little religious background. She was an Australian whose English husband worked in Oxford. Elizabeth recalled:

> I never darkened the door of a church at that time, but I started to wonder about God and eventually went and knocked on the vicarage door, not knowing what I was going to say when it was opened. I can't remember how it went, but Stuart asked me in and he kept in touch with me in a very gentle sort of way over the next few months. He never pushed or harangued me – which would have sent me flying. But he always managed to make another appointment and eventually I realized I had to make a decision about it. I thought that would make me very miserable indeed, but it was anything but that. I remember the joyfulness, the laughter, and also of being asked to do things that I hadn't the faintest idea how to do, like lead a Bible study. But he always encouraged me to do it and to write things for the parish magazine. That was the beginning of my Christian life.

Jennet Blake also knocked on the vicarage door. She was a villager who had moved away but been forced to return home for four years because of glandular fever. Those years coincided with Stuart's ministry in Eynsham. Perplexed by the turn life had taken, she walked up the vicarage steps and knocked on the door: 'I remember very clearly his study, I think almost more than anything. It was lined with books. And he kept on feeding me books to read the whole time and I particularly remember his great love and respect for William Temple. I bought quite a number of books which I still have which I owe to Stuart's recommendation.' Jennet remembers a feeling that came upon her unbidden one day: 'When he was looking for the right book for me his hands would wander over the shelves and then he'd pick out a book which was the right book at that time – I still remember sitting there thinking "One day he's going to be the Archbishop of Canterbury". I never told anybody about it because it was so "way out" but I was absolutely convinced of it at the time. It was very plain and I think it arose out of his very spiritual selection of what I needed.' Equally accessible was Brenda, who was often sought out by those who particularly needed a woman's ear.

Eynsham was not allowed to become an ecclesiastical island, though. There was a range of neighbouring villages along the banks of the Thames and connections began to be made between them. It soon became customary for each village church to take an interest in the rest, combining choirs and congregations to visit each one on the appropriate patronal festival. They called themselves the Rivers Group, and began to run their own ecumenical magazine. Stuart was a prime mover in this and in August 1955 he rented a school at Burnham-on-Sea for a sequence of week-long holidays for people from the Rivers Group. Eynsham was well represented. Forty years later one holiday-maker remembered it as 'the most impressive holiday of my life'.

Other people went to Lee Abbey for holidays, and the vitality of that community had its effect on parish life, with members helping in the run-up to an ecumenical mission in Eynsham which was conducted with a flair and imagination to match the dedication of the missioners. In one eye-catching parable – performed outdoors – the clergy, apparently newly released from jail, publicly appeared in mock prison garb adorned with a pattern of arrows and bearing on their backs the slogan 'Just Out'. The village got the message: the gospel has to do with release from slavery to self and with the freedoms of forgiveness, and that in this fundamental matter clergy and laity were on the same footing. In a paperback published in 1956 called *The Lee Abbey Story*, Jack Winslow tells the story of its first ten years, and on page 56 in the original edition he introduces an unnamed vicar to illustrate how 'where new life has come to a parish it has led to a remarkable degree of co-operation between the different Christian bodies in the place'. The anonymous vicar was Stuart.

Among the groups of people who sought Stuart out was the thriving Christian Fellowship at the Nuclear Physics Research Centre in Harwell, which had built its own church and where Stuart was a welcome speaker. One young nuclear research scientist called Eric Jenkins, with his wife Pru, was contemplating a secure financial future offered by work in the USA. Eric and Pru, however, were also feeling the call to Christian ministry and talked this through with Stuart, coming on one occasion to visit him at Eynsham. In due course Eric and Pru exchanged comfortable quarters at Harwell, a rising salary, and financially golden prospects for the near penury of theological training. Stuart was a calm and reassuring guide on the way. Their path was to take them to the diocese of Liverpool where they eventually arrived for Eric's ordination with two small children and remaining funds of £15. Many years later Canon Jenkins was Stuart's adviser in social and scientific issues in the Liverpool diocese and secretary to the national Society of Ordained Scientists.

Amid such scenes of parish life, however, Stuart maintained the discipline of daily study. He was well launched on what was to be a life-long study of the New Testament, and in particular of the Gospels. The ample margins of his copy of Souter's edition of the Greek New Testament – a Phelps reading prize awarded to him at Wycliffe in 1946 – is richly decorated with his own notes, as is his edition of Huck's synopsis of the first three Gospels in Greek, and this was to be the basis of considerable published and unpublished work in later life. He also studied Hebrew and made time to read widely. Meanwhile, his 'first' in theology had not gone unnoticed farther afield – and as early as 1954 he was invited to Durham to discuss a post at a theological college there, with he and Brenda both travelling up for the interview. However, as Brenda put it, 'nobody felt it was right and Stuart did not want to leave Eynsham so soon', adding: 'we assumed that he would stay at Eynsham for the rest of his ministry'. The year of 1956, though, brought one innocent-sounding invitation, seemingly better suited to Stuart's idea of being the scholar parson, and it came from Wycliffe Hall.

The Principal was now the Revd F. J. (John) Taylor, who combined academic ability with major parochial experience; he came to the post from running a large urban parish in Birkenhead and was destined to become Bishop of Sheffield. One urgent temporary need of his in 1956 was to strengthen Old Testament studies in the college. Stuart's principal research interest had been in the New Testament, and he was somewhat taken aback by a request to give a series of lectures on the Old. But he had long regarded the Old Testament as vital to a proper understanding of the New, and the opportunity to lecture on the subject at academic level simply brought forward the challenge that had been lying in wait since the days in India when he had drawn his own interlinked maps of Old Testament thought and history and sought to immerse himself in the world in which Christ grew up. Stuart burned the midnight oil in preparation for these lectures and in order to deliver them made the 16-mile round trips to Oxford on his bicycle. Hidden from view was John Taylor's impending need to appoint a new Vice-Principal, a post that would have to include Old Testament teaching.

Another straw in the wind was a letter Stuart wrote to Canon V. A. Demant towards the end of 1956 about the subject of a thesis he proposed to write for the postgraduate degree of Bachelor of Divinity. It was a development of the theme of his priest's essay of 1950 concerning the differences between evangelical and catholic spirituality, now bearing the fruits of his years in Eynsham. It represented a concern that was to abide, and one that would bear rich fruit in high office.

Stuart's first incumbency, which was also to be his last, was by any standards a resounding success – reviving a local church, creating ecumenical life, renewing a community, influencing a wider region, and attending to prayer and study. He certainly enjoyed it.

VICE-PRINCIPAL DAYS

John Taylor duly invited Stuart to become Vice-Principal. Stuart nowhere records his thoughts about the invitation, but clearly it was not an easy choice. The dreadful old vicarage had become a handsome and comfortable home, Brenda had conquered the garden, a young family was happily growing up and had many friends, the parish was humming with life, and Stuart was in the full bloom of his thirty-ninth year. Critically, he now knew the powerful reciprocal love between a vicar and his flock and the bonding of family life with place and people. Brenda remembers how they realized that this would be a movement from one kind of ministry to another, a setting out along a different path, a major change. Clearly, it was a struggle. But his love of study was insatiable and he was a born teacher, with a teacher's sense of creating community by imparting knowledge. Not ambitious in a worldly sense, he nevertheless was ambitious to achieve his natural potential and find spheres in which to do his best work. Eventually, in Brenda's words: 'God seemed to be pushing us to Wycliffe so finally we went.' After what was to be remembered as four and a half joyous years, it was time to pack up house once more. In January 1957, Stuart took up his college appointment.

The change brought difficulties. From living in a large house with a constant procession of people to – and often through – the front door they were once more in a private dwelling. From being known to everyone in the village they had become relative strangers in town. And instead of having father sharing mealtimes, the family had to get used to him working and dining in college. Their new house – number 4 Blackhall Road – did not help. Brenda hated it:

> It had four floors, two rooms on each floor, a basement kitchen and dining room, and no heating. Endless stairs, and as the top floor was occupied by a married student and his wife, for the first year all five children had to sleep in one room. Stuart had to turn the cloakroom into a study. I felt like a ghost at first. I knew very few people; Stuart was out all day and evening, but free sometimes in the afternoon. There was only a very small garden. We had no car, so I was stuck there. Once a week we invited students in for coffee. I missed Eynsham and parish life and so did our dog Toby – he kept walking back to Eynsham and once turned up there for the Parochial Church Council meeting. It was not my happiest time, but I think Stuart enjoyed the stimulus of college life and it proved to be an essential preparation for what followed.

The older children went to Headington School (the junior part) – paid for by my father. Timothy went to Crane's Court and we used to take him there on the back of a bicycle and fetch him back. On Sundays we went to St Giles Church where Canon Diggle was Rector. Occasionally friends visited us. For holidays we went to our caravan in Swanage – I was often cooking for ten on two gas burners.

We sometimes played tennis at Wycliffe. Very occasionally we went punting. I used to play the piano for the family to dance to. Stuart and I tried redecorating a room in the house, but it was not a success! I took part in some things at Wycliffe – but not much. I had no help in the house and no one to be with the children. It was a very confused time for me. However, sometime during our time in Oxford we were asked to take a German girl who was reading theology at Bonn University and wanted to do a year at Oxford. So Hilda Knoblauch came to live with us and was great fun, and became a good friend.

It was during these years, in 1955, that Stuart's and Brenda's fifth child, Alison, was born.

With regard to academic life, the requirement to teach the Old Testament made Stuart increasingly aware of the overlap and interplay of spiritual truth with political life. He believed the Old Testament revealed the ground plan and pattern of God's involvement in human affairs, embodying truths he believed to be for all mankind. This was to become a source of much wisdom in his own thinking. The appointment was critically important for his future work and he took to college life like a duck to water. The Principal's wife, Margaret Taylor, remembered how his years 'with us at Wycliffe Hall were extremely happy ones – his deep faith and ready wit were so much a part of him. I know he was very much loved and helped by staff and students.'

Involvement of students in parish life for pastoral experience and outreach was something he entered into with gusto. John Morris recollects one such occasion when, now himself a vicar, he played host to Stuart and a party of students at a baptismal service at St John's, Longbridge: 'On this occasion there was somewhere between a dozen and twenty babies and their families gathered at the font with a large congregation. Stuart was assisting me and I must have asked him, when we got to the individual baptisms, if he would like to do some of them. Thinking no doubt that this was a privilege best left to the parish priest, he tactfully declined. "No, no", he said. "You wash and I'll dry."'

As he got into his stride with his lecture programme he began to find space for research and decided to pick up the threads of the BD thesis. His proposed title at Eynsham would have made most of his congregation blink. It was: 'The controversy between John Wesley and William Law studied as a point of reference for the understanding and more accurate differentiation of the two elements in Christian spirituality commonly called Catholic and Evangelical'. Getting to the heart of any such difference was for him a matter of prime importance for Christian unity and effective mission.

Two things lay at the heart of this concern. One was a development in his own experience and practice of prayer. This appears to have stemmed from the great enlightenment at Christmas 1942, when prayer became a workable blend of penitence and thanksgiving which had nothing to do either with earning God's favour, or with a (self-defeating) pursuit of personal excellence. The other was a passionate desire for the unity in Christ of all believers. He believed that by examining the roots of different traditions – and particularly the less well documented and insufficiently studied roots of evangelical prayer – he would help in the work of Christian unity.

In the summer of 1957 Stuart broached his thesis idea with his friend Leslie Sutton of Lee Abbey. Stuart knew Leslie to be well versed in the writings of William Law and John Wesley and to know something of the difference that developed between them. Leslie modestly disclaimed academic distinction, but Stuart well knew that this seasoned missionary-evangelist-pastor was a man of deep prayer, wide reading, strong mind, and clear perception. His heart as well as his head knew a good deal about the inner journeys of Law and Wesley. He was also nurtured in the long tradition of evangelical piety which has sometimes gone 'underground' in society and has lacked the kind of devotional literature created by the catholic approach. The correspondence is worth quoting.

Stuart wrote to Leslie on 3 June 1957:

I think we often misunderstand the real nature of the issue between Catholic and Evangelical and often, too, maintain a curious dichotomy in our minds between the experience of justification and its dogmatic expression on the one hand and the actual practice of the spiritual life on the other. . . . There does, I believe, exist a genuine evangelical mysticism which is distinct from the Platonist type which so early made its mark in Catholic thought. They are distinct but I hope we should not find that they are antithetical, and it should be possible to approach a theology of the spiritual life which is at the same time evangelical and systematic (i.e. catholic). What is more I doubt if it could be done anywhere else but in the Church of England in which the two traditions do at least rub shoulders. . . . It has always seemed to me that it is at the devotional level that Evangelicals and Catholics find each other incomprehensible.

Stuart got a very prompt reply from Leslie: 'Now I don't want to put you off your stride but I do wonder if the difference is not between the Evangelical and Catholic but between the evangelist with his "subjective discovery" of the scriptural doctrine of justification by faith and the writer-mystic whose emphasis was on the obedience of love. (His growth is from law to love.)'

After a learned discourse on Wesley and Law, Leslie Sutton battened on to a theme close to his heart as a layman. He believed that the problem of the day lay in a clerical attitude that

> wants to ignore the fact that the gifts of the Spirit: faith, knowledge, prophecy, discernment (all these in the Holy Ghost and so in the Eternal Realm), may be given to the lay folk as well as the clergy. But the supernatural gifts of the Spirit, waited for, expected and received and used in the church, is not spoken about by the Clergy as a whole and by very few Evangelicals. If they did we would have revival groups springing up all over the Church and the truth would dawn upon the poor blindfolded bemused laity that Christ the Son of the living God dwelt within them to be manifested to the world. Tell your Wycliffe boys this. Don't let them become a closed shop Levitical class. Tell them you old rascal!

Eighteen months passed before Stuart again broached the idea of submitting a thesis. In the interval some new connections had been made between his abiding interest in its theme and the amount of attention he was now paying to the Old Testament. This quiet marriage of concerns became profoundly influential in his work and on 6 February 1959 he wrote to Canon Demant: 'The material seems to be collecting round some such title as the following: "The history of Christian spirituality reinterpreted in the light of the Biblical experience of the Remnant".' Pressure of work, and in due course another change of job, eventually closed down work on the thesis and it was not completed. The work was not lost, however, but formed an influential part of his outlook, and years later he would lecture on different aspects of prayer in Old Testament times as perceived before, during, and after the exile.

Here then was Stuart, busy with the 'technicalities' of college life, ever deeper into the serious study of the Old Testament while not neglecting the New, seeking to apply what time was available to tackling a theme lying at the heart of ecumenism. But that was not all. One vicar of his acquaintance recalls asking which contemporary theologians were producing the best insights for the new day. Stuart surprised him by saying that some of the best theological insights were coming from some certain modern poets. He was full of surprises.

His time as Vice-Principal also brought him an invitation to conduct a mission in America in 1959. This was at Corning in New York State and ran from 16 September to 6 October. It was a many-sided experience. In one of his six letters home, this veteran flyer said of his journey 'it was strange to be off the ground again for the first time after fourteen years'. Characteristically he counted the number of passengers: 'There were 76 on board and a more cosmopolitan crowd it would be difficult to imagine. . . . However the crew was very distinctly English – and aircrew RAF at that, so I felt reasonably at home.' Then for two and a half absorbing weeks he was plunged into the sort of wide-ranging programme that came to characterize the style of much of his later work. The ground plan was what his hosts called an 'institute' and showed the local church taking its teaching role very seriously. In addition to preaching at services, he gave three lectures on the Bible, three on church history, and undertook smaller-group work on Mark and Luke. Meanwhile, the enterprising rector behind the visit contrived occasions for Stuart to speak to college, business, and social groups of great variety, and with small groups and individuals, sometimes late into the night. He attended a diocesan conference and had lunch with the Bishop, and had an introduction to American church life that was to serve him well in years to come. It also marked the start of his last academic year at Oxford.

A NEW COLLEGE'S FIRST WARDEN

In the 1950s increasing numbers of older men were offering themselves for ordination, many of them non-graduates from industry and commerce, many of them married and with young children. Providing for their needs was a major challenge of the day and few felt this more strongly than the chairman of Wycliffe Hall's governing body, Christopher Chavasse, Bishop of Rochester.

Chavasse's interest in the matter doubtless owed something to family and personal circumstances. The son of Frances James Chavasse, second Bishop of Liverpool, he was brother of First World World double-VC Noel Chavasse, and had himself been wounded in the war. He believed his own cathedral community and precincts would make an ideal base for a new-style college. Founded in AD 604, the diocese was deeply rooted in English Christianity with a cathedral at the heart of the industrial Medway towns of Rochester, Strood, Chatham, and Gillingham. When a new dean, the Rt Revd William Stannard, a former Bishop of Woolwich, chose not to live in the huge old deanery, Chavasse seized upon it as the ideal home for a new college. CACTM (the Bishops' Central Advisory Council for the Training of the Ministry) sanctioned a trial year with Dean Stannard as temporary warden and the college opened in the autumn of 1959 with 21 students in a successful first year. Acting Principal was the Revd Alan Robson, a 29-year-old Oxford graduate in theology, who was helped by members of the cathedral chapter. Examination results satisfied CACTM inspectors, and so the search for a full-time warden and strengthened staff was authorized.

So far, so good. Then developments took a quirky turn. Alan Robson writes: 'In characteristically autocratic fashion Chavasse approached Stuart Blanch and the appointment was made without consulting the governing bodies of either college – in spite of his being chairman of both! I recall being told of the appointment by a delighted Bishop Chavasse who added with some relish: "I'm in hot water with both College Councils but if you really know what needs to be done do it yourself and then face the music!"' Brenda Blanch wryly recalls a different angle to the affair at Wycliffe Hall: 'Fury all round!'

Robson was anxious: 'Never having heard of Blanch,' he said, 'I was particularly apprehensive about the appointment of a man from a definite evangelical college to this college which provided for men of all shades of churchmanship. My wife Liz still remembers vividly how, having sought a meeting with Stuart at the earliest opportunity, I drove off to Wycliffe Hall one summer morning full of foreboding – and how that same evening I returned radiant with joy and bursting with enthusiasm for "this splendid man and his lovely wife and family".'

In the matter – if not the manner – of his choosing Stuart, Bishop Chavasse knew exactly what he was doing. The Oriel Canonry at Rochester had formerly been linked to an academic post in Hebrew at Oxford, and the new college itself was dedicated to men whom Stuart was well qualified to understand. His grasp of the situation was evident in the four-point strategy he brought to bear from day one – tackling community needs and family pressures as well as academic requirements and corporate worship. Alan Robson recalls how at their first meeting 'he wanted to introduce a form of the ancient monastic institution of the "Little Chapter"' – a daily 15-minute meeting of the whole college, staff and students, after breakfast. Other immediate aims were to provide local accommodation for men with families, and the organization of an annual 'Wives' Week'. These were essential parts of achieving a rich life of worship, and the best, most suitable, academic programme where the goal was to devise a format that challenged the most able while empowering the less academic.

The daily 'Little Chapter' was a great success. Everyone was free to make a complaint or suggestion and then a member of staff or a student would give a five-minute exposition of Scripture as a 'thought for the day'. 'It was Stuart who gave it the magic we all came to associate with it,' says Alan Robson. 'There was always an air of expectancy as we gathered in the common-room and awaited the arrival of the warden.' At the end of Stuart's first year, the college had 41 men in residence with numbers set to grow. With the college secure and led by the man of his choice, Bishop Chavasse retired in 1961 and was followed by Bishop David Say.

For Stuart and Brenda, now living in the adjacent gatehouse, the new college was a congenial sphere from the start. Cathedral life, however, was new territory. Canon Douglas Vicary, his one-time tutor at Wycliffe, and now headmaster of the city's King's School, says that in cathedral chapter meetings it was said of Stuart that 'he never opens his mouth except when it has to do with the college. I told this story to a friend – a practising psycho-analyst – and he said "Well, it's a bit like the King in Chinese drama mythology – he doesn't do much but everything goes well around him".' Among things that 'went well around him' was the early creation of a college chapel in the crypt.

The new chapel, immediately accessible to the college via a tiny garth, gave the college a beautiful chapel 'in the round' or, as Stuart put it, 'a chapel on the "table in the wilderness" principle'. Here students could lead their own services, something not possible in the cathedral services, advantageous though these were in other respects. Students rubbed shoulders with bishops, dean, archdeacons, and canons, and encountered moments to trea-sure, as when Archdeacon Laurie Harland reached the end of a beautifully read passage from the Old Testament, paused, and then said, 'Here endeth the wrong lesson', or as when a newly ordained deacon, having read the Gospel at an ordination, announced, 'Here endeth the Gospel'. 'I hope not, laddie, I hope not,' the Archdeacon was heard to mutter.

Stuart provided students with a startling introduction to their new life by setting an examination on their first day. The Revd John Green recalls: 'Stuart entered, dressed in sports gear, gave us an exam paper – and walked out telling us that we would not be shown the result of our efforts until we left Rochester . . . it was the subtlest, kindest, most diplomatic way imagin-able of cutting us down to size.' The two papers were devised to reveal what people knew or didn't know (a) about the world (b) about the Christian faith. Most of the questions were either multiple-choice or one-word answers. The first paper was about history, literature, art, science, and politics. The second tried to see how much a man knew or understood about his faith and the ministry. One question was: 'The priest in his ministry is found standing in a number of places: the pulpit, the pub, his study, the market place, the altar, the sick room, the classroom, the committee room. Place these in what you believe to be their (descending) order of priority.' Newcomers were then introduced to all the subjects of the full syllabus. Greek and Hebrew were included to help provide a 'feel' for the original languages of the Bible. In this the college had the tuition of Laurie Ford, a minor canon of the cathedral who provided the texts out of his own pocket.

Alan Robson recalls:

The size of the syllabus left us with little latitude for radical experimentation, but Stuart was determined that these students needed a different approach from the standard lectures and essays. Most of the work was covered in seminars. Members of a group would be given a 'work sheet' on the subject for the week. It would outline the nature of the subject, and main works to be read and the sort of questions to be answered. All students would be required to cover the whole subject, but each would be set one of the questions to deal with in detail. With the handful of men over 40 – and therefore excused from taking the General Ordination Examination – Stuart was able to experiment more radically. His most interesting project was what he called the 'Comprehensive Curriculum'. He worked on particular themes, largely doctrinal, and related each to the major areas of theological interest. So, for example, in a fortnight's work on the subject of the incarnation, the work sheet would be set out something like this:

OT: Genesis 1, 2 and 3, Proverbs 8, Wisdom of Solomon 7.
NT: 1 John 1, Philippians 2, Colossians 1.
History: The Arian Controversy.
Doctrine: The Nicene Creed, the Church as the Body of Christ, Sacrament as visible 'Word'.
Liturgy: Propers for Christmas.
Church's mission as 'continuation of incarnation', the Church in the world.
Incarnation and life of prayer.

To this outline would be added a reading list and a number of questions to be discussed. This 'thematic' structure of study has since become the great educational orthodoxy, but without a sufficiently critical acceptance of its limitations. Stuart used this scheme for men whose training had perforce to be condensed. It could also be used for men doing a full course, but not at the expense of acquiring the necessary disciplines.

Stuart taught the Old Testament, and Alan Robson taught the New. Two local vicars lectured on a part-time basis: Dr Ray Selby on doctrine, and the Revd David Cox (Chairman of the Jungian Guild of Pastoral Psychology) on the more clinical side of pastoral studies. Laurie Ford taught Hebrew and Greek. Canon Ross Hook, later to be Bishop of Bradford and chief of staff at Lambeth, lectured in church history. Dr Ashfield, the cathedral organist, instructed individuals in the proper singing of the services. 'Under Stuart,' writes Alan Robson, 'we were all primarily friends and colleagues in a common purpose. Each of us came from a different ecclesiastical tradition and we differed quite markedly in our theology. This made for some interesting and sometimes quite intense discussion, but one recalls not a single instance of anyone taking offence or of our fellowship being disturbed.'

This was the team, and this the method, encountered by students from all walks of life. The Revd Tony Smith, who came to the college from life as a farmer, writes: 'Previous sermons in our parish churches could hardly have prepared us for the excitement that Stuart conveyed, the wish to know more. It wasn't until much later that it became apparent that his intention was to break down wrongly based faith and replace it with something based on true scholarship and an excitement for the gospel.'

Stuart's personal style as a teacher is remembered as 'different and refreshing'. This recollection of John Green is typical: 'One day Stuart blew, a little late, into the common-room where the seminar was to be held. Without introduction he said dramatically: "'And David danced before the Lord with all his might, and he was girded with a linen ephod' (2 Samuel 6.14). What's this all about?" He then proceeded to extract from that one verse astonishing pearls of wisdom about sacral kingship, the significance of the ark and of the covenant, of Jerusalem and the ritual of worship. . . . He continually warned about being dogmatic. I was taught to read the accepted authors, but continually to think for myself. "It is accepted that . . ." was out. "Some/most scholars are of the opinion that . . ." was in. As a result the books on the first shelf above my desk are reference books, concordances, various versions, and lexicons.'

Having to uncover the foundations of their own beliefs and then having to dig deeper was a requirement that brought distress to some. Stuart had a very sensitive nose for anxiety and had ways of dealing with it. One was at the daily 'Little Chapter' and another was in his compline address on Friday evenings. One such address is remembered in this way:

We were approaching the end of term, the men were getting tired and it was at such times that morale began to suffer and the more sensitive began to wonder whether faith was going to survive. Stuart took as his text a verse from the resurrection stories in the fourth Gospel: 'They [the angels at the tomb] said to her: "Woman, why are you weeping?" She said to them, "Because they have taken away my Lord and I know not where they have laid him"' (John 20.13). Mary had come to the tomb *certain* of where Jesus was and how things were with him. She was distraught to find that he was not there. She ascribed his disappearance to some hostile 'they': 'they have taken away my Lord'. She had not considered the exciting possibility that Jesus was not to remain bound up in grave clothes and sealed in the tomb. Always he breaks free – to meet us where we are (Jesus is at Mary's side) and to give us a wider and deeper vision. ('Do not cling to me . . . go and tell my brethren, I am ascending to my Father and your Father . . .')

'Such sermons as these,' says Alan Robson, 'were not merely ad hoc sermons applicable to a particular situation. They came across with real force because they expressed something that was clearly central to Stuart's own religious life.'

Stuart sent periodic newsletters to help families feel part of the community and each year organized a 'Wives' Week' when wives and children could reside in or near the college, share in its life, and take part in the lectures and discussions. Two or three clergy wives would try to prepare the wives for what lay ahead, and in all of this Brenda played a leading role. Special attention was given to the children who had their own programme of games and outings while at the same time discovering something of what Daddy was up to while away from home. One former student records that his children were in tears when the week came to an end.

The world and its problems, on the doorstep of the college, were regarded as an educational asset:

Every student experienced the life and worship of parish churches varying in churchmanship, sociological setting and strategy, and all were given hospital experience. In addition to small teams appointed to the local hospital, St Bart's, all students were on a rota which provided two men each day to say evening prayers on the wards. Several students found themselves attached for a period to the chaplain of Borstal, of the training ship *Arethusa*, or of the oil refinery. At least one who had the Borstal experience was later to serve as a prison chaplain and a number of men were later involved in hospital and industrial chaplaincies. Maidstone Prison was only a few miles away and, while we did not attach students to that chaplaincy there were several men who actually shared life in the cells for a few days.

Meanwhile, the net was cast wide for speakers to talk at Wednesday evening lectures and discussions. Among the visitors were MPs, parliamentary candidates, Foreign Office officials, civil engineers (engaged in building the M2 bridge over the Medway), and police chiefs. Games also were encouraged. Cricket on a local school field had an element of 'needle' when the opponents were Wycliffe Hall, and volleyball and croquet were played with gusto in the college grounds.

Stuart had been at Rochester for little more than a year when the Principal of Wycliffe Hall, John Taylor, was appointed Bishop of Sheffield and the hunt was on for his successor. One day Stuart approached Alan Robson with disturbing news:

> He told me he was being hard pressed to accept the post, and that very morning had received a letter from Archbishop Donald Coggan urging him to return to Oxford. He asked me what I thought. In spite of my dismay I think I told him that if he were at all ambitious he would certainly do well to go, but all of us at Rochester would be very sad. To my great delight he then told me that he had just written to the Archbishop saying that if the Almighty had intended him to come to Rochester he couldn't possibly be wanting him to move so soon.

College life is probably best summed up in its worship. Stuart introduced variety by alternating compline with 'home-grown' experimental services that encouraged creative thinking about liturgy. Those that proved to be of continuing value were eventually assembled as a book of 'Community Prayers', all vividly relating Scripture's ancient imagery to contemporary needs. Friday compline included an address – a 'college sermon'– bringing the week's work to an end, and was looked forward to with keen interest by the community and, according to Alan Robson, 'never more so than when Stuart was to be the preacher'. The content was often prompted by the sort of questions and concerns he knew to be current in the community at the time.

The last task set by Stuart was to ask the men to complete a questionnaire about the course. Two years later, in the light of their early experience of ministry, they were invited to re-evaluate their views. In general, the first response complained of too much academic theology, the second showed a wish for more. Clearly, Stuart was making a major contribution both to the method and spirituality of theological education.

Involvement in the college community made the Blanch family life much easier than at Oxford. They did not have a television of their own, but would watch the set with the students in the common-room. And there were games. Tim Blanch recalls: 'When I was younger it didn't take much to get him out of his study for a kick-around. I used to go and say "Do you fancy a game?"' The reply would be, 'Yes, give me five minutes and I'll be with you.' For the children, the family habit of playing games indoors and outdoors continued into adulthood, with table-tennis always a firm favourite. Brenda and Susan were both pianists and they would play duets together, while Susan also played the viola and flute, Hilary played the violin, Angela the cello, and Tim the clarinet. Stuart, who had taken piano lessons as a young man, joined in and later tackled the flute. For a brief period of time they would play together, but movements away to university imposed its own time limit on the fun. Holidays, however, presented a challenge. For their first two years they went to France, but when holiday plans for the summer of 1963 fell through, the college secretary mentioned her brother's cottage between Marloes and St Brides in Pembrokeshire, which happened to be free. They took it. The five beaches, the abundance of birds, the proliferation of flowers, and the fine walking country made it an ideal location. In 1965 they were able to buy a tumble-down cottage with a lot of ground round it at the west end of Marloes, and live alongside it in a caravan while they gradually transformed it into a comfortable home. With Susan by this time at Durham University and the rest of the family variously occupied during vacations, they told the family: 'During the holidays this is home and if you want to come home you must come here.' Brenda said, 'Marloes was ours and we could do what we liked with it. Stuart loved it. . . . He used to do the sandwiches for lunch if we were going out, pretty good doorsteps. He would read, and we played cricket on the sands and swam. We'd always have a swarm of people down there – the family's friends. The catering wasn't too easy. I exchanged one sink for another, nevertheless I loved it.'

Gradually they fell into an annual pattern of visits that was to mark most of their working life, going for a week after Christmas, a week after Easter and, when not abroad, for four weeks in the summer. Among their friends in the small community was the local rector, Peter Davies, and his wife who, in a parish well removed from major ecclesiastical goings-on, enjoyed this wider contact.

They were enjoying life to the full, but 1965 brought another call for thoughts of a move. Again John Taylor was involved in it. As Bishop of Sheffield he was keen for Stuart to look at the vacant post of provost at Sheffield Cathedral, though in the event the appointment went to another. Then in 1966 the much-loved and long-serving Bishop of Liverpool, Clifford Martin, announced his retirement. In his diocese was the Huyton

constituency of the then Prime Minister Harold Wilson, whose first choice
for Martin's successor he is said to have made personally. The appointment
was declined. Soon afterwards the Bishop of Sheffield's wife took a phone call
for her husband who was away. It was from Canon Reginald Lindsay of Liverpool, asking questions about her husband's former Vice-Principal. She
remembers speaking of his high estimate of Stuart and it was part of a process
that resulted one day in a phone call from Number 10 Downing Street to the
Bishop of Rochester. David Say was informed that there was a letter in the
post for Stuart, and recalls that he was told 'rather firmly' to make sure that
they did not have another refusal. The Bishop writes: 'I waited half an hour
or so after I knew the post had arrived and went down to call on Stuart. He
opened the door to me himself and was surprised to see me and could not
understand why I had come.'

Unaware of Liverpool's episcopal vacancy Stuart had already opened his
mail, and coming across a letter purporting to come from 10 Downing Street
had been exploring the possibility of a student prank. (Recently a student had
walked into Stuart's study and run a tape measure over him before leaving
without a word, a ritual resulting in the presentation to him of a priest's
cloak.) It isn't clear where Stuart's enquiries had got to when the Bishop rang
his doorbell, but David Say recalls: 'When I told him I thought he might have
had a letter from the PM his off-hand response was "Oh that!"' The fact was
that he did not keep a list of episcopal vacancies and hadn't been aware of
Liverpool's need for a new bishop.

In later years Stuart spoke of his unpreparedness for episcopal office. He
had always wanted to have spheres of maximum influence for the sake of the
gospel, but that wish does not seem to have included thoughts of a bishopric,
a job carrying duties that might impede the use of his particular range of gifts.
It was clearly something he had not thought about a great deal. Comments
during his days in India had included a heartfelt wish that bishops be
approachable, friendly, and hospitable, and their homes a meeting place for
disciples and seekers. Beyond that, he had said little on the subject. But his
spirit was ready on the day the call came. Recalling his early morning visit to
him, Bishop Say said: 'He never questioned for one moment that it was his
duty to say "Yes".'

~ 4 ~

Numbers:
A Bishop's Many Tasks

LIVERPOOL

Nothing pleases a Liverpudlian more than to observe that if you draw a circle round a map of the British Isles, its centre – give or take a mile or two – would be Liverpool. Certainly its remarkable history as one of the world's great seaports has given the city and region a powerful sense of identity and helped to create the distinctive mixture of its population. A survey carried out in 1998 showed that 20 languages are spoken in the city. The resultant blend is probably unique. In 1966, however, the city of Liverpool was busy knocking much of itself down and rehousing thousands of people, both in the tower blocks that replaced streets, and – more numerously – in the city's growing fringe of housing estates and new towns.

Coming into Lime Street Station through its daunting, smoke-blackened, underground approach tunnels, Stuart and Brenda would have emerged into a city still bearing many scars of wartime bombing. The blitz had claimed over 2,000 Merseyside lives and was still a powerful part of community memory. Children still played on 'bombdies' – their name for areas of residual destruction – and people being moved from long-term homes for new-build areas accused the council of 'finishing Adolf's work for him'. Thirty years later cliché-ridden national newscasting is still apt to pick out areas of dilapidation as Merseyside's badge of recognition, while Liverpudlians themselves are keen to point to the city's spectacular waterfront, its great buildings, fine parks, leafy suburbs, splendid orchestra, theatres, universities, and strategic location.

In the 1960s, though, the home-grown phenomenon of the Beatles succeeded in reviving Liverpool's image around the world. It was at a time when the prospect of travel to the moon was becoming a reality and the tingle factors of Beatlemania and space travel combined on Merseyside to create a mental cocktail that transformed the local outlook on the grimy sprawl of a struggling city. It also seemed to inspire the city's two great football teams, Everton and Liverpool, with the latter, under Bill Shankley, embarking on a long period of dominance in the game. In the world of time and space, Liverpool mattered. That, at least, was how it felt. It was a stirring feeling, and it affected Merseyside church folk as much as anyone else.

Liverpool's church life vividly reflected the city's distinctive history. Deep-rooted Roman Catholic, Anglican, and Free Church communities had long lived cheek by jowl and not always happily. Before the war there were bitter rivalries between Catholics and Protestants. Helping each other in the shared tragedies of the blitz and other wartime sorrows did much to put old differences into a human perspective, but strife of sorts there still was. Other faith communities were also part of the city's spiritual life. The strong Jewish community had a distinguished history and creative energy, and Moslem and Hindu communities were putting down roots that were to see the arrival of temple and mosque ten years later. Stuart's new diocese, however, comprised far more than Liverpool. It took in a semi-circle of south-west Lancashire and Cheshire which included the wealthy resort of Southport, the ancient market town of Ormskirk, the industrial town of St Helens, the coal-mining region around the vigorous town of Wigan, the chemical centre of Widnes, and the ancient and newly booming town of Warrington. There was also a good number of rural parishes with farming communities. For Brenda, who had never been north of Birmingham, it was a new world.

Symbolic of the whole was the unfinished cathedral, already dominating the Merseyside skyline, and well on its way to its present status as the largest cathedral in the Anglican Communion and the fifth largest church in the world. Already it had the world's highest and heaviest peal of bells, and one of the world's biggest organs. But in 1966 a decision still had to be taken about whether or not to complete it. Meanwhile, at the other end of the aptly named Hope Street, the Roman Catholic Metropolitan Cathedral was rapidly approaching completion. These two buildings and their linking road were signs of the times.

Bishops are used to commiserating with their clergy about the problems of moving. For the Blanch family, the move was as awkward as for any. Happily, Susan was now settled at Durham, reading music, but Hilary was about to do A-levels and so, being in the same form as the Bishop of Rochester's daughter, Anne, stayed on with the Bishop's family in Rochester for a year. Angela, who was boarding at Headington School and had just done O-levels at 15, also stayed on and was joined for a while by 11-year-old Alison, while Tim, due to go to King's at Canterbury, remained in Rochester at King's, with Alison subsequently coming up to Liverpool to be a day girl at Huyton College. Such matters weighed heavily on Stuart's and Brenda's minds as they came to their fifth house in 20 years. Bishop's Lodge was, and is, in the prosperous and pleasant suburb of Woolton where the quarry bites deeply into the hillside below St Peter's Church, itself built of the rock on which it stands. The same quarry supplied the stone for Liverpool Cathedral and gave to the Beatles their original name of the Quarrymen. Also in Woolton was the home of George Andrew Beck, the Roman Catholic Archbishop of Liverpool.

Waiting to welcome Stuart and Brenda was a seasoned and talented diocesan staff. The suffragan Bishop of Warrington, Laurence Brown, was an older man who had come to his own post from being Archdeacon of Lewisham, and in due course would go on to be Bishop of Birmingham. For these first crucial years his great experience, ebullient good humour, and robust common sense would be there in friendship and support. A wealth of experience was embodied in the two archdeacons, Hubert Seed Wilkinson, Archdeacon of Liverpool, and the widely travelled Eric Evans, Archdeacon of Warrington. Completing the inner staff was the lay diocesan secretary, Jack Todd, who would himself be ordained in middle age by his new bishop. At the cathedral a new dean, Edward Patey, had arrived from Coventry in 1964, exchanging one twentieth-century cathedral for another. In taking on a building of such controversial scale and grandeur, dauntingly yet to be completed in days seemingly out of key with Gothic splendour, Edward Patey had taken the long view of a man of faith. From a splendid base that was still partly a building site, his work proved to be radically ecumenical and directly related to the great social issues of the day.

CONSECRATION AND ENTHRONEMENT

Stuart's consecration was in York Minster on 25 March 1966, the Feast of the Annunciation. On that day he was given a leather-bound five-year diary with the date of his consecration stamped on the cover. His entries began at once with the bald statement: 'Consecration in York Minster'. But at some point he made an entry on the date of 2 January where he wrote: '"I looked and there was none to help and I wondered that there was none to uphold" (Isaiah 63.5).' Maybe he was feeling the need for the kind of induction course not to be available to new bishops for some years to come. But he went on to add: 'God needs mighty men – the Abrahams, the Moses, the Isaiahs, the Augustines, the Luthers of this world.'

In asking Canon Geoffrey Rogers, former warden of Lee Abbey, to be the preacher at his consecration, Stuart was reflecting the important role of Lee Abbey in the early years of his ministry. Canon Rogers, in 1966 Diocesan Missioner in Bishop Cuthbert Bardsley's Coventry diocese, had been a missionary in India before coming to Lee Abbey, and there was little for Stuart's comfort in what he had to say in his sermon about a bishop's job. The workload of a modern bishop, he said, was such that no man in his right senses would want it. But he had good things to say about God's grace and God's man.

At Bishop's Lodge they inherited the services of chauffeur-gardener Joe Kelly, and his wife Muriel, who lived in the cottage in the grounds of the Lodge. They formed a happy partnership, and for non-driver Stuart, one of special value. 'I've tried driving two or three times,' he once said to a friend, 'but I never mastered the co-ordination of hand and foot and after bumping into things quite a bit I decided not to go into it seriously.' Having managed his clerical duties by bicycle for 17 years, he had no intention of letting his brand-new Moulton bicycle (a gift from Rochester) rust in the Lodge's ample garages and so regularly cycled downhill to Church House, returning chauffeur-driven with the bike in the boot. Brenda, however, had learned to drive at Rochester and they now bought a Morris 1000 Estate. Its registration letters TUD provided a ready-made name and 'TUD' was soon to be seen all over the diocese with Brenda at the wheel and the bike in the back.

The enthronement was set for a date of special significance for this lover and student of the earliest Gospel. It was 25 April, St Mark's Day. Edward Patey remembers that Stuart had entertained some anxieties about it: 'He greatly disliked the idea of being "enthroned" and I had to assure him that the entire service would have a strong emphasis on servanthood. . . . He was relieved to know that he was not expected to wear a mitre in the cathedral – and never did. In fact, I never saw him wearing this somewhat bizarre form of headgear until in York Minster – and even then I think he put it on with diffidence.' The service was to start in traditional style with the Bishop hammering with his staff upon the great doors of the Rankin Porch. Situated on the south side of the nave, this was in those days the main entrance. Standing on the otherwise deserted area outside the great door, he turned to his chaplain and said: 'I do hope we've come to the right place.'

The first years of his episcopate were lived against the background of war, both in Vietnam and Biafra. Europe witnessed the fate of Czechoslovakia's fight for freedom. The American civil rights movement was passing through epic days. Space travel was expanding human knowledge, imagination, and aspirations. Drugs, the hippie culture, and sexual licence pervaded the public imagination. And brooding over all was the Cold War. Family life was awash with images of the world's troubles and thrills, delivered into the home on a tidal wave of television. The excitement of change, shot through with images of tragedy and overshadowed by the threat of nuclear war, marked the way most people were experiencing life in the developed world.

His enthronement sermon struck a resounding note. The needs of the world and the challenge to the Church were gigantic, and on the scale of Goliath. But Goliath had to reckon with David. Edward Patey comments: 'I think that in some ways Stuart saw himself as a little David fighting against the giant forces of the secular world. And he was certain of the effectiveness of the stones in his sling.'

Stuart's friendship and co-operation with Edward Patey was important to both of them. It also benefited the diocese and the cathedral, and became a vital factor in the region's ecumenical life. Local wartime experience had led to the first steps in ecumenical co-operation, and in 1944 a committee of Anglican, Roman Catholic, and Free Church members was formed to tackle the work of rebuilding bombed churches. That body's work ended in 1950, but it was the basis of a group reconstituted in 1963 under the chairmanship of Bishop Laurence Brown to help promote co-operation in planning. Bishop Brown was also chairman of an active ecumenical Churches' Youth Advisory Committee. Things were already moving when the Liverpool Churches Ecumenical Council was formed in 1966 with Edward Patey as its first chairman. Plans to build the new Roman Catholic Cathedral on a fine and long-established site among some of the university's older buildings gave a high-profile focus to ecumenical interest. The two great buildings – one nearing a more than 70-year process of construction and the other starting out on a spectacular two-year building programme – were situated at either end of the aptly named Hope Street. The dean and the Catholic Cathedral administrator were only too pleased to respond to encouragement from their respective bishops to develop close links between the two.

A PATTERN OF WORK

In thinking out his own pattern of work Stuart inherited the help of Bishop Martin's long-time secretary, Pamela Edis. It was immediately clear to her that, though very much in tune with Bishop Martin's style and spirit, Stuart would go about his business in a different way. He elected to do most of his administrative and interviewing work at Bishop's Lodge, coming into Church House on an ad hoc basis for board meetings or for any interviews more conveniently held there. He would usually be in Church House twice a week. Once there, however, he had the knack of somehow pervading it, taking a stroll through the offices and having a word with anyone who came across his path. He and Laurence Brown were often to be encountered conversing, with habitual chuckles, wherever they met each other between rooms on public corridors.

Bishop Gordon Bates (Bishop of Whitby 1983–2000), then diocesan youth officer, recalls a characteristic event and the effect it had on him: 'My office was on the very top floor . . . in the attic, I suppose. The Bishop's suite was on the first floor. . . . Shortly after Stuart's arrival I needed to talk with him about a particular youth project in the city and went down to ask Pam Edis to book me a time . . . half an hour later there was a knock on my office door and in walked the new Diocesan Bishop with the words, "Gordon, I hear that you want to see me".'

Pam Edis found him to be a man of discipline who 'had a terrific inner life of thought, and awareness'. She also discovered that he was a teacher, becoming aware that she was herself being taught as she worked: 'He was concerned with structures and with using consultants. He was a thinker who would get his thinking transformed into action by other people – he was an enabler.' He was also a rapid administrator. Colleagues in York observed later that his years in insurance made for a clean desk! Clergy and others were used to getting a reply to or acknowledgement of their letters by return of post. But his daily session with correspondence reached a cut-off point at 11 a.m., which was the deadline for his appointment with study. And study for him meant the Bible. He used to say that he spent an hour with the Bible to make sure that he was living in the real world. Another fixture in his day was a spell of quiet before the evening journeys to services or meetings.

Two days after his enthronement he was tackling something of a log-jam when he conducted the first of his confirmations at St Anne's, Wigan. With so many to do, and with as yet no built-in variety in his stock of suitable sermons, he promptly rethought his approach to an endlessly repetitive task which he knew was a vital once-in-a-lifetime experience for the confirmees. His preconceived idea of an 'improving discourse' for young Christians was replaced by the attempt to pass on the message God urgently has for all mankind when so many are in church. Of that his tongue would never tire. On that understanding he was to thrive. He seemed to feel that he was properly launched, when on 3 May, eight days after his enthronement, he wrote in his diary: '"I will thank the Lord for giving me counsel" (Psalm 16.8) – the beginning of things in Liverpool.'

Family life was beginning to find its new pattern and pleasures, and among them for the menfolk was football – Stuart and Tim going together to watch Liverpool play at Anfield. 'Dad absolutely loved football,' Tim recalls. 'Cricket, in a low key sort of way. But, with football, getting very excited – shouting and jumping up and down! We watched the 1966 World Cup. We didn't have television, we watched it in Joe's [the chauffeur's] house – Joe was away. The electricity coin-meter ran out at a critical point in the match. We couldn't find it – we were rushing around with the coin – and when we found it in a cupboard under the stairs we had missed a goal. So we got a telly soon after that.'

Entries over the next few weeks of 1966 give some idea of the undercurrent of Stuart's thought during those early days. Was it right to feel pleasure in the exercise of his new powers? Were there dangers in feeling strong? What was his real job? How does God work in the lives of human beings? (7 May): '"The Lord hath pleasure in the prosperity of his servants" (Psalm 35.27). A liberating view of God – we need not be afraid of success'; (10 May): '"To give knowledge of salvation unto his people" (Benedictus) – the comprehensive function of a minister of the Gospel, to make His people aware of what He has done for us'; (20 May): '"The spirit of the Lord began to stir him in Mahanehdan between Zorah and Eshtaol" (Judges 13.25). What strange hidden portent was given to him that he should become aware of powers at work in him? When was my Mahanehdan?' (28 May): '"I will pour out my spirit on all flesh" (Joel 2.28). Strictly irrelevant to Pentecost when God poured out his Spirit on some flesh, but it expresses a glorious hope, a rationale for mankind, an end-product of this mysterious life-process'; (9 June): '"The Lord of hosts . . . the God of Jacob" (Psalm 46.7). What a strange magnanimity – and yet not to the Hebrew mind. The high and lofty one who inhabits eternity is the friend of every little man who grapples with himself and with his circumstances.'

Thoughts like these ran like threads through his days, and with them he pondered the contents of two letters sent to him shortly after his enthronement. They, and his response to them, would – with their consequences – prove to be historic. In his pamphlet *Future Patterns of Episcopacy*, written in 1991, he describes what happened:

Only a few months after I came to the diocese I received two letters by the same post. One was from a distinguished Roman Catholic educationalist in Norfolk and the other from an evangelical clergyman in Cornwall. They wrote clearly without prior consultation, but their message was almost identical: 'Isn't it time that the churches in this country ignored their differences and worked together in united mission to the nation?' . . . My first reaction was to write a courteous letter to them both, saying that I would give their suggestion some consideration – later. And then I would have put them in my 'too difficult' file. But I paused (there is much to be said for a pause). Was it just a coincidence that I should get two letters on the same day on the same subject from such different sources? So I wrote a holding letter and promised to write again when I had taken counsel. But how to take counsel and where? It occurred to me that the northern convocation would be meeting in the next few weeks. With Donald Coggan's encouragement I proposed to submit the letters to the northern House of Bishops. They were received with interest but, it has to be said, with little sign of response. We had other things on our mind.

The Archbishop suggested that I should take the letters home and broach the subject with the Roman Catholic Archbishop of Liverpool on the obvious principle that if such an approach could work in that strife torn city it could work anywhere. But the omens were not good. I hardly knew my counterpart in Liverpool, although he was thought to be a somewhat conservative churchman. Our houses were separated by a park and when our respective dogs met there they invariably fought each other. However, I went to meet him. I found him a gracious, hospitable man, with whom it was easy to converse. When he said goodbye, he made what was for me a very significant remark: 'If this is of God we must do it.'

LEARNING AND TEACHING

Having arrived without the prior experience of being a suffragan bishop, Stuart whimsically talked to his diocesan conference about learning to be a bishop. This was typical of his disarming informality. But the sense of a fine mind in control of a wide range of material created instant respect and the attention won by his talks. Amid the huge changes of the 1960s and 1970s he was able to provide the diocese with a powerful sense of the present moment both in history and mission and his presidential addresses to diocesan synods were listened to with delight. Once, before the diocesan synod discussed its financial business, he devoted ample time to expounding a psalm. It shed new light on the business agenda, which was then tackled with clarity and despatch. Another time a group of clergy asked that for a certain synod all business be transacted in the morning so that he could lecture to them in the afternoon. He agreed, and that afternoon there was a full house with no defaulters.

An early priority was to plan a series of lectures in the cathedral for the spring of 1967. This was the first chance most people had of hearing him talk in ordered length about the world they lived in and of the God who made it. With the new space exploration programme affecting perceptions of the world, his theme – 'Faith in a Space Age' – met a special need. His opening words, 'Faith lost in a space age will only be recovered in a space age', at once set the present day within the story of mankind.

In 1967 people were aware that their mental landscape was being redrawn and Stuart's task was to link that landscape with the world of the Bible. He showed orthodoxy to be endlessly inventive. The disciples of Jesus, he said, saw Christ as the hinge on which the universe turns. What does the life of Christ say to us now if we treat it as a genuine incarnation of reality? The creed makers, he said, were grappling with phenomena so real that they 'could not bend them to their philosophy'. They had concentrated on the person of Christ rather than his function, thus 'providing what the educated Englishman thinks he believes'. Consequently, popular Christianity was struggling with two wrong ideas, namely: that God cannot suffer, and that human beings cannot be perfect. This double error, he pointed out, makes the idea of the incarnation impossible and divides grace and nature, sacred and secular, Church and world. In the space age such thinking produces a sense of acute isolation and friendlessness. But a real incarnation has something to say about the possibility of human perfection, which in Christ is not in his avoidance of error, but in his relation to the Father. He is the summary or climax of human evolution, that to which we all move if we are willing. And mankind is called to be the body of this Christ – a thought that he contrasted with some modern novelists 'shut up in their own experience, bounded by the horizons of a single human life'. Second, with regard to God's nature, he is not by nature remote, though there is the possibility that 'we want him dead in order that we may control our own lives'. He is the 'one in whom we live and move and have our being'; he is 'in the midst'; he is personal, and the Christ-man is our best guide to God.

With the coming of the space age our cosy world had gone for ever. 'The "mind" of the universe is revealed in events rather than cosmic or natural patterns.' This poses problems for the Greek view of pattern and order, and for the humanist view of man imposing his pattern upon the universe. But the Judaeo-Christian view sees man as the locus of ultimate reality and all history finds its significance in an event that makes sense of all other events, the incarnation in Christ of the logos – the 'explanatory word'.

Creation is God's work. Contingency is real. The universe is violent in heaven and on earth, but it is 'the womb of love', and we are the victims and the masters of it. Mankind is the agent of a cosmic process – 'homo laudens'. God may be thought of as a composer and conductor – composing as he conducts, with the universe as his orchestra, and man – temperamental, brilliant, capable of improvising and making terrible mistakes – is the soloist. God is involved. Indeed, he 'changes', inasmuch as suffering is change; he 'becomes', inasmuch as he achieves his ends (a reference to process theology), but he is supreme. While this may all seem to be far removed from the desperate problems of daily life as experienced by many local citizens, winning this ground among people who attended cathedral lectures had much to do with helping the masses of people who would never think of going to such events. He was moving them towards involvement with the God who is involved with the world. There were large and attentive audiences, including many Roman Catholic priests and nuns.

Stuart was well launched upon his work of giving people a framework for their thinking, and his capacity for doing so was to be widely sought. One of the concerns of the day was to think out Christianity in the secular terms of unchurched people, an endeavour that seemed to expect little help from the Bible. Stuart, however, found in the Bible the very tools required for the job. In October 1967 he was invited to give the prestigious William Temple series of lectures in Coventry where the theme was 'The Revelation of God through the World', and his three lecture titles were 'The Church and the Secular City', 'The Church and the Affluent Society', and 'The Church and the Establishment'.

AFFIRMING AND PLANNING

His approach to his work combined long-term strategy with swift response to signs of life and to initiatives not of his own planning. He had his own clear objectives and plans that he believed to be of God and he pursued these with tenacity. But he was keenly aware that God was active in many people and ways of which neither he nor his watchful staff could be aware. Looking for signs of life was part of his understanding of a bishop's job. Planning what to build depended at least in part upon the living stones available. He took improvisation seriously, and it was in fact an important part of his method.

John Higham was a young incumbent who wanted to create a home for young offenders newly released from prison. 'I'll need a small parish with a big house,' he said. Stuart co-operated and the result was a home where four or five ex-offenders at a time were in residence for extended periods of up to a year, a facility that continued to operate for over twenty years. Hard at work in the racially mixed and deprived district of Liverpool 8 was the energetic GP Dr Leslie Bruce, who was feeling strongly drawn to carry on his medical work as a priest. Before the days of non-stipendiary ministry and non-residential clergy training, Stuart's decision and direction was unfussy, direct, and enabling. He required Leslie to give 18 months to doing the Archbishop of Canterbury's Certificate of Religious Knowledge and said: 'Do this for 18 months and then I will ordain you,' adding, 'You'll find that certain clergy will be against you. But don't worry. If it should be a problem come and see me and we'll sort it out.' Leslie, in fact, encountered no criticism at all. People in Liverpool 8 took him and his dog-collar and stethoscope to their heart and the day before his ordination a passing Liverpudlian said to him in the street: 'Hey Doc, I hear you're going to be ordained tomorrow. That's a bloody good idea!'

His response to requests for help from clergy was equally prompt and frank. Chaplain Superintendent of the Mersey Mission to Seamen was former wartime RAF pilot, the Revd (later Canon) Bob Evans. With a problem requiring episcopal help, he rang Church House, was put straight through to the Bishop, and the following conversation took place: 'Bishop, I've got a problem.' 'Is the problem personal?' 'Yes.' 'Is it your own?' 'No.' 'We don't really know each other. I'll come and have lunch. Don't mention your problem until after it. Let's get to know each other first.' At lunch the former pilot and the former navigator boxed the compass of conversation before dealing with the matter in hand. Bob Evans said: 'I felt I was dealing with a Father in God, and I don't use the term lightly. He was one of the very few bishops I knew in over fifty years' ministry whom I felt I acted for vicariously.'

The then vicar of Holy Trinity, Wavertree, Malcolm Forrest, was making out his list of Easter Communions for the sick. He had invited a dying parishioner who was not confirmed to receive Communion with his regularly communicant wife on Maundy Thursday and met the response: 'What I'd really like is to be confirmed.' Malcolm phoned the Bishop on Monday of Holy Week. Stuart arrived on that Maundy Thursday morning en route for another appointment, confirmed the man, then celebrated the Eucharist. 'It transformed Maundy Thursday for me for ever after,' said Canon Forrest. As an example of one-to-one episcope among the laity it did not stand alone. Brian Harris recalls his special home visit to confirm and then give Communion to a 90-year-old former suffragette in Kirkby. He could not, of course, respond to every pastoral opportunity in the same way, but it was high on his list of priorities to do so when possible. One Friday night fire largely destroyed the handsome church of St Luke, Great Crosby. On the next Sunday, services were held in the church hall. The following Thursday, the vicar, Raymond Lee, gathered his PCC to face the future. On that evening, following a confirmation service, Stuart said to Pam Edis, who was driving him: 'Let's go and see Raymond.' He walked unannounced into the solemn assembly and spoke individually to each member. 'It lifted our spirits at once and we never looked back,' said Canon Lee.

Backing enterprise was also important to Stuart. A few hundred yards inland from the cathedral, close to the university and in the faded splendour of Falkner Square, five large terraced houses – of which one was a vicarage – had been 'knocked together' to make a Christian hostel for overseas students. Done with the blessing of Bishop Martin, ably backed and properly financed, it was the zeal and practical skills of its founder, the local vicar, Sydney Goddard, and his wife Cicely that made it work. The house thrived and was to have a long and fruitful history. Prophets of doom, however, predicted that it would not long survive a change of bishop. Stuart promptly gave it his backing. Addressing a diocesan conference he said that World Friendship House 'could not have been organized by a committee'. It was there 'charismatically'. Sydney Goddard was soon made a diocesan canon; he was an evangelical. Another new canon to be appointed early in Stuart's Liverpool years was Frank Sampson, the long-serving vicar of St John's, Tuebrook, the most advanced Anglo-Catholic church in the diocese. Frank Sampson was to be vicar of St John's for over forty years, and today is portrayed in one of the church's windows. One of his many curates, whom Stuart ordained, was David Hope, himself to be Archbishop of York some time after Stuart.

Stuart's seemingly spontaneous support of sound individual initiatives had a place amid clear goals requiring long-term planning. The relocation of people from inner city to housing estate or new town developments called for much redrawing of parish boundaries. The future of churches bereft of their old parish population had to be thought through, redundancies or amalgamations decided upon, and care for new housing areas provided for. It was a problem characteristic of the time, and one that imposed heavy burdens. A way had to be found to help the work forward but at the same time lighten the episcopal load in that area. The perception of the need was characteristic of the new bishop, and so too was the manner of its solution. On a parish visit he was impressed on one occasion by the good order of its vicar's study and of the way in which timetable, tasks, and information were effectively analysed and portrayed on wall charts and in a filing system. He noted a man of warm pastoral gifts who knew how to order his business, a combination of attributes not always present in clergy. So it was that the Revd Frank Harvey was asked to become the diocese's first ever planning officer, a job he pioneered with distinction until he became Archdeacon of London.

Other new forms of ministry were coming to birth. In 1967 local radio made its national debut, first in Leicester and then in Liverpool, where Radio Merseyside took to the air in November. Preparations had begun some months earlier as the BBC contacted a wide range of community organizations, which importantly included the churches.

An ecumenical three-day course for clergy and leading laymen was held in the Western Rooms of Liverpool Cathedral, led by some heavyweights of the broadcasting world, including Grace Wyndham Goldie and Eric Blenner-hassett, and members of the Church's TV and Radio Centre at Bushey. On hand were the first members of Radio Merseyside's staff, including manager Michael Hancock, and Roman Catholic journalist Bob Azurdia, destined to become its first religious programmes producer. Together with fellow church leaders, Stuart invited a number of clergy and laity to make attendance a high priority. As if under fire, friendships were forged as small ecumenical groups struggled to produce magazine-style programmes within a limited time span under critical eyes. This baptism of fire was a learning process for all concerned, and in itself was an event of major ecumenical importance – with some participants still involved in broadcasting 30 years later.

Local radio was to be a potent and enduring element in Merseyside's ecumenical life and church people were to be a potent factor in its general development. Significantly, Radio Merseyside, and later the local commercial station, Radio City, were to provide Stuart and other church leaders with a new platform and a new forum. Their voices were to become 'household voices', recognizable to members of the general public as well as to churchmen. It also provided them with experience of broadcasting not easily come by before and prepared them for better participation in nationwide broadcasting. Stuart, who had an ideal broadcasting voice, sat behind a microphone with aplomb and was to become increasingly sought after on radio and television. It was at this time that he appointed two of his clergy to 'do what they could' to help with the media – the first appointments of their kind in the diocese.

One of his senior clergy, however, initially found Stuart a bit of a puzzle. Canon John Hunter was field officer of the Diocesan Board of Education and had put Liverpool in the vanguard of new approaches to this work, with a series of successful residential conferences introducing clergy to group dynamics. 'He had me to lunch, as was his way when he wanted to get to know you,' John Hunter recalls, 'it was in his club – the Racquets Club in Upper Parliament Street – and I found it extremely difficult. I couldn't make him out. I felt I was ploughing through treacle, and I saw my job coming quickly to an end. He was, however, very keen on the lay training side. Here he was excellent. He was keen on promoting big teams for lay visitation. His principle was to look for areas where the Holy Spirit was working and homing in on them.'

Whatever Stuart's own understanding of that conversation may have been, he was quick to meet one particular need and instituted the diocesan practice of holding 'first incumbency' conferences. These were for clergy in their first posts as rector or vicar. John Hunter's job was not finished, but something was to happen at Stuart's first Lambeth Conference that would have a bearing on the course that John Hunter's job would take.

THE 'BIG PICTURE': UPPSALA AND LAMBETH

The year 1968 brought the fourth Assembly of the World Council of Churches (WCC) in Uppsala. It also brought the tenth Lambeth Conference. Little more than two years after his enthronement, Stuart was to attend both. Following Liverpool's popular Lay Diocesan Conference on the last weekend of June, Stuart joined Archbishop Ramsey, Archbishop Simms of Dublin, Bishop Oliver Tomkins of Bristol, and Bishop Williams of Bangor. Other members of the Church of England delegation to Uppsala included Canon John Bickersteth, a parish priest from Rochester. Brenda followed on 11 July, much concerned about her father's failing health.

The WCC was itself slowly achieving greater ecumenicity by growing links with the Roman Catholic and Orthodox Churches. Nine Roman Catholic theologians were among the 135 members of the Faith and Order Commission. Also from Rome were messages from the Pope (Paul VI) and Cardinal Bea, and from Constantinople there was a message from Ecumenical Patriarch Athenagoras II. The theme of the Assembly was 'Behold I make all things new' and the key words were 'Renewal' and 'Revolution'. Kenneth Kaunda spoke on rich and poor nations, Professor Barbara Ward, of Columbia University, New York, spoke about international economic development, and James Baldwin – the black American novelist – spoke on the theme 'White Racism or World Community?'

There was no doubting Stuart's enjoyment of so great an international gathering, its provision of such a large window on the world, and its point of reference to human need on a global scale. But he also had a wider frame of reference. On 12 July he wrote in his diary: '"We are strangers before thee and sojourners as were all our fathers. Our days on earth are as a shadow and there is none abiding" (1 Chronicles 29.15) – the one note which is entirely absent from the Uppsala symphony.' The next day (13 July) he wrote: '"I stick fast in the deep mire where no ground is" (Psalm 69.2). Uppsala emphasises the helplessness of the church when the first commandment is forgotten: "Thou shalt love the Lord thy God".'

During the days of the Assembly Brenda's father's condition deteriorated drastically. On 17 July a phone call from Pam Edis brought news that called them back to England. On 19 July Stuart wrote, '"Their minds were fixed on what they achieved instead of what they believed" (Romans 9.32) – the perennial temptation of the church, of Geneva as well as Rome.' Later that day he added: 'Dad died 6 p.m.' In the strange days that separate a death and a funeral, and with a mind doubtless still echoing to the speeches, discussions and small talk of Uppsala, he wrote on 20 July: 'Only the minister who takes time to hear will have anything significant to speak – the systole and diastole of ministry'; (23 July): 'Dad's funeral. "I stand amazed at the unfathomable complexity of God's wisdom and God's knowledge" (Romans 11.33). Bewilderment for Paul was not an occasion for doubt but an invitation to praise.'

Returning to the northern latitudes of Uppsala, they arrived at 2 a.m. to find that it was already daylight. At its conclusion, the Assembly produced a four-point message under the heading 'But God Makes New'. It spoke about mankind as neighbours – but neighbours not knowing how to live together; it spoke about scientific advance and revolutions, their potentialities and perils – but observed that 'man doesn't know who he is'; it spoke about the gap between rich and poor, and mentioned armament as the crucial point of decisions for the day. And it concluded that these matters demand the attention of the worldwide community, recognizing that in the WCC only 'the beginnings of such a community has been given to us'.

Then it was time for something else. Stuart's note for 25 July read: 'Opening Service of Lambeth Conference, Canterbury'.

A BISHOP'S WIFE

These first years in Liverpool had been busy ones for Brenda. While her first priority was home and family, she was also concerned to engage more widely. She had found many tasks awaiting her. Clifford and Margaret Martin had overseen the diocese rather on the lines of a vast parish in which the vicar and his wife, in traditional roles, were closely identified with key central structures. Margaret Martin had been the much-loved diocesan president of the Mothers' Union, chairman of its then younger partner, the Women's Fellowship, chairman of the Moral Welfare Committee, and chairman of the Church Missionary Society's Women's Committee. Brenda confessed that she'd never belonged to the Mothers' Union, pointing out that this was the consequence of never having lived in a parish with a branch. However, she began membership as diocesan president, work that proved very fruitful: 'With the MU I had to go to all sorts of places, and in the process was often on the receiving end of people's ministries.' On one such outing Brenda remembered being impressed by a young vicar in Southport and mentioning him to Stuart. In due course the Revd John Waine was appointed team rector of the vast new-town parish of Kirkby from which he successively went on to be Bishop of Stafford, of St Edmundsbury and Ipswich, and of Chelmsford.

Brenda believed that there were plenty of able people ready to take on her various roles, and by degrees they took her place – vicar's wife Muriel MacDonald became the highly competent president of the Mothers' Union, and another vicar's wife, Esme Bell, took over the Church Missionary Society work with similar ability. Brenda, however, decided to stay on as chairman of the Board of Moral Welfare where Marguerite (Sally) White was the indomitable moving spirit. She had developed the work from scratch under Bishop Martin, and was deeply involved in frontline work for which she was later awarded the MBE. In that exposed and costly work, Brenda wanted Sally to have her immediate personal support. Jobs handed to others, however, were apt to be replaced by new ones, and one day Dr Geoffrey Barnard, Principal of St Katharine's College, a teacher training college conveniently situated near Bishop's Lodge, invited her to become a governor. These were critical days for the college, with great changes on the horizon involving historic developments in Liverpool's educational life. This was work that Brenda grew to love. She also became a governor of St Hilda's Church of England High School for Girls, forming firm friendships with headmistress Sister Mary Grace and other sisters on her staff at that time. In due course Brenda also became a magistrate, becoming more closely acquainted with the more difficult side of city life and some of its casualties and trouble-makers: 'I met a lot of people not connected with the Church, and so I used to tell Stuart about them.' Stuart and Brenda were both keen on meeting people outside the Church and making them a natural part of their hospitable networking activity, including them on the guest lists for dinner parties and other social functions at Bishop's Lodge.

LAMBETH 1968

Lambeth 1968 was a 'new-look' Conference. Two years after Stuart first wore gaiters, it went down in history as the first 'gaiterless' Conference. The Archbishop had set the trend by turning up at a Buckingham Palace garden party in a cassock; the bishops quickly took the hint and gaiters and episcopal apron swiftly became a thing of the past.

Inevitably, the planning reflected the international life of the Church in the previous decade, which had included two Assemblies of the World Council of Churches and the great Anglican Congress held in Toronto in 1963. Toronto 1963 had seen 2,000 delegates from 78 countries speaking 200 languages in (and around) one hotel for ten days. Those involved found their image of Anglicanism radically changed by participation in the fellowship and activities of this passionate, multi-lingual, multi-coloured throng. The sheer preponderance of black and brown faces, the constant sound of other tongues, the variety of costume, vestments, traditions, and political and economic backgrounds, all combined to produce a potent mind-shift for many. This found expression in the Congress appeal for Mutual Responsibility and Interdependence in the Gospel (MRI). For those who had not yet shared this kind of experience, these altered perceptions were waiting in the wings of history ready to register in the minds of new leaders. This was to make its mark on Lambeth. Presiding over the Conference, as he had at many of the sessions of the Anglican Congress in Toronto, was Archbishop Michael Ramsey.

The Conference theme – 'The Renewal of the Church in Faith, in Ministry and in Unity' – was all of a piece with the new look that Michael Ramsey was encouraging. One aim was to create a structure in which every bishop had a chance to speak. With 462 bishops present compared with the 310 of 1958, and with 26 consultants and 76 observers, this was an important aim, especially if, as executive officer Bishop Ralph Dean said, 'some, with becoming modesty, refrain from speaking at plenary sessions'.

As the British bishops converged on Canterbury they had plenty on their minds about life and thought in their own homeland. In the realm of theology, John Robinson's latest book, *Explorations into God*, had been published the previous year, while a year before that a more orthodox note had been sounded by John Macquarrie's *Principles of Christian Theology*. Academic issues of another kind were also on the minds of many. The future of English theological colleges was being scrutinized, while Sir Bernard de Bunsen's committee thought about their reorganization. Meanwhile a report on synodical government in the Church of England had been published in 1966, and thinking was on course for its eventual introduction in 1970. Another report, on diocesan boundaries, had appeared in 1967. The Church of England had a lot of domestic business to attend to. But it was also increasingly aware of the sort of question that had been heard at Toronto 1963 and increasingly thereafter: 'When is the Church of England going to join the Anglican Communion?' In the event, the relationships underlying that serious joke were to be addressed in a decision to create the Anglican Consultative Council, and the replacement of an executive officer by a secretary-general. Those decisions were taken after the bishops – divided into 33 groups – had grappled together at considerable depth with matters involved in the renewal of the Church in faith, ministry, and unity. The approach bore the marks of an Archbishop of Canterbury who was also a theologian and teacher – a genuine doctor of the faith. It was an important occasion in the history of Anglicanism.

In the Conference's division of labour Stuart found himself at the heart of a discussion that was to have far-reaching effects. He was assigned to that third of the Conference membership chaired by the scintillating H. Lakdasa J. De Mel, Archbishop of Calcutta and Metropolitan of India, which was concerned with 'Renewal through Unity'. Within this section Stuart was a member of sub-committee 31a, whose brief was to look at Inter-Anglican structures. It was from this section, and in the first instance from this committee, that there came a recommendation to create the Anglican Consultative Council. He was therefore closely involved in a major development in Anglicanism. The linked sub-committee, 31b, had the task of examining the role of the Anglican Communion in the families of Christendom. Work that Stuart was about to set in hand in Liverpool, and some later work when he chaired the General Synod's Partners in Mission working party, was to be well served by this experience.

While he enjoyed them, Stuart did not mistake such gatherings as something larger than life. His diary notes the undercurrent of his thought at the time:

(31 July): Prayer and witness – the two indispensables of Church life – the practical interpretative factors of my existence; (1 August): 'He shall be like a tree planted by the water side' (Psalm 1.3). The world desperately needs such – men who are content to be rather than striving to do; (7 August): Call to Renewal is the theme of the Conference and seemingly, too, of my own inner life – the all importance to me of God Himself. Uppsala, Dad's death, the Lambeth Conference, Finchley, London, Focolare, our Silver Wedding. All passes, only God abides.

On 8 August Stuart wrote to Brenda who had gone to their cottage in Marloes, whimsically opening for her a window on the proceedings: 'We spent the afternoon having our photographs taken, but at least the weather was good and Marloes did not seem too many miles away. We have plenary sessions this week, but there are consolations. This afternoon's session was cancelled to give one of the sections time to repair their report which was badly mauled in the morning.' And then he mentioned an event that was not a scheduled part of the programme, but which had its own bearing on events to follow in the north of England: 'Tomorrow Donald, Cuthbert and I are having lunch with two others to discuss the possibility of a nation-wide mission.'

Archbishop Donald Coggan had strong convictions about the Church's primary task of preaching the gospel, so too did Cuthbert Bardsley, Bishop of Coventry, himself a colourful, talented, and enthusiastic preacher with broad sympathies and great personal gifts of communication. Together with Stuart they met informally to ponder what could be done to make the Church of England more evangelistically engaged in its homeland. As they talked together it came to be felt that a particular region was needed to kick-start the process. Stuart left the meeting having said that he'd see what he could do. On 14 August Stuart's diary records the words: '"But Jeremiah the prophet went his way" (Jeremiah 28.11). So every prophet needs to attend to the voice of the world – then go his way and wait for the voice of God. What happens after Lambeth may be more important than what happens at it.'

NEW DAY DAWNING

Back at last in Liverpool, Stuart called on Archbishop Beck, the Methodist District Chairman the Revd Rex Kissack, a Manxman born and bred, and the Moderator of the Presbyterian district. Together, these four men agreed to meet monthly on a regular basis. Stuart then contacted John Hunter, his Board of Education field officer, and appointed him secretary to the group – instructing him 'to sit in the corner, say nothing and take notes'. As the four leaders thought together about how best to communicate the faith, John Hunter remembers the spirit of their meetings: 'Stuart said from the start that all should be done from an ecumenical point of view and he coupled this with his vision for the north.' Suddenly, as if from nowhere, an immense agenda was under serious discussion. One consequence among many was that for John Hunter the uncertainties surrounding his own job fell away and a new role took shape.

The group continued to meet monthly through the autumn of 1968 and into the new year, careful not to go public either about their meetings or about ideas that still had to be worked out, and for which, even in general terms, their respective churches were not yet ready. Stuart's concerns, however, were not confined to his own diocese, as indicated by a note in his diary for 9 October 1968: 'CTN discussed in the Upper House, Convocation of York'. Even at this seminal stage and before the 'Call to the North' was decided upon and received its name, Stuart was already referring to it by the initials that were to become its logo: 'CTN'. The subject was soon to resurface in the same body. On 15 January 1969 his diary note read: 'the commissioning of the Twelve has in view not episcope but evangelism – suitable portent for the meeting of the Upper House today?'

February 1969 brought a major development arising from a feature of Liverpool life – the annual series of lunch-time addresses given during Lent at the parish church of Our Lady and St Nicholas, Pier Head. Knowing that Dr Coggan was to preach there on 19 February, Stuart invited him to attend a meeting of the Liverpool group. He wanted to broach the idea of a northern initiative that would be totally ecumenical and embrace the whole province of York. 'At this point,' says Hunter, 'Stuart had the brilliant idea that the exercise should not be in the traditional evangelical form, but for church leaders to say "We will [ourselves] be active in mission".' This was a major point of departure for new thought and action. It was to test the belief that if the leaders acted together in concert and with conviction, the enterprise would find its own way of being effective. No well-worn patterns of denominational 'mission' would be unthinkingly taken 'off the peg' from the storerooms of church history. The leaders themselves would take the lead in finding the way. They would be leaders in mission.

Dr Coggan was keen on the idea and agreed to invite church leaders of all denominations to a meeting in Bishopthorpe. The resultant gathering was to be a watershed in ecumenism in the north and a landmark in missionary thinking for English churches considering their homeland. Those are, of course, very large claims very little reflected in current histories of twentieth-century religion in England. But the structures to be set up across the north of England during the following years, and many of the people involved in them, entered into the deepening ecumenical life of the Church. Their contributions are streams that had their spring in 'Bishopthorpe 1969'. Its effect has been incalculably effective for good and has yet to be properly assessed for history and as a pattern for future work.

The landmark meeting itself took place on 28 May and was held in the great dining-room at Bishopthorpe. Every denomination, including the Salvation Army and Quakers, was represented at its most senior level. Dr Coggan presided, and with some church leaders perched on window-sills, more than every seat was filled. For John Hunter, 30 years later, it was to be remembered as 'the most striking meeting I've been to in my life'. For Stuart – although a key day in his ministry – it attracted the following comment in his diary: 'The strongest impression was of the poverty and confusion of the Church, but the most enduring impression may well be of the strange, secret triumph of God's will over ours. Alleluia.'

Certainly not all participants were keen on the idea of a practical programme for proclaiming the gospel together. But it was early days. As a practical step forward Stuart suggested that Anglicans, Roman Catholics, and Free Churchmen appoint an officer to represent the project to their own brethren in the north. John Hunter was to fill this role for the Church of England, and Archbishop Beck secured the winsome and able services of Father Dennis Corbishley for the Roman Catholics. The Free Churches, although not structured for making a similar appointment, were to be involved with equal commitment in every other way.

Such a venture could not be rushed. The Bishop of Durham, the brilliant and learned Ian Ramsey, counselled that they make haste slowly. So too, from a different perspective, did Archbishop Beck. But that counsel did not prevent shoulders being put to the wheel. It encouraged the search for workable ways and means.

Embarked upon his new role, John Hunter suggested that the enterprise should have a small directorate comprising three church leaders from each of the three traditions – Anglican, Roman Catholic, and Free Church. This was agreed and the resultant nine-man committee, known as the Committee of Nine, has continued to function with changing tasks ever since. The 14 Anglican dioceses of the northern province were taken to provide the geographical basis for a convenient organizational pattern. Upon this pattern each diocesan area formed its own three-man committee by bringing together a member of each tradition. The resultant 14 groups of three began to meet quarterly – a 42-member body surveying progress, reaction, thought, prayer, and insight across the north of England. Anglican deaneries at grassroots level matched the process by forming their own three-person committees. In this emergent scheme, Hunter and Corbishley were key figures of great industry, with Hunter himself visiting every church leader in the north.

With this amount of needful infrastructure in place it was possible to tackle the very wide range of questions raised by the attempt to preach the gospel ecumenically and in concert. When it was decided to issue the 'Call to the North' during Holy Week 1973, a broadly based process was already in place and active at many different levels. It was a fine piece of tactical planning to accompany a historic development in strategy. With the hindsight of history, entries in Stuart's diaries in 1969–72 show how the CTN and all its concerns overarched his years in Liverpool – 14 June 1969: '"O how unlike the complex works of man, Heaven's easy, artless, unencumbered plan". Wycliffe, St Aidan's, Huyton, CTN'; 26 September: 'CTN is simply the slow, laborious way God has given us for expressing a similar concern for our countrymen'; 10 October: 'The Wycliffe motto stands out against the fog – Via, Veritas, Vita – a way to follow, a truth to believe, a life to enjoy. It could be the simple comprehensive theme we need for CTN.'

Nowhere were the early fruits of CTN more evident than in Liverpool's response to the failure of the Anglican–Methodist Reunion scheme on 5 July 1969. Stuart and Methodist District Chairman Rex Kissack had been meeting regularly for over a year. Both had been dismayed by the Church of England's failure to get the two-thirds majority required to match Methodism's willingness to proceed. In September 1969 they wrote to their respective constituencies to say that 'pending the emergence of a national policy we would "draw together our governing bodies as far as the law permits"'. Following that suggestion it was agreed by the Bishop's Council and the Methodist Superintendents Meeting to call a first-ever joint Anglican–Methodist Synod for the Liverpool diocese and Methodist District.

The timing was brilliant. In 1970 the Church of England was to embrace synodical government. Explanatory posters were up in every church, with special meetings being held to explain, advise, and answer questions. The Liverpool idea of holding a joint Anglican–Methodist Synod in the very first year of Anglican synodical government had immense appeal. It sent out a message that was prophetic in style as well as content. A committee was set up and work began on planning an event that would require some careful preparation and hard work. The Synod was duly scheduled for 27 February 1971, a period of 18 months later. Here, then, was another project that overarched what could have been a negative period of church experience. It gave a sense of initiative, purpose, and consequent meaning to troubled people in both traditions, and on the wider ecumenical scene ran in parallel with the creation and building up of the 'Call to the North' structures.

As 1969 came to an end so too did Laurence Brown's time as Bishop of Warrington. He had been appointed Bishop of Birmingham where he was to be enthroned on 10 January 1970. Laurence Brown's departure broke a major link with Clifford Martin's regime, but by this time Stuart was well established, settled, and secure in the affections and structures of the diocese and there was widespread pleasure at the preferment of a popular and powerful suffragan.

His successor was to come from Stuart's old diocese of Rochester. He was Canon John Monier Bickersteth, vicar of St Stephen's, Chatham. Like Stuart, he had served in the forces during the war, ending up as a captain in the Royal Artillery. Unlike Stuart, he was a member of a distinguished clerical and literary family and was not the first of them to be a bishop. He brought 20 years of parochial experience with him, which had begun with a four-year curacy with Mervyn Stockwood at Moorfields in Bristol. Unusually he was consecrated in Liverpool Cathedral, together with Richard Watson, who was to be suffragan Bishop of Burnley, on 7 April 1970. John Bickersteth brought a buoyant, outgoing, and engaging personality swiftly to bear on the rapidly moving scene of church life on Merseyside and proved to be an ideal episcopal colleague for Stuart.

TIMES OF CHANGE

The year 1970 brought changes of government in both Church and state. Following June's General Election, the Conservative Party under Edward Heath replaced the Labour government of Harold Wilson, while for the Church a more permanent change occurred in July when the old Church Assembly met for the last time before the inauguration in November of synodical government. Meanwhile, among the Church's concerns in the north-west had been the need to provide ordination training for married candidates, specifically for those who, because of family commitments, could not undertake it in residential colleges. Other courses had been pioneered in the south of England – notable examples being Dr Alex Vidler's 'Doves' at Windsor, and the Southwark Ordination Course. This was a concern close to Stuart's heart, and he was glad to respond to a Manchester-based initiative involving the dioceses of Blackburn, Chester, Manchester, and Liverpool aimed at making suitable provision in the region.

The history of this Manchester-based concern dated from 1962 and gathered momentum from 1967, the moving spirits being Professor Ronald Preston, Archdeacon Hetley Price (later Bishop of Doncaster), and Canon Gwilym Morgan. In 1970 the time for action had come and Stuart attended the first formal meeting of north-west dioceses hosted by the Bishop of

Manchester, Dr Greer. The ability of those most closely concerned with the project meant that his contribution was not required to be great, but his input stemmed from relevant experience and his needful support of the project was unreserved. So began the distinguished history of the Northern Ordination Course, later to become the North West Ordination Course, which currently serves nine dioceses.

Another major cause of concern was the burgeoning power of the media, concerning which Harold Wilson's Labour government had planned to set up a committee of enquiry. In its last-ever session, the Church Assembly had decided to set up its own commission to prepare evidence for the planned committee. However, changes taking place in broadcasting caused the new government to drop the project, considering the enquiry likely to be of more value nearer the 1976 expiry date of the BBC's charter and ITA's constitution, both of which dated from 1964. In its first-ever group of sessions, however, General Synod decided that in this matter it would stick to its guns, believing that government interest might well revive and that widespread discussion would in any case serve the nation well. Early in 1971 it appointed an 11-member commission representing a wide spectrum of Anglican life under the chairmanship of Sir William Hart, and served by two secretaries, the Revd Michael Saward, the Church Information Office's Radio and Television Officer, and Mr Lionel Wadeson, the General Synod's assistant Secretary. From 1967 to 1970 Stuart had been chairman of the BBC North Regional Advisory Committee and was appointed to serve on the commission as its sole episcopal member. So began the 26 meetings – eight of them residential – that were woven into the fabric of his next three years. These gave him a close acquaintance with the character and working of the contemporary mass media, introduced him to many of its practitioners, and involved him in the commission's ecumenical consultations and its enquiries in nine selected dioceses.

The purpose now was no longer to prepare the sort of tightly argued unanimous report best suited to a parliamentary committee of enquiry, but to stimulate public discussion by reflecting the commission's own range of views and convictions in the light of their research. The question they asked was what has the spirit and ethic of Christianity to contribute to mass media programme planning? The Church of England is a broad Church, and nowhere was its breadth more visible than in response to such a question. Some argued in favour of stricter censorship, provision for Christian proclamation, and for the Church to appoint people to the television companies' advisory posts, rather than follow the current practice of allowing the companies to choose their own. Others argued for artistic licence, a need for the world to be seen as it is, and an open forum for the presentation of any faith, with religious advisers selected by programme makers. This division of opinion was present in the commission's membership and reflected in its discussions, and the hope was that by passing on an account of these a wider debate would be most effectively encouraged. It was scheduled to report back in 1973.

It was not the Blanch family's only involvement with the media. When possible, Stuart and Brenda attended concerts of the Philharmonic Orchestra and during the interval would be guests in the Green Room. Here Brenda was one day approached on the subject of the proposed new commercial radio station currently attracting the attention of media-minded business-men. A member of the consortium gathering to make a bid for the franchise asked, 'Would you consider serving with a group of us on this board? We need a statutory woman!' Brenda took time to read their submission before agreeing, then said, 'If we're going to apply for the franchise we've got to know each other and know what our strengths are.' Consequently she invited the members to dinner – 'And Stuart couldn't be there! It was maddening! I was left with all these men.' The consortium was awarded the contract, and Radio City duly took to the air with the Bishop's wife on the board. She did it with conviction because all its members lived and worked in Liverpool: 'We really wanted to make it work for Liverpool.'

ANGLICAN–METHODIST SYNOD

Liverpool's Anglican–Methodist Synod was duly held on 21 February 1971 in the city's old College of Technology Building, a few hundred yards away from the mouth of the Mersey Tunnel. Four working parties had prepared workshops on the themes of the mass media, social responsibility, youth, and the ministry. The aim was to discern lines of practical work in each area and synod members signed up for participation in one or other of them. It was very much a working synod with most of the programme devoted to the workshops themselves and a plenary session concerned to authorize further practical work along these lines. There was a notable absence of rhetoric. The failure of the Anglican–Methodist scheme in the face of so much work for the churches to do in society made for serious practical intent. Nevertheless, the gathering picked up a sense of quiet elation as some attainable targets came into view. Among the resolutions accepted was one presented jointly by Stuart and Rex Kissack, calling upon the churches 'to consult jointly at circuit, deanery and parish levels with a view to common action in commending the Christian faith more effectively to those outside the Church'. It was a significant emphasis. The leaders were not directing church folk into structural, liturgical, or ministerial reform, but to the shared task of carrying out the Church's first and fundamental mandate to preach the gospel. It was the same principle as that of CTN, and – like CTN – it found appropriate structures to carry out the purpose. At the end of the day the committees behind the synod working parties were charged with ongoing tasks that were to enjoy a healthy span of years and contribute much to the ecumenical life developing on Merseyside. The working party that had the longest unbroken life from that date was the one concerned with the mass media, which evolved into a permanent part of local church life.

WORK OVERSEAS

By this time Stuart was beginning to get invitations to conduct missions and speak at conventions or other gatherings overseas. The start and conclusion of the process that created Liverpool's Anglican–Methodist Synod began and ended with trips abroad. The period of 8–21 November 1969 saw him addressing gatherings in Alabama, and there were engagements in Bermuda from 16 to 27 April 1971. Halfway between these two trips, however, came an event which, in church circles, brought him to national attention. The tenth anniversary of the College of Preachers was celebrated by a 'Festival of Preaching' held on the campus of York University during the week of 14 September 1970. The title was, perhaps, a trifle misleading. What was on offer was a sequence of lectures to preachers about preaching, and the lecturers were a formidably endowed quintet.

Archbishop Michael Ramsey spoke about theology and the preacher, and of 'the whole gospel for the whole man'. Father Hugh Bishop, Superior of the Community of the Resurrection, spoke of the nature of faith – Christ's and ours ('there is no such thing as untroubled or untested faith'). Alan Richardson, Dean of York, spoke about the resurrection ('without Easter, Christmas has no meaning'). Professor C. F. D. Moule spoke about the 'finality' of Christ – 'what Israel was meant to be Jesus succeeded in being'. And Stuart was to give what were advertised as three Bible studies. Small wonder that the occasion attracted an attendance of hundreds – all of them preachers. The campus was crowded.

Even in such glittering company Stuart shone. His fellow speakers gave serious thought to the challenge posed to Christian preaching by the many changes in life and thought characteristic of the time. In that context, Stuart's way of expounding the Bible was to take three popular and powerful contemporary novels and to link them to major themes of the Bible. So the themes of *Animal Farm* by George Orwell, *The Castle* by Kafka, and *The Spire* by William Golding provided the routes by which he led his audience into the heart of Scripture. Although the method was novel, his introduction to each talk was one of simple piety, using for an opening prayer the words of a familiar hymn: 'Break thou the bread of life, dear Lord to me; as thou didst break the bread in Galilee'. It was an event – a happening. In church life he had taken the stage as a national figure, and there was a swift request for a book based on his talks. Hence he added some writing time to his daily study and on 26 July 1971 his diary bore two words: 'Completed book'. Under the title *The World Our Orphanage*, the book was originally published by Epworth in 1972, the first of his nine books.

'CALL TO THE NORTH'

Plans to launch 'Call to the North' were coming to fruition, and as Easter 1972 approached a letter was 'offered for public reading' in all the churches of the north of England. It was the fruit of much prayer and labour, a unique document calling for a unique enterprise. It read:

We, Donald Coggan, Archbishop of York; George Andrew Beck, Archbishop of Liverpool; John Marsh, Moderator of the Free Church Federal Council 1970–71, leaders of the main Christian traditions in the North of England, speak together at this Easter season to the people of the North.

For four years leading representatives, concerned for the church and for society, have been meeting for prayer, discussion and planning. Three things have led to our meeting and so to our addressing you; FIRST, we must together speak a word from God to men and women in their need of an understanding of the meaning of life. God lives. God reigns. God cares. He has spoken to men – supremely in the life, death and resurrection of His Son, Jesus Christ. His Spirit is at work in the Church which Christ founded and in the world for which He died. SECONDLY, men and women today need to hear what God has to say, and to accept His will. More than that; man as an individual and society as a whole, cannot be healthy till God's word has been heard and obeyed. THIRDLY, we grieve over the past and present disunity. We thank God for a growing unity. We seek to move forward to a deeper unity.

In the light of these positive convictions, we call upon every member of our churches: 1. To use the coming twelve months to learn the meaning of the Christian faith, and how to relate it to mankind's needs. 2. To join in prayer for this purpose with fellow Christians of all traditions. 3. To work out ways of making the Christian faith intelligible to those at present out of touch with Christian worship and activity. 4. To plan some definite acts of witness to the Christian faith, beginning where possible in Holy Week 1973. God is calling His people to action everywhere. In His name we make this CALL TO THE NORTH.

For Stuart and Brenda, 1972 was notable for another reason. Their son Tim was spending his 'year out' between school and university on a kibbutz in Israel and together with their eldest daughter, Susan, Stuart and Brenda made their first visit to Israel. It was a two-week tour that affected their spiritual life in a way that was soon obvious to all. Stuart's speaking and preaching immediately took on new colour and fresh excitement as his knowledge and love of the Bible encountered the climate, terrain, language, and life of its homeland. It was to be the first of six visits over the years. Talking to his diocesan synod soon after his return he provided them with a picture of the worldwide Church, of which ecumenical life in Liverpool was a part, simply by recalling an afternoon in the Jerusalem garden of a rabbi with whom he had an appointment. The garden was set in a courtyard round which a richly luxuriant vine spread in every direction with great beauty and variety of foliage. Thus he described the Church. Then he added, 'But you know, as I waited for the rabbi, I passed the time by tracing the rambling branches of the vine to its source and there I discovered that this great and wonderful thing had just one single root.' There was no need for him to explain that particular parable.

The reading of the 'Call' was a green light for the production of more literature focusing on the work of Easter 1973. Study and prayer groups that had been meeting throughout the north during Lent had been fuelled by leaflets and other material produced by 'CTN Working Party Number 5' – the literature committee – based at Church House, Liverpool, which now got on with the next stage of its work, with much thought being directed towards the interconnections of social and political concerns, worship, and evangelism. A wide debate was rising among people whose emphases had lain in different areas. Evangelism in a social or cultural vacuum was an idea that got short shrift. So too did emphasis on social action or worship that was divorced from evangelism. The effect was to create a growing sense of mission that comprised worship, social action, and evangelism in one indivisible life.

In his privately circulated paper *Unity, Theology and Mission,* John Hunter reflected on the overall process: 'We become concerned for Jerusalem the city as well as the individuals within it, the flock going astray as well as the lost sheep within it. It is the corporate goal of the gospel to the whole nation that gives something of a new look to evangelism today. Once the gospel is seen to exercise a saving power over not only individuals but the cultures within which they live, it excites and unites the Churches as they speak to the community.'

The Bible Society was now much involved. Its popular *Word in Action* tabloid (number 4 of 1972) carried the major headline: 'Nine Thousand Churches in Call to the North' and continued:

Take the North of England, all of it, from Nottingham to Berwick, Chester to Carlisle. It's a big chunk of country, covering as it does the great industrial complexes of Lancashire, and Yorkshire, the Mersey, the Humber and the Tyne. Think of cities like Liverpool, Manchester, Leeds, Newcastle; think of the mills and factories, the high rise flats, the suburbs, the manufacturing towns. That's a lot of people. Then take a little book called *Good News for the North by a Man Called Mark.* Attractively produced, illustrated with line drawings, this is a special edition of Mark's Gospel in Today's English Version, *Good News for Modern Man.* Then state your aim: to place a copy of this book in as many homes as possible during Lent 1973. That's the scope of the 'Call to the North' . . .

A project like this can't be tackled by one church nor even by one denomination. This is a joint effort running right through the denominational spectrum. Nine thousand churches are involved. It's as ambitious as that. The churches of the North have asked the Bible Society to produce half a million copies of this special Mark's Gospel.

And so in the Lent of 1973 ecumenical twos and threes, drawn from the different traditions of 9,000 churches, went from door to door in their neighbourhoods with their gift of a Gospel.

Preaching in the cathedral on Easter Sunday 1973, Stuart said:

Easter is not a lonely peak but part of a range – the resurrection of Christ is congruous with the inner history of the universe and the church . . . the 'proof' of the resurrection resides not in the 'evidences' but in the nature of God elsewhere revealed in Scripture. . . . The Church is dead, tangled in its own structures, immovable, reactionary. But we do not rest on the virtues of the church but the promise of God. Therefore we are capable of resurrection.

Lazarus (in his graveclothes) did nothing! The words 'Loose him, let him go' apply to the church. We shall never be effective witnesses to the resurrection of Christ until we know something of that experience in ourselves.

In the wake of the activities of Holy Week 1973, the 14 regional ecumenical committees created under the aegis of CTN across the north were to have an ongoing life with an overview of the enterprise provided by a two-tier system of annual consultations at Scargill House. One was the church leaders' conference, and the other was a similar gathering of ecumenical officers and other people active in the field. CTN structures were to be dissolved in 1977, with the ecumenical officers' annual gathering coming to an end a little later; but under the name of Northern Consultation for Mission, the church leaders' conference continues to this day as an invaluable part of church life in the north.

It was now a long time since the start of Stuart's time in Liverpool and the day when he had received two letters asking why the Churches could not speak their message together. These letters, and his response to them, had helped launch important work in church life across the north of England. Its influence was to last for decades and helped the churches form a view of mission that embraced evangelistic and social concerns. Its effects are with us today and the churches have much to learn from it.

BROADCASTING AND THE CHURCH

As 1973 wore on, it became time for General Synod's working party on broadcasting to present its report. The cover of the 119-page document carried a grainy black and white picture of Liverpool Cathedral's massive tower glimpsed beyond a small forest of television aerials of the then neighbouring chimney-potted house tops. It was an eloquent ikon of an important enquiry. When in November 1973 Stuart presented it in General Synod he was able to refer to his 'batch of typescript ten and a half inches thick, 54 booklets, 12 books, 128 submissions, 57 interviews, 27 meetings, and two and a half years of work' that he had shared with his fellow commission members. The report, however, met a strange fate.

For Christians, the crucial consideration at issue was embodied in the first of the report's general conclusions: 'Broadcasting does not simply reflect the attitudes of society but helps to form them. It follows that producers cannot be neutral or disclaim responsibility for the attitudes they help to propagate.' In other words, how can Christian people, and how can the organization of the Church, best share in the life of the nation – in the milieu and at the points where 'everyman's' life is variously portrayed in the mass media? This was the debate the report sought to promote. In his speech Stuart said:

What is reflected in the report is something which is integral to the Church and has been from the beginning – a division in the Church as to its relationship to society, and therefore necessarily to broadcasting. There have been from the very earliest days of the Church two dominant attitudes towards society, one the world-denying aspect and the other the world-affirming aspect. . . . On the whole I incline to the second view.

The most important thing, I suppose, and the greatest danger, is the propagation of unrealistic life objectives. . . . [these] leading to false hopes and ultimately to discontent, violence and 'dropping out', are the dangers of the medium. . . . I believe that the Church as a whole has a far more dynamic and positive thing to offer: that is to say, it has a responsibility for making television what, by the grace of God, it could surely become, for co-operating with men of good will in exploring and encouraging the positive aspects of the medium, for helping broadcasters to help society to grope towards moral, spiritual and cultural values which are identifiable, explicit and beneficial.

Among the six questions proposed for discussion in churches nationwide were: 'Is the prevailing neutralist philosophy one to be supported, or ought some more distinctive position be adopted by the broadcasting authorities? If the latter, then what sort of philosophy ought this to be?' 'What action ought the churches to be taking to equip their members (a) both to listen and to view more intelligently, and (b) to participate more effectively in broadcasting, and how can sufficient resources be provided for the task?' And on the heels of that were proposals for the creation of diocesan communications committees, diocesan directors of communication, and consideration of creating a communications resource and training establishment.

Of the 16 speeches in the subsequent debate, 10 were favourable to the report, three were noncommittal as to its recommendations, and three were critical. Among the critics were two future archbishops, Robert Runcie, then Bishop of St Albans, and the newly appointed Bishop of Durham, John Habgood. John Habgood spoke against its reception and voted accordingly. In the event the report was received by 162 votes to 108, but argument about its general philosophy had left little time or energy to address its practical recommendations and the motion calling for these to be referred for consideration by the standing committee met a sad fate. Sir John Lawrence, who had said, 'I do not think that ever before in this Synod we have had a report which was as important as this one', but disliked the three proposals mentioned, moved an amendment to exclude them. After a five-hour debate, the chairman put the amendment without asking the authors of the report to respond, so increasing the likelihood of that amendment being passed, as indeed it was. So while the report was sent on its way to the dioceses for discussion, work on the appointment of diocesan communications committees and diocesan directors of communication was delayed for some years. Nevertheless, diocesan discussions of the report spread awareness of the issues around the country and some dioceses pressed on with their own arrangements. Liverpool was one of them.

TERTIARY EDUCATION

By the end of the twentieth century, Liverpool had become home to three universities. In the 1960s there was only one. The 1960s, however, were crucial years in the history of tertiary education in Liverpool. Its College of Technology became Liverpool Polytechnic, en route to becoming the John Moores University. Meanwhile, local teacher training colleges were experiencing the radical effects of a prolonged nationwide review, which in their case was ultimately to lead to the creation of Hope University College.

The Church of England's St Katharine's College, just a short bike ride from Bishop's Lodge, had quickly engaged Stuart's attention and he was to play a key role in shaping its future. The introduction of the Bachelor of Education degree in 1960, together with planned growth in numbers, and the admission of male students in 1966, were the local effects of a nationwide development that had a lively and sometimes confusing course to run. Among the many ideas abounding in the next few years was one advanced in 1973 by St Paul's College, Cheltenham, suggesting that the country's 27 Anglican colleges consider forming a federated Anglican University. Meanwhile, in 1964, the Roman Catholic Christ's College of Education had been relocated in handsome new buildings just across the road from the Oxbridge collegiate-style complex of St Katharine's. At first there was little contact between the two communities, but that was soon to change.

In 1965, a matter of months before Stuart's arrival, the college had appointed Dr Geoffrey Barnard as its new Principal, and he and Stuart soon formed a warm working relationship. While working in Tanzania Geoffrey Barnard had got to know William Scott Baker, Bishop of Zanzibar, who was now approaching retirement and had mentioned that he was wondering where to spend it. On a day when both Stuart and Laurence Brown were ill and nobody was available for a confirmation, Geoffrey Barnard had an idea. St Katharine's was growing in size and

> we needed all the chaplaincy help we could muster. We were in the position of having some money to finance a part-time post and I was struck by the thought that William was used to big cities (Newcastle), was used to young people (as a former chaplain of King's College, Cambridge) and was devoted to music, as was his sister Nona who trained as a concert pianist, so what better than the Phil? William was one of the last great 'Catholic' colonial bishops from what was one of the highest of the high dioceses.

Geoffrey wondered how Stuart would feel about such an appointment? Thus Stuart was carefully and cautiously consulted. He need not have worried; there was no problem. For Stuart, churchmanship was entirely secondary to a firm faith, a missionary commitment, and a pastoral heart. There was nothing but a warm welcome to the arrival of the man from Zanzibar who would become an assistant bishop in the diocese. 'We at the college', said the Principal, 'had great cause to be thankful to Stuart for having the courage to take on a bishop from a quite different background. And William held Stuart in the highest esteem. No bishop normally thinks of retiring to a place like Liverpool – except William, who loved every minute of it. He was a tremendous success with our students and I am sure that his great spirituality brought quite a handful of our young men to test their vocation to the priesthood.'

There was typical gaiety about the new working relationship. As well as bringing full episcopal regalia William also brought the bow and arrow given to him by some of his African flock 'to make sure I could always find fresh meat to eat in Liverpool'! And, says Geoffrey:

> Stuart's total lack of pomposity manifested itself when, at the college, we had a grand 'do' to celebrate William's thirtieth Consecration Anniversary. We had planned a more than splendid High Mass in the old style with Stuart as preacher – Stuart, of course, in 'Choir Habit' plus crozier, William vested to the hilt also with crozier. William suddenly registers this impropriety and the following exchange ensues: William – 'I'm so sorry. Would you mind, as it's rather a special day for me, if I carried my crozier as well?' Stuart – 'Why on earth not, Bill? Carry two if you like, but why do you ask?' William – 'Well, you see, really only you should carry your crozier in your diocese. I used to be very

particular about that.' And they both did. This for me was so typical of Stuart's total lack of concern with the minutiae of such things whilst at the same time being never other than dignified and a presence.

It was in a happy set of personal relationships that difficult decisions were made. Plans for expansion required fund-raising and on 8 October 1970 Stuart and Brenda, together with Bishop Baker, joined 450 students and 50 staff members and governors on an eight-hour sponsored walk. Significantly, it was in the actual outreach year of the 'Call to the North', 1973, that the governing bodies of Liverpool's three voluntary colleges (St Katharine's, and the Roman Catholic colleges of Notre Dame and Christ's College) responded to the *James Report* by setting up a joint committee to discuss federation. The following year, 1974, was to be remembered by Geoffrey Barnard as 'the year of meetings' – the most critical being in February 1974. This was the moment that set in process a sequence of events that was eventually to result in the creation of Hope University College. Archbishop Beck, Stuart, Bishop John Bickersteth, and Dr Barnard gathered to meet the representative of the Government Department of Education and Science (DES). The government's policy was conditioned by a much proclaimed concern for economies of size and scale, and as this could not match the real needs and opportunities of every situation there was the fear that the proposed federation would fall foul of such thinking. Anxiety was in the air.

The meeting developed in an unexpected way. The DES representative began in jolly mood with enquiries about the sartorial differences of the bishops – the black of the archbishop and varied purples of his Anglican colleagues. 'You tell him, John,' said Stuart, turning to his suffragan. Then, with a characteristic beam to partner characteristic directness, he said to the man from the Ministry: 'Now then, what's all this business about size and scale?' Geoffrey Barnard says: 'I could expand a lot on the meeting that sealed the fate and survival of the voluntary colleges. Stuart's great good humour, mastery of his brief, wit and urbanity totally disarmed a not readily won over man from the Ministry.' While formal DES approval was awaited, the first meeting of the Federal Academic Council took place on 1 May. Ten working parties began to tackle practicalities of aims and ideals, and dates of terms for 1974–5 were federally agreed.

'I was brought up, as it were, by George Bell,' writes Geoffrey Barnard, 'and it always seemed to me that Stuart had so many of George Bell's qualities. He was a considerable scholar in his own right; he touched the world at many national and international points; he always seemed to be at peace; he

Stuart's parents, William and Elizabeth, with their eldest child, Will (1901)

Stuart with Rover, the first of his many dogs, *circa* 1922

The choirboy, *circa* 1930

Stuart and Brenda, 1944

Eynsham Vicarage, mid-1950s

Brenda, brushing out at Eynsham Vicarage

The Vicar at work: a baptism
at Eynsham

Stuart and Richard Hamper dressed
as escaped convicts during a parish
mission, Eynsham 1956

St Valéry-sur-Somme: a family holiday in France, early 1960s
(l. to r. Susan, Tim, Brenda, Stuart, Alison, Hilary, Angela)

The family on the day of Stuart's consecration as Bishop, 25 March 1966
(l. to r. Hilary, Tim, Brenda, Stuart, Alison, Angela, Susan)
Photo: *Yorkshire Press & Gazette & Herald*

Off to work: the Bishop of Liverpool heads for Church House, October 1974

After a balloon flight over Yorkshire, 27 September 1977

Blessing the boats
at Whitby, 1977

With Prime Minister Harold Wilson and
Mrs Sheila Hunter at the Northern Church
Leaders' Consultation, Scargill, 1977

With the Queen Mother at Bishopthorpe,
29 June 1978

Lambeth Conference 1978

With Her Majesty the Queen at the service to mark the completion of Liverpool Cathedral, 25 October 1978
Photo: *Liverpool Daily Post and Echo*

With the chief rabbi, Dr Immanuel (later Lord) Jakobovits, 31 October 1978

A familiar sight to parishioners: the Archbishop visiting one of his churches – this one at Withernsea
Photo: *Holderness Gazette*

At Dr Coggan's retirement: presenting a book containing the signatures of all General Synod members, November 1979

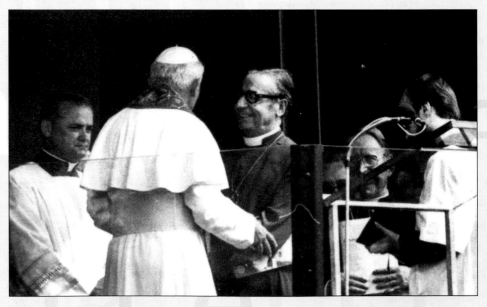

Whit Monday, 31 May 1982: greeting Pope John Paul II before 210,000 people on the Knavesmire, York

always appeared to have time for the greatest and the least and the famous bicycle photograph seems to say it all. Stuart and Brenda, who was my wonderful vice-chairman, were great good friends to me and my wife and St Katharine's College owes them both far more than can ever be told or known.'

Another critically important ecumenical event took place at much the same time. On 15 March 1974 the Merseyside Churches Ecumenical Council was ready to appoint its first full-time ecumenical officer, funded by grants primarily from the Anglicans and Roman Catholics. 'It was a notable day,' writes Edward Patey, 'when the Ecumenical Council Executive, meeting in my office in the cathedral, was ready to appoint David Savage, a Baptist minister. His appointment was proposed by Stuart Blanch and seconded by Archbishop George Andrew Beck.' The appointment was made during a series of six Lent talks given by Stuart on Radio Merseyside which were being used as material for ecumenical house-groups. His title theme – 'Modern Dilemmas' – employed his insights into the biblical themes of six modern novels.

Between 1972 to 1974 the range of Stuart's lecture programme increased. His themes included 'The Use of the Bible' (for the Readers Board at Salford University – July 1972), another series of cathedral lectures, 'The Church in 1984: its Structures, Religion and Theology' (November 1972), 'The Experience of Prayer in the Bible' (Belfast – December 1972), 'Ministry Today and Tomorrow' (PCC reps – Altrincham, March 1973), 'The Bible and the Institutional Church' (three lectures given in Oxford to Gloucester clergy, July 1973), 'The [Hospital] Chaplain and his Faith' (at St Katharine's College, Liverpool, September 1973), 'Religion in Society' (Liverpool City College of Education, November 1973, and in revised form at Down and Dromore in December 1973). In December 1973 he also concluded a week-long series of talks and discussions related to marriage guidance counselling by giving a lecture on the theology of marriage. 'The Church and the Kingdom' was the theme of his lectures to a clergy fraternal at Wrexham and at Grassendale in February 1974.

It had been a momentous eight years for the diocese: the decision to complete the cathedral had been made and the appeal launched; parish boundaries had been extensively revised; the role of a planning officer had been established; ecumenical team ministries had been established in the new growth areas of Halewood and Skelmersdale; a major team ministry had been created in the new overspill town of Kirkby; new churches had been built, synodical government had been introduced, and so had the new Series Two and Series Three services; ecumenical life had been transformed within a frankly missionary spirit and intent; a first-ever Anglican–Methodist Synod had been held; the 'Call to the North' had found its origin and much of its back-up servicing in the diocese; and critically important ecumenical steps had been taken to secure the combined future of previously separate teacher training colleges.

As was said of Stuart at Rochester, 'Like the King in Chinese drama, . . . everything went well around him.' Yet his voice was often that of a prophet laying the axe to the roots of a selfish society. Years later this was the voice remembered in General Synod on the eve of his retirement when Professor J. D. McLean recalled him speaking to General Synod during his Liverpool years. Speaking of the ravages of unemployment, 'Stuart called for a new concept of wealth in place of the false god of profit; materials are cheap, he said, and therefore we use them; men are expensive and therefore we keep them unemployed – the voice of the pastor and prophet.'

~ 5 ~

Deuteronomy:
The Archbishop's Concerns

THE CALL TO YORK

The early months of 1974 brought to a head the long-running conflict between government and trade unions which in December had resulted in a three-day working week. Prime Minister Edward Heath called a General Election on 28 February, following which neither major party commanded an overall majority. Mr Heath resigned and Harold Wilson came back to power with the words 'All I can say is my prayers'. It was a train of events which led to another election in October, which gave Labour a three-seat majority, and saw Margaret Thatcher replace Edward Heath as Conservative Party leader a few months later. Meanwhile in early 1974 the Vietnam war still had another tragic year to run and in America the Watergate affair was rumbling relentlessly on with things looking increasingly bleak for President Nixon. Britain, meanwhile, returned to a five-day working week on 8 March.

It was against such a background that, on 11 March 1974, Archbishop Michael Ramsey announced his retirement. Ramsey's qualities of intellect and saintliness, together with his engagingly striking appearance and demeanour, helped to make him a well-loved and recognizable emblem of Christianity in Britain and around the world.

On 6 May Dr Coggan, spending a busy working weekend in Cambridge, was summoned to 10 Downing Street and invited to let his name go forward to the Queen as Ramsey's successor. He was 64, and would be 65 before he could take up the post. After a medical check-up and a quiet day at their intended retirement house at Kettlesing, he accepted and the appointment was announced, at which point the usual Church of England parlour game of primate-spotting suddenly switched from Canterbury to York. It proved to be a long game. Many names were mentioned and it later became known that Robert Runcie, the Bishop of St Albans, was one of those who had been approached but had declined.

Eight years after Stuart's and Brenda's arrival in Liverpool the diocese was busy and happy. Working closely with Stuart, however, John Bickersteth noticed that he was showing signs of fatigue, and suggested that he and Brenda take sabbatical leave. They agreed, and built into it their third trip to the Holy Land in three consecutive summers. They did the month-long course at St George's College, Jerusalem, and then – joined by daughter Susan and her friend Alice Nissen – stayed on for a fortnight's holiday, the high spot being their walk together from Jerusalem to Jericho, which Brenda once said 'has always been a highlight of our lives'.

Refreshed and invigorated they returned to Liverpool. 'Soon after we arrived,' Brenda recalls, 'at about 10 p.m. – there was a call for Stuart from Donald Coggan, who told him that a letter about York would be arriving tomorrow and he hoped that Stuart would say "Yes". This was an awful blow to us after a lovely time in Israel! We went to bed very depressed! In the morning the letter arrived. We prayed and thought long and hard and in the end decided that Stuart must say "yes". We could find no good reason for not going, much as we loved Liverpool.'

About ten days later their daughter Angela was married to Timothy Ambrose in Liverpool Cathedral, after which many guests filled Bishop's Lodge and gardens with Brenda and Stuart absorbed in family matters and showing no sign of the impending move. But the man who had enjoyed the thought of being a scholar parson in the country and had come to love caring for a busy diocese was now confronted with a concertina-like expansion of duties. To become Archbishop of York was to take on five roles in one. He would be Bishop of his own diocese of York. He would be the Provincial, convening the Northern Convocation, caring for the bishops of the province, visiting its various dioceses. He would be Primate of England as distinct from Primate of All England (the designation of Canterbury), and as such he would have national responsibilities. He would be Metropolitan, available for public duties in the city and expected to extend hospitality to distinguished visitors who may not conveniently be accommodated in the city itself. He would continue to be a member of the House of Lords. Although the fact that the Northern Convocation's role had largely been taken over by the workings of General Synod meant an easing of one burden, this was countered by additional responsibilities in Westminster and having to spend more time travelling between York and London.

The announcement was made on 13 September and a cloud passed over the diocese. True, it had the silver lining of pride – but there was the sense abroad of the end of an era. 'Eventually we went to look at the house [Bishopthorpe],' Brenda recalled, 'No one was there. We had taken a picnic lunch with us and amused ourselves by sitting at either end of the long table in the medieval hall! There was no carpet in the main entrance hall, and hardly any equipment in the kitchen.' The tradition was for each Archbishop to supply his own kitchen equipment, crockery and cutlery. A welcome thought at this point was all the large cooking pans they had bought when Rochester Theological College had closed down in 1970 and which, with their own crockery, had been used for entertaining in Liverpool. 'Later in the day,' Brenda recalls, 'we called on David and Dorothy Blunt – feeling rather tired and depressed. They were marvellous – took pity on us – and Dorothy "stretched" their meal to provide enough for us. They have always been a great support.'

David Blunt was a former public school master whom Dr Coggan had invited to become his lay chaplain. It had been an inspired appointment. His father was the much publicized Bishop of Bradford, whose carefully expressed concerns about the underlying issues of Edward VIII's proposed marriage to Mrs Wallis Simpson had precipitated the 1936 crisis that ended with the King's abdication. But the Bishop was also a noted biblical scholar with a number of published works to his name. David Blunt shared his father's love of Scripture, understood the pressures of episcopal life, was knowledgeable about public affairs, and had a gift for friendship. He and Stuart were well suited to each other.

On the Sunday following the announcement, Stuart's diary showed an appointment at the cathedral that was not reflected in the cathedral's published programme. Knowing that one of his clergy was ill, Stuart visited him. In hospital, suffering from hepatitis, was Canon Owen Eva, whose son Peter was also there with meningitis. For Owen's wife Joy and the whole family, it was a time of maximum stress and anxiety. Owen recalls Stuart giving the glad impression of having a morning off in order to spend time with them, as both patients slowly began to recover. Perhaps they reminisced about the occasion when Stuart had arrived at Halewood for a confirmation service having lost his voice, and Owen had conducted the vocal parts of the service, celebrated Communion and preached, and Stuart had laid on hands to confirm the candidates.

Among his October engagements was delivery of three lectures at the Royal Institute on the theme of 'The Concrete City', a term much in use to denote secular society in an urban age. Not much of what was being said on this subject at this time found its starting point or substance in the Bible. Stuart, however, approached the whole field of concern via the Old Testament. What he said clearly shows his thoughts about the interaction of Church and state and his ability to light the way for Bible-loving evangelicals, chiefly concerned for the salvation of individual souls, to see and welcome the social, economic, and political implications of their faith. Bible writers, he pointed out, are well-nigh unanimous in asserting that the Church has by the very nature of its calling (as of Abraham) a responsibility not only for individuals, but for individuals in relation to each other – that is, society and its structures. Church and society should be seen not as two spheres of activity, closely or remotely connected with each other, but as modes of God's relationship with us – the one in law and judgement, the other in grace and mercy, with each being equally God's. It follows that concern for the world rather than alienation from it should mark the Church's attitude to the world.

The November group of General Synod sessions were Stuart's last as Bishop of Liverpool and also the last to be attended by Michael Ramsey as Archbishop of Canterbury. It was also the first time that members knew the identity of both new primates. Two aspects of these sessions give something of the flavour of the Church's thinking about itself and its task at that particular time. One was a report on episcopacy in the Church of England by the standing committee and the other was a debate about evangelism. In presenting the report on evangelism, Canon Colin Craston spoke about the confusion of thought surrounding the word 'evangelism' and welcomed the signs of greater clarity that seemed to be emerging:

Those who used to see mission and evangelism as co-terminous areas of concern and activity – as, in fact, synonymous in meaning – have with penitence acknowledged their previous limitation of vision. Notably the International Conference of World Evangelization at Lausanne in July witnessed a frank admission by Evangelicals from all over the world that evangelism without a concern for social justice and caring service is untrue to the Biblical revelation in general and the ministry of Jesus in particular. On the other hand more liberal Christians, scandalised by much apathy of the church at large towards injustice and appalling human need, who have been emphasising the social and political aspects of God's mission, are now welcoming the concern for proclamation of those traditionally most involved in evangelism. And Christians of all traditions have been convinced of the organic relationship between the Gospel and the Church Catholic. The church is an essential part of the Gospel, and incorporation into it an essential part of evangelism.

Stuart did not take part in the debates of this group of sessions. The contribution he could well have made was provided by Donald Coggan and Cuthbert Bardsley. Cuthbert Bardsley spoke about evangelism, the social message, and mission as all belonging together, but each being distinct. Dr Coggan's contribution brought evangelism together with the search for unity in the Church: '"Call to the North" has, I believe, made it clear that when the Church is obedient to Christ in the matter of evangelism, he of the greatness of his heart throws in as a kind of bonus a growth in unity.' He then made some remarks that hinted at what, with Stuart's backing, he would be doing himself a year later and something of the spirit in which he would be doing it: 'It is often said, and I am getting rather tired of it, that we are not ready to go out in evangelism. . . . It is far better to take risks and to do something wrongly than not to do it at all.'

When Stuart came to address his diocesan synod for the last time, he said his years at Liverpool had given him a larger faith in the Church, its base in history, and its mission: 'The life, death and resurrection of Jesus Christ are the only explanation we have of this extraordinary church consciousness', with mission being the task of the whole Church all the time. Warning against too restricted a view of what that mission is, his last words to the synod were, 'The Church's history demonstrates, I believe, that it is always winning strange and unexpected victories out of seeming defeat.'

After a trip to Belfast where he spoke again on the experience of prayer in the Bible, he and Brenda confronted a Christmas charged with regret and excitement. The leaving of Liverpool entailed a round of local and regional farewells. An early celebration at St Peter's, Woolton, was followed by a parish breakfast attended by many people and involved the pattern of farewells that were repeated in many other places until the great farewell Eucharist at the cathedral on 8 January 1975. The vast cathedral that they had come to love was packed to capacity and it was typical that he should begin with sharp concerns of the day, and equally typical that he should set them in a larger context: 'Modern society's worst problem is not inflation,' he said. Today's society bore the burden of 'meaninglessness . . . a wasting, enervating disease far worse than inflation'. Mankind's need for purpose was not met by such a creed as Marxism with 'its trivial, partial understanding of history's meaning. Only he who receives the grace of Christ sees the world as it really is, and it is God's world, not the devil's. He came unto His own and if, tragically, His own received Him not it is still His own.' Stuart said that he did not fear for the Church because it had a humble part to play as a channel of God's grace and 'it is of the essence of God that He must reign'.

After the service he was presented with the portrait by Dawn Cookson for which he had been sitting. This was a sensitive study in pastels, showing him in convocation robes with the manuscript of one of his books on his lap. It was an attractive and informal portrait, out of the run of most such studies adorning diocesan and episcopal buildings, and was to hang, eventually, alongside the more traditional ones of his predecessors in the conference room of Liverpool's Diocesan Church House. Among other gifts, Stuart and Brenda were presented with the highly practical gift of large carpets for their new home. 'Pity they weren't Axminsters,' grumbled one reporter, losing the hoped-for headline of 'By Axminster to York Minster!'

A PRIMATE OF ENGLAND

As Liverpool adjusted to being without a diocesan bishop, York was preparing for its new Archbishop and his wife. Among those waiting to welcome them was the Very Revd Alan Richardson, KBE, DD, the redoubtable scholar Dean of York. Like Michael Ramsey, he himself had been ordained in Liverpool where he and Ramsey had been fellow curates – Michael at the parish church, and Alan at St Saviour's, Falkner Square. Later Alan had been a chaplain at the cathedral under the redoubtable Dean Dwelly where he had met his wife Phyllis. This Liverpool connection added to the warmth of their anticipation of working with the Blanches, and this meeting of such formidable and devout minds promised much for the future. First signs of it were evident in preparations for the enthronement with an attempt to make the service as accessible as possible to all sections of a vast congregation in a huge church.

All was going well with arrangements when tragedy struck. Disrobing after evensong on the 23rd, the Sunday before the enthronement, Alan Richardson suffered a massive heart attack and died in the vestry. For all concerned, there could hardly have been a worse blow. Writing about this in 1995 Lady Richardson spoke of Stuart's and Brenda's immediate presence: 'They were so very kind and supportive. They came at once to the Deanery. I do not remember much about that but I know I was deeply aware of their loving support and this went on afterwards and helped me to go on. For example they took all the Deanery furniture into Bishopthorpe while I waited for a home in Durham. Of course I had to leave the Deanery as soon as possible and my housekeeper and I waited in my little Yorkshire cottage. The Blanches came to see us there.' She continued: 'Stuart was a bishop whose loving counsel helped me through the worst days of my life.'

Although his days as Archbishop began with crisis there was no sign of this in Stuart's public appearance and manner on the day of his enthronement. For people in what was now his old diocese of Liverpool, a special train had been chartered to take to York the 300 people who had tickets for the service; a tape recorder from Radio Merseyside picked up the sounds of the guard's whistle echoing along the platform at Lime Street, recorded excited conversations among groups of travellers on board, and eventually the hubbub outside the Minster as the Archbishop's procession wound its way round the south side of the nave to the great west door. Stuart wore the simplest of white copes, and also, for the first time, a mitre. Dignified and relaxed, he seemed almost to stroll along, using his crozier with the ease of a shepherd wielding his crook on a country walk. As he came into sight there was a burst of applause and he directed an affable smile and nod to its source. Those close to him noticed with amusement that the mitre was slightly askew and that a wisp of hair had escaped from its clasp. The service itself wonderfully combined the splendour of humble pomp required of the business afoot with the movement of its action to places where most could see and be near to significant parts of it. It was a poignant tribute to Alan Richardson's work and hopes for the future.

Stuart took as his text 2 Corinthians 4.7: 'We have this treasure in earthen vessels', words that summed up his attitude to himself and his great office and also – realistically – to those he would serve. After speaking about the power of the gospel in the life of the individual he went on:

If there is one thing which we in the church have learned to see in the past twenty or thirty years it is that the Gospel is not simply a message for the individual; it is a message for society, and a message for mankind. . . . We have had our fill of easy recipes and quick solutions and comprehensive cures and we know that there is nothing we can do to save ourselves. The schools and universities have patently failed as centres of social engineering. How did we come to believe that they would succeed? Why should we have imposed this burden on them? The medical profession with many triumphs to its name finds itself still baffled by diseases of the body and the mind which seem to yield no solution. Social workers who may have imagined with some justice that they could cure the hurts of mankind find themselves baffled over and over again by the complexities and the irrationalities of the human heart. Economists who might once have imagined that the redistribution of the earth's resources was simply a matter for good will and better legislation run hard up against the ingrained self-interest which is characteristic of us all. Idealistic politicians who have had a genuine vision for society, socialist or conservative, capitalist or communist, lose their way in the corridors of power and learn the hard way that politics remain the art of the possible . . . whatever particular form society may take, I see no hope for it without the Gospel. For the Gospel both in the Old Testament and the New offers a way of life which we either accept or deny, either we live by it or we die in the absence of it.

Giant Despair stalks the land. But if the Bible is to be believed hope never depends upon our own skills or on our own foresight or on our own goodness. It depends in the end upon the unfailing will of God – or to put it another way, on the inner compulsions of the universe. As the tide flows up the beach and the sun rises over the horizon so there is an order in spiritual affairs, a process which is in the end irresistible. He must reign till He has put all His enemies under His feet. The time will come when the kingdoms of this world will become the kingdoms of God and His Christ. . . . We have only just begun. What is the history of the Israel old and new? A mere four thousand years in the history of God's dealing with mankind. What matter our little reverses, our paltry disappointments, our misunderstandings about the Bible, our divisions in the Church? What do all these count in comparison with the glories of knowing Christ and discovering the riches which dwell within Him? Earthen vessels we are and shall remain, but we have a precious and inexhaustible treasure.

And so he went out through the great west doors to speak God's blessing to the city and to start his new work.

Three days later came the solemn hour of Alan Richardson's funeral. It was from there that he went to Scargill for the first 'Call to the North' conference of church leaders which he now chaired for the first time. Two days later he was broadcasting on the BBC's *Woman's Hour* programme from a studio in Leeds before making a trip to Oxfordshire and his old parish of Eynsham to conduct a confirmation service and, together with Brenda, receive presentations from a congregation that had been represented at the enthronement. His official diary was of course far fuller than his five-year diary entries, but the latter in March 1975 include entries with regard to having Mrs Phyllis Richardson to supper on the 16th, being sworn in to the Privy Council on the 18th, and attending General Synod's standing committee on the 19th. In such ways, an archbishop's programme of relentless travel and endless meetings quickly took hold. April brought a visit to Windsor, then a retreat that he conducted for members of Oak Hill Theological College in Southgate, followed by the first of two trips made that year to Ireland, on this occasion for a consultation of the British Council of Churches at Newcastle, County Down. He returned to London at the end of the month for a meeting of what he called the 'evangelism group'.

In the course of these days Stuart was also making time for finishing a book begun in Liverpool. *For All Mankind* was about the Old Testament. Published by the Bible Reading Fellowship early in 1976, it was reprinted immediately, being reprinted again the following year. It was a striking accompaniment of his transition from Liverpool to York and set out some of the ways in which he helped people relate the Bible to their own lives. In his introduction he wrote: 'It is a book which is meant to throw some light on our path, to put a spring in our step and a song in our hearts. . . . But [it] is not concerned just with the individual believer; it expresses the mind of God for communities and nations; it is a book for all mankind.' Later he sheds light on his own work as a teacher when addressing teachers who would be using the book for work at school or church: 'The greatest contribution a teacher can make is to provide perspective, to relate the apparently unrelated in a meaningful way – Athens to Jerusalem, politics to theology, the culture of ancient Egypt to the culture of the modern West, the novels of Camus to the story of the Fall, the decalogue to current jurisprudence. It is a tall order but the diligent teacher of the Bible can expect to have windows opened not only in heaven but on earth.'

One early and urgent priority was consultation about the appointment of a new dean. This resulted in the installation later in the year of Dr R. C. D. (Ronald) Jasper, another distinguished academic to follow Richardson, and a man to be deeply involved in the creation of the 1980 Alternative Service Book.

Stuart's first diocesan synod at York was on 14 June when he spoke about leadership:

We are being asked to offer to our people a total view of reality which cannot in the nature of things be any different from that reality as it was understood and imparted by our Lord himself. . . . The obligation of the church is to teach all nations. We might make a modest start by endeavouring to teach our own nation. Teaching in the Bible is never an academic exercise or just a means of conveying information. It is a process by which the whole heart, mind and will of men are formed in accordance with the will of the Creator. . . . Maybe this is the only kind of leadership that will make any sense in the twentieth century.

During these days Dr Coggan was thinking about the kind of lead he should be giving to the Church from Canterbury. The way his mind was working became apparent in July during a BBC Radio 4 interview on the *Sunday* programme. Here he indicated the sort of questions to which he would like to give some answers, and consulted Stuart about a direct and immediate initiative. He suggested a 'Call to the Nation' by the two Archbishops to be read in every church throughout the land with simultaneous and maximum media coverage. It was to centre on two questions: 'What sort of society do we want?' and 'What sort of people do we need to be in order to achieve it?' It was to encourage debate and to invite people to write personally to Dr Coggan.

Stuart readily agreed. It cohered with the ongoing 'Call to the North' activity. It would provide a focus for the many questions abroad in the nation. It would engage church leaders in debate at the highest levels and bring church folk into wide-ranging local discussions in which they could speak with their neighbours about their own beliefs. The 'Call' was to be read in the churches on 19 October 1975 and would be heralded at a press conference chaired by Dr Coggan in London on the 15th.

Meanwhile, life in Liverpool was adjusting to the arrival, on St Barnabas Day (11 June), of Stuart's successor on Merseyside. David Sheppard, Bishop of Woolwich, was already famous as a Test and County cricketer long before he was ordained, and long before becoming a bishop had done major work as warden of Canning Town's Mayflower Family Centre in London. Here he and his wife Grace had developed an urban Christian fellowship where every effort was made to relate Christianity to a deprived and unchurched inner city community. His evangelical experience of conversion at Cambridge and his curacy with Maurice Wood, later Bishop of Norwich, at St Mary's, Islington, lay at the heart of his wish to select and concentrate upon an area of need and a sector of society in which the gospel is most needed and church life least effective. Making this bold priority became a life-long choice that was to mark his journey in years to come. It was here that he had attracted the attention and enthusiasm of the colourful Bishop of Southwark, Mervyn Stockwood. Stockwood was of a different temperament and churchmanship, but was passionately committed to relating the Church to the political and social structures of its immediate context. He wanted David Sheppard as a suffragan bishop and got him. From this very different mentor, David Sheppard learned the ropes of episcopal life and political relevance, and with this background came to Liverpool alert to the measure of Merseyside's deprivation and opportunities.

'CALL TO THE NATION'

Stuart's diaries during the summer of 1975 included for the first time some brief notes of bodily ailments: 26 July: 'In bed with gastric flu'; 3 August: 'Damaged back'; 13 September: 'A troublesome leg'. It was in the midst of these unpleasant but minor ailments that he and Brenda bought the modest house that was to be their first retirement home in Oxfordshire. 'Little Garth' was in Bloxham and for Stuart – living in a palace – it brought a sense of freedom and security that he openly mentioned to others. September, however, brought a hectic autumn programme. Immediately before the trouble with his leg came a television broadcast for Tyne-Tees in Newcastle, and after the onset of the leg ailment a second trip to Ireland to speak at the Irish College of Preachers in Dublin, from which he returned for an ordination service. October brought the installation in the Minster of Ronald Jasper as the new dean, a helicopter flight to another television appearance for Tyne-Tees, and his first consecration of a bishop – that of David Galliford, who became suffragan Bishop of Hulme in the diocese of Manchester.

Then came the reading of the archbishops' pastoral letter in all parishes, a day he spent in the large dockside and residential parish of Drypool, Hull. The 'Call to the Nation' initiative was not without its critics. These in general belonged to three camps. There were those who thought it too high-handed and lacking in the sort of consultation required for an adequate response at all levels. Moreover, unlike 'Call to the North' it was not made ecumenically, and was thus deemed to be out of step with the spirituality of the nation. There were also those who felt that it was not sufficiently informed about the social and economic causes of human need. The criticisms had weight, but it was widely felt that the Archbishops' action was timely, proper and helpful, embodying the truth that broad-based outreach will by its very nature reveal areas where the Church is not ready for its primary task.

Although Stuart did not hold centre stage in 'Call to the Nation' his role was influential. One justifiable criticism of the venture was that of a lack of preparation, including scant provision for response and co-operation at ground level. Aware of this, Stuart turned to a familiar source and contacted John Hunter in Liverpool where the 'Call to the North' literature committee had just produced draft material with a directly relevant theme for forthcoming ecumenical Lent discussion groups. The committee drove up to Bishopthorpe in response to Stuart's invitation, and over a cup of tea on the terrace agreed to release its material for an enlarged role in life. Certainly the provision had all the hallmarks of haste – a note of the material arriving in vicarages and rectories sent in the post, together with clergy payslips at the end of September – but it was there, and the take-up was widespread. The group from Liverpool would have liked time to improve its presentation, but it met the moment and they got the job of producing something further (and better) for the following year as the effects of the 'Call' continued to be felt in a broad spread of house-meetings up and down the land.

Stuart's other move was a landmark in his ministry. He invited newspaper and radio station editors in the northern province to a reception at Bishopthorpe. They responded in strength, and it was a great occasion that bore fruit for years to come. It also quickly brought a lot of work on to Stuart's desk, and his response made him something of a favourite with the media. He did not treat journalists as a race apart to be viewed with suspicion and kept at a distance, but as friends and neighbours with burdens and needs of their own. Immediate consequences included his writing an article for the *Yorkshire Post*, a series of three articles for the *Manchester Evening News*, one for the *Sheffield Star*, and one for Darlington's *Northern Echo* – and he continued to write for these papers throughout his time at York.

His articles give something of the sense and spirit of the 'Call'. Writing in the *Sheffield Star* in October 1975 about the permissive society, he said, 'A society which permits its members to do anything they like at any time ceases to be a society in any significant use of that term. A democratic society requires that its members not only vote but think.' Writing the same month in the *Manchester Evening News*, he said:

> What sort of society? One in which whatever our adversities we remain free – not 'free' to do what we like regardless of the needs of others, but free in the sense that a great artist or a great musician is free, free to express the gifts great or small which God has given us. We can pay too high a price for security or universal education or unfailing social services if the price is subservience to an omnicompetent state which provides all we need but at the same time destroys what we really are. God's glory was perfectly revealed not in a system or a philosophy but in a man. Good people can make a bad system work, bad people can make a good system unworkable.

He was also quickly in demand for television and radio, programme planners recognizing that rare sparkle of star quality in someone who managed to be the same person in front of camera, in the pulpit, and in a one-to-one private chat with a hard-pressed journalist. He always managed to find the universal in the particular and often that 'particular' was the individual with whom he was talking.

Following the 'Call', Dr Coggan received 27,000 letters and his office sent out 25,000 copies of the prayer cards requested in them. The prayer thus spread abroad in the land was: 'God bless our nation, guide our rulers, give us your power, that we may live cheerfully, care for each other, and be just in all we do'. He then invited the Revd John Poulton to distil the correspondence into a book that was published under the title *Dear Archbishop* and helped to create the profile of religious consensus in the nation that was hoped for by both Archbishops.

The pattern of primatial tasks continued unabated. November brought the inauguration of the newly elected (and second) General Synod. Then came attendance at a state banquet for President Nyerere, followed by another television appearance – this time with Jimmy Savile in the programme *Speakeasy*, where the theme was 'Life After Death'. His lecture programme took him to Lincoln Theological College on 26 November and to the Humberside Council of Churches on 6 December, where on both occasions, though with different introductions, he spoke about Church and society in the Old Testament with a conclusion that was firmly down to earth: 'Your attitude to the social services; your involvement in local politics or ministry to the Church; your attitude to grants by the World Council of Churches; your view of the General Synod and the appointment of bishops. These all presuppose, if they do not articulate, a theology of the kingdom.' Old Testament theological method, he argued, involved a search for the significance of the 'Church' in the world. How God's chosen people related to society as a whole occupied by far the largest place in the Old Testament. The options were seeking a role of dominance, or of service, or of guardianship of truth, or maintenance of tradition, or of existence as leaven, salt, or light. He pressed the view that modern society is coextensive with Old Testament society, that our Lord's own teaching presupposed a kingdom theology, and that the Church has to adapt to it.

The date of 11 December found him in Newcastle at the university chaplaincy where he spoke about the mass media. As a bishop, he regularly heard complaints about sex and violence in the media as well as criticism of the underlying philosophy, assumptions, and values of many programme makers and the company policies that they exemplified. He believed these criticisms to be true, but they were not, he said, the whole truth. They had their good companions: quality programmes in drama, art, science, history, nature; the work of the Open University; and the public discussion of important issues alongside the basic work of good news reporting.

Stuart's own relations with media people was the first element of his personal approach to the moral mixture that is the media. The second was his awareness of the negative forces within every organization, including the Church itself. Thinking of the media as an industry, he observed that 'the same dangers reside in any human institution: industry as a whole, the civil service, Church House, the great international combines, the EEC, the Communist Party. They can all transcend, condition and corrupt those who belong to them.' Mass media, he said, are an indispensable element in any participatory democratic system, where they must be free not only of proprietary control but also of union control; he ended epigrammatically: 'The medium is always the message' – as in the case of the incarnation where the Word was made flesh. The Church itself is a 'mass medium par excellence'. The problem, and the challenge, is matching the medium to the message rather than vice versa.

The 'Call to the Nation' undoubtedly opened many doors for Stuart and he walked through them with wisdom and assurance. This made him known throughout the north in ways not available to most of his predecessors. It also increased the demands made upon him as a speaker, with many calls coming from secular groups who wanted to hear the Church's voice. This was a form of mission and dialogue for which he was ideally suited and he gave it priority, never satisfied with a routine recycling of old material. He was clearly in good form and enjoying the work, but an entry in his diary on 16 December 1975 indicates the critical way he ran his eye over himself in a job he was doing well: '"The man whom thou has made strong for thy service" (Psalm 80.17) – and beware the man who presumes upon that strength for his own self-satisfaction or aggrandisement.'

He and Brenda and the family enjoyed their first Christmas at York but found themselves missing the rich pattern of their Liverpool celebrations. His year ended at a conference for theological college principals and their staffs on 30 and 31 December at which he lectured on the theme of 'The Vanishing Clergyman'. In thinking about the declining number of clergy in a Church full of change, he said, 'We need to read the signs of the times' and study what exists. Current trends were for the diversification of clergy roles, with a blurring of the edges between ordained and lay ministry which, he said, occurs whenever the Church recovers its proper role of ministering to society. Clergy were exercising responsibility for public and civic life and the common factor of current trends was leadership of mission in the community over against the old, almost exclusively pastoral and liturgical, tradition: 'The status and function of the professional ministry alters from age to age.

132

What constitutes its identity is a call to leadership in God's Name on the basis of God's authority with a view to the fulfilment of God's purpose for the world.' 'We are on our own with the Holy Spirit!'

While there is need for lay ministry and for congregations to be trained in the care of their own members, there is also a need for professional ministry requiring a high degree of full-time, life-long commitment aided by increasingly specialized on-the-job training and calling for intellectual and management qualities. It calls for theology to have a prime place in training: 'It is failure here [in theological ability] that is most noticeable to lay people.' And he ended by stressing the importance of theology for creating parish policy.

It had been a good start to the York years, as he reflected in a letter to Edward Patey on 10 January 1976:

> Our household has just dramatically contracted from 10 to 2, so we feel a certain 'leisure' – but it has been a happy Christmas for us all, and Brenda and I are off to Marloes next week to recover. The Christmas festivities at the Minster, alas, compare rather unfavourably with Liverpool, as the family were quick to point out, but Ronald is, I think, bent on reformation. In other respects the crossing of the Pennines was less disturbing than we might have expected. Church life here has, I suspect, missed the trough and sails on, if not serenely at least sturdily unaware that the church has had a crisis! The people have been most welcoming and I have been introduced, sometimes against my will (!) to many 'interesting' aspects of Yorkshire life; but we have enjoyed: – the RAF, the lightship (less so), the international sheep-dog trial, the N. Moors national park, a carpet factory and the inside of many (too many) TV and broadcasting studios. As for Bren she has survived many parties, numerous luncheons at home and abroad, innumerable bun-fights, increasing conversation, and even the management of this house and the household that goes with it – gardeners who bring in vegetables by the barrow load, who require us to walk on the grass, not on the paths and look darkly at the infamous Benjamin [the current dog] and the tender plant he has just desecrated. . . . But, the mallards swim on the river, the pheasants rise from the grass and the owls challenge each other outside our bedroom window. It all helps to keep us sane if ever ecclesiastical matters threaten to occupy our minds. And there are marvellous, real things happening in the Church; while the mill clacks on we grind our wheat.

On 27 January came the consecration of two more bishops, Clifford Barker for Whitby and Michael Henshall for Warrington, the former to be a close colleague as suffragan, and the latter to succeed John Bickersteth at Liverpool following his move to Bath and Wells. Thus Stuart came to his first anniversary at York on course for a two-week series of addresses in Canada from 31 March to 12 April.

BISHOPTHORPE

Such a range of activity rested upon a happy home base. When they left Liverpool for York, Stuart and Brenda invited chauffeur-gardener Joe Kelly and his wife Muriel to accompany them; they were happy to agree and so helped provide life with a welcome bit of domestic continuity. Helping him settle in was Donald Coggan's former domestic chaplain, the Revd Colin Still, whose company Stuart enjoyed until it was time for him to move on a few months later. In seeking his successor, Stuart again turned to Liverpool, and in January 1976 appointed the Revd Bob Lewis, a former theological college tutor who was then a team vicar in the large parish of Kirby. With long-serving senior secretary Daphne Woods, it was a happy set-up. Bob writes, 'There was a staff of four – two chaplains, two secretaries (with part-time secretaries in addition from time to time). We worked upstairs in what was grandly called the "Secretariat". Approached by a staircase these were pleasant premises which had been sacrilegiously carved out of the old Archbishop's study where Temple had written "Readings in St John's Gospel". There were two gardeners. So it was a small and intimate set-up.'

David Blunt recalls the change of style that Stuart brought to Bishopthorpe: 'From the strict, even hectic, ten years working with and for Donald, the change was great. Stuart was a more relaxed man, his work schedule was more measured, and he husbanded his strength . . . otherwise he would not have done so much; though part of his genius was to enable his team and colleagues to develop their initiative in the shared work and for the agreed aims. Together with his gift as a great encourager he was a great gift-giver to his close team.'

The Archbishop's senior staff (the three suffragan bishops of Hull, Selby, and Whitby, and the archdeacons of York, East Riding, and Cleveland) met once a month for a day, the two chaplains also being present. These were Bob Lewis's favourite days: 'The fellowship was deep and there were lots of laughs. Brenda was wonderful with coffees and teas, and always a superb lunch. We began with Communion in chapel, taking it in turn to celebrate (Stuart never hogged anything like that). They were happy days when vacancies were discussed and appointments made. We worked in Stuart's study and always sat in exactly the same places (e.g. there was one sofa always occupied by the Bishop of Hull and the Archdeacon of the East Riding).'

Morris Maddocks, Bishop of Selby, recalls Stuart's first staff meeting when 'he intimated to us his method of working: "Except in an emergency or for parish visits try not to arrange anything for me in the morning when I try to pray and read; 5.30 p.m. to 6.30 p.m. each day is a quiet hour before I go out to my evening work. Monday is my day off. I'll let you have a note of my holidays." And still,' he notes, 'the work was done, including answering up to 1,000 letters (extra to the normal mail) whenever he spoke on television. He also had a little table made at the back of the car so that he could read and write while travelling.' Even though he had Mondays off, 'he would come into the office to do the essentials before going off to walk on the hills with Brenda. He had great ability to actually hand over a task. This could be somewhat alarming for his staff.'

Stuart's day began early. His regular pattern was to take a walk around the grounds first thing and this is when he would do his weather measurements and record them in his special book. Then, at 7.30 a.m., he would go to the chapel for Morning Prayer where he would be joined by Brenda, the chaplains, and sometimes other staff members and overnight visitors. Staff prayers as such were held at 8.45 a.m. just before the day's work began. Holy Communion was on Wednesdays. The regular round of daily worship is remembered with affection by the chaplains: 'Stuart appeared in his cassock and occupied the grand archiepiscopal stall with its carved angels,' recalls Simon Wright (chaplain 1979–84), who also came to his post from a parish in the Liverpool diocese. 'What we all really liked was to hear him read the lessons, particularly the Old Testament, in which he discovered all sorts of meaning and often humour that none of us realized was there. An example is Genesis 18.33, "The Lord went his way, when he had finished speaking with Abraham". Stuart could make it quite clear, by the way he read it, what a mighty figure Abraham was in that it was the Lord who "went his way" after his interview with Abraham was finished.'

Clifford Barker, Bishop of Whitby, later to follow Morris Maddocks as Bishop of Selby, was also keenly aware of his devotional life:

I suspect he was most at home with contemplative prayer, with the Bible and nature as starting points. A prayer which he sent me when I had a long spell in hospital after an accident suggests that Celtic spirituality had a particular appeal for him. He was not so keen on formal worship though the Eucharist was of great importance to him. Twice yearly when the rural deans attended, midday prayers were invariably led by Stuart and were always carefully prepared and very relevant to the time and the work of the participants.

Administration began with tackling the huge daily correspondence, which totalled 10,000 letters a year. Simon Wright observes that 'he had a bit of reputation for not liking administration. In fact he was very good at it. He always left his desk completely clear at the end of the day with everything filed or put away in its proper place. Prompt at 10 a.m. his chaplain and the senior of his two secretaries would join him in his study for the daily meeting when he would go through his diary and hand out tasks, many of which arose from the day's post. Then each of us in turn would raise any issues we had.' As Archbishop he was, of course, the end of the line for intractable problems. David Blunt recalls 'two words of wisdom I got from him which I have found invaluable – "Not everything matters!", and "There is not an answer to everything".'

Not all his correspondence was administrative or replies to letters received. Simon Wright remembers that

> he wrote thousands of letters to all sorts. He congratulated people and thanked them and sometimes took issue with them. For instance he congratulated the Chief Constable of West Yorkshire when the Ripper was caught. He commiserated with Keith Joseph when he was pelted with eggs when he was Secretary of State for Education. He told Arthur Scargill off for advocating 'extra parliamentary action' before the miners' strike. Many of the recipients wrote back to express their genuine gratitude that he had taken the trouble to write to them in this way. His letters were often witty and generous. Many of course were replies to people with something to get off their chest. Stuart reckoned that they only wrote to him when all else had failed and when nothing could be done, but his kindness and interest was often very important to the writers. Stuart exercised a real ministry through his letters and it was something that the general public never saw.

A charming example of his aptitude for adding to his own work in this way came when he spotted a newspaper item about a local choirboy who had been selected to join the choir at St Paul's Cathedral for the wedding of Prince Charles and Princess Diana. He wrote to him, wishing him well and saying that they might see each other there!

The 'secretariat' kept Brenda well supplied with problems of her own. Sometimes the plans being laid 'upstairs' would make hospitality demands upon the household that Brenda, 'downstairs', knew could not be met: 'They would send down and say, "We think so and so would be a good day to have such and such and could they come to lunch?" And then I would have to work out whether we could do this or not. Because we had a very small staff. So I used to say, "No. You can't do that!" Of course they were gaily planning all sorts of things.' But the right moments were quickly found and the great house was regularly and frequently used to good advantage.

Stuart kept to his regime of daily study and would get down to his books from about 11 a.m. or 11.30 a.m. each day for a full hour, making a clear distinction between study and preparation of his sermons, talks, and lectures for which he kept a special drawer. He made it plain that this was something all his clergy should be doing. He repeatedly told them that if they didn't study they would soon cease to have a ministry. When instituting new clergy to their parishes he would say to congregations in a humorous way (but with serious intent): 'If you see your vicar out and about in the morning let him know he ought to be in his study.' His love of study was infectious, and the first to feel the benefit of it were his senior colleagues. Morris Maddocks writes:

> His example in reading gave me a desire to get back to regular reading and he made suggestions and encouraged me in this. He also encouraged me in the writing of my first two books.
>
> The warmth of his relations with the senior staff meant that diocesan occasions, as with staff meetings, while serious, were fun. He knew his staff and their families, just as he and Brenda enabled us to know theirs. His Christmas gifts to each member of staff, invariably books which he had himself bought while browsing in bookshops on his day off, were carefully chosen to reflect each individual's background and interests.

In a time of family illness Donald Snelgrove (Bishop of Hull, 1981–94) found Stuart a close personal comfort and guide as they talked together about family illnesses. As a wartime naval man, he also sensed in Stuart the dimension of understanding shared by men who had lived with physical danger. Leslie Stanbridge, Archdeacon of York (1972–88), notes some of his Christmas presents with their inscriptions. Among many were: Dillistone's biography of C. H. Dodd – 'To Leslie, with many thanks for all you do for us and just being with us', and Austin Farrer's *The Brink of Mystery* – 'To Leslie, with thanks for his unfailing help amidst many mysteries'.

Men about to become bishops were invited to stay overnight at Bishopthorpe on the eve of their consecration, and in the case of married men their wives were also invited, and sometimes their families too. One bishop-to-be enjoyed a game of table-tennis with the Archbishop on that particular evening, another recalls the Archbishop bringing him an early morning cup of tea on the great day. And the wives found a special friend in Brenda. 'These were always very convivial occasions,' remarks Simon Wright. 'On the day of the consecration there was further hospitality for all the bishops and their wives and lawyers who were taking part. Many of them had travelled long distances following a very early start, so Stuart and Brenda decided to turn the midday refreshments into a full-scale luncheon in St William's College.' Brenda was to remember it as 'a wonderful time for fellowship – you didn't need to make a special time for bishops and their wives to meet other people, they all used to stay until four – a wonderful natural opportunity'. Simon Wright felt a strong sense of unity among the bishops of the northern province and believed it to be the fruit of the northern leaders' overnight meetings at Scargill and the warm hospitality at the time of consecrations. Part of the chemistry was the tradition, carried on by Brenda, of having all the diocesan bishops' wives of the northern province to stay for three days every three years, when the wives of the suffragans would also come on the third day.

At meetings of General Synod held in York, the staff of Church House, Westminster, enjoyed a welcome of their own. Its secretary-general, Sir Derek Pattinson, recalls the run-up to the first such York Synod after Stuart's appointment. Having noticed that on previous occasions the 20 or 30 members of Sir Derek's staff had not interrupted proceedings by starting to clear up before business was complete, needing therefore to stay on an extra night, Stuart approached him one day in London and said, 'Do you think they'd like to come to Bishopthorpe for the evening?' 'They would!' was the reply, so after being shown round by Stuart and Brenda they were entertained to dinner, an arrangement that became a regular event until Stuart's last Synod in July 1983 when the staff reversed the roles and themselves played host to Stuart and Brenda.

Hospitality was also a key feature of ordinations. The retreat took place at Bishopthorpe and Stuart spent the whole of the time with the ordinands, often walking around the grounds chatting to individuals he met. He saw clergy very much as preachers and teachers and his 'charge' was always a Bible exposition of some great theme.

In the diocese he took most of the institutions and licensings himself, with journeys to places like Hull, Cleveland, and Whitby after a full day in York.

His chaplains thought he delivered his finest sermons on such occasions. He also took on about a quarter of all confirmations in any given year, as well as many anniversaries, and so was well travelled, well known and well liked throughout the diocese. 'His visits to parishes were memorable,' says Leslie Stanbridge. 'With Stuart you could relax! I remember the wardens at Bubwith in their very cramped and overcrowded vestry waiting with apprehension for the new Archbishop. Eventually Stuart appeared with a great smile on his face, and set everyone at ease. "Well, Archdeacon, what are we doing tonight?"'

Informality was an instinct that he developed into something of an art form, retelling anecdotes of his minor embarrassments to help people feel comfortable together. He enjoyed telling of the day when, slowly coming to earth after a balloon flight over the North York moors, he was greeted by a passing horseman calling out, 'Good morning, your Grace.' The same words greeted him on a train while unwrapping a packet of home-made sandwiches. On holiday in Israel, feeling free of officialdom and far from pomp, he dived into a swimming pool only to hear, as his head broke the surface of the water, a nearby head saying, 'Good morning, my Lord.'

Clifford Barker observes that he was much loved for his approachableness, humour, and care: 'The quadrennial clergy conferences at Swanwick were welcomed rather than dreaded by the clergy, and this was largely due to him. His daily Bible studies and talks, as well as his informality and willingness to be involved in the less structured parts of the programme, helped to create a strong sense of identity and family spirit. I well remember him joining in an impromptu cricket match and bringing it to an end when he hit the ball a prodigious distance. It was declared lost among much banter and laughter.'

CROSSING BOUNDARIES

Stuart's strong inclination to cross boundaries between the Church and the rest of society was matched by an ability to do so with ease. In the best sense of the word he was a 'canny' soul. This was as much appreciated by church folk as by the many people he met who had little contact with church life. Canon Geoffrey Hunter wrote, 'Stuart was remarkable among all his contemporaries for his ability to reach beyond the boundaries of the Church into the wider community and to speak a word which appealed to non-Christians with humour and power.' A magistrate recalls him talking to the Magistrates' Association and holding them 'spellbound for nearly an hour on the Ten Commandments'. The Revd Paul Rathbone, a long-serving incumbent in the diocese and vicar of Bishopthorpe from 1983, writes: 'Those were really wonderful years in the diocese. His preaching, his teaching at clergy gatherings, his relaxed and humour-filled chairing of synods were refreshing and renewing. I always thought his giving priority to engagements outside the Church was absolutely right, giving a lead in getting the Church turned inside out.'

He found much common ground with the Jewish community in York, where memory of the twelfth-century massacre of Jews in Clifford Tower is part of city history, and also in Leeds, enjoying warm relations with all. It is thought that his commitment to such friendship had much to do with the generous donation made by the Jewish community in Leeds towards the repairs of the Minster following the fire of 1984. His knowledge of the way of the world probably owed as much to earliest influences as to his chequered career. But it came also from his close knowledge of the Old Testament in which the way of the world is so fully portrayed, analysed and illustrated, and this was undoubtedly the key to his good relations with the Jewish community.

His affinity with the Old Testament seemed almost intuitive. He resonated with the close dependence on land and livestock of its foundation characters, their strong personalities cast in dramatic situations, their domestic and public life closely intertwined, their evolution into a nation linked with the development of their law, their story shot through with the subjectivities of human experience, their history bound up with the destinies of nations, and the wisdom of their centuries carefully stored. His experience, temperament, and imagination made for a special response to its detail and overarching pattern and he read it in Hebrew to catch its resonances and sound its depths. His wide reading in the Classics and world literature had early come on stream when he read the Bible. But perhaps at some deep level of the mind there was a spark between it and his childhood experience of country life, of animals, farm and farmhands; of its great figures, of his beloved father, his own innocent encounter with tragedy, the sorrow of his mother, the strength of his elder brothers, and the ongoing life of which he eventually found the underlying pattern. He studied the Scriptures with academic rigour, but he read them as life-giving literature. Somehow it lay at the heart of his ability to cross boundaries and discuss social, cultural, and political matters with a whole range of secular organizations. It was the context in which he thought about the things that worried Church and society. It provided him with a long view of the human and divine forces at work amid history's constant recapitulation of humanity's central problems.

It was also close to his ecumenical vision. He had long been concerned to track to their sources the differences experienced in Christian spirituality – Catholic, Protestant, evangelical, systematic, charismatic – and had begun to find clues in the Old Testament, noting how the experience of the 'faithful remnant' during their time in exile contrasted with that of the larger body of Israel that preceded and followed it. He was intrigued that Daniel's and Ezekiel's experience of prayer was as different from the secure and triumphant worship in the temple at Jerusalem, as was Elijah's at Horeb. This opening up of the Bible's theological landscape was part of what made him such a breath of fresh air to Christian ecumenism. For him, ecumenism was not a tinkering with ecclesiastical machinery inside the walls of a permanent religious factory, but family life exposed to the wind of the Spirit within the broad sweep of history. But while Christian ecumenism was a big challenge to the Church in all its parts, that was not, for him, the end of the Church's agenda. Always the convinced and dedicated follower of Christ, he regarded the Church itself as a family stemming from Abraham's response to God's call. Here were grounds for faith between two pilgrim peoples and he delighted in his warm relations with the Jewish community. Writing in the December 1975 edition of the CMJ magazine *Shalom*, he mentioned four aspects of Jewish life that he particularly valued: '1. Worship in the home; 2. The significance of history – it has a meaning; 3. The God of righteousness; 4. Unflinching witness to God under most adverse circumstances.'

On 11 October 1977, towards the end of his second year at York, Stuart gave the St Paul's lecture to the Council for Jewish–Christian Understanding. The lecture was delivered in the Crypt of St Paul's Cathedral and his theme was 'The Kingdom and the Law'. He was in fine form: 'The "Promised Land" always lies on the other side of Sinai: that is, it is not conceivable to think of society except in terms of a freely recognised, willingly obeyed Law of God. . . . I see no hope for society unless it is prepared to recognise universal law, binding upon all mankind, which society infringes at its own peril.' He pointed out that his subject, 'The Kingdom and the Law', was related to the question ('What kind of society do we want?') raised two years earlier by the Archbishops' 'Call to the Nation'. 'How is the kingdom to be achieved? Is the Law integral to it or an interim stage on the way to it?' Such questions require a definition of the Law, for which views vary from 'universal principle' to 'temporary regulation'. By this route Stuart came to consider the relationship of the Law of God, on the one hand, and the kingdom of God on the other. Two trends emerged: that exemplified by a rigorous devotion to the Law, as at Qumran, and that of 'humanist' Jews

141

trying to make the Law intelligible in the dominantly Greek civilization in which they were scattered. In Jesus we see one who assents totally to the Decalogue, but dissents fiercely from many laws and regulations, distinguishing between the Law of God and the law of man.

This lecture was one of a series that he slowly developed over the coming years dealing with the relevance of the Old Testament to contemporary affairs and uncovering areas of concern and potential co-operation between Christians and Jews. One expression of this came 11 years later when he called on Christians and Jews to 'concentrate on what we share: viz (a) monotheism; (b) the doctrine of creation; (c) belief that man is made in God's image, fallen but capable of salvation; (d) a shared view of the future as being in God's hands; (e) belief that history has meaning; (f) the same attitude to God's commandments'.

In other lectures he argued that for Christians there is only one theology and that is a Hebrew theology. 'A young Jew sits on the throne of the universe', is how he once put it, and in lecturing about Jesus as prophet, evangelist, and shepherd he observed how little, in practical terms, the ministry of Jesus is taken by the Church to be a model for training its own ministry. In his comments on justice and international affairs his frame of reference was the Law of God given at Sinai, expounded by the prophets and most fully expressed in Christ. For Stuart, this was something given in history and alive through all ages. Here was the ground plan of the universe in its relation to humanity. On this basis he urged that Christians and Jews should make common cause against 'materialism, exploitation, destruction of family life, etc.' 'Differences', he said, 'should be seen not as obstacles but as opportunities to learn from one another.'

That he wanted such friendship and its insight to be spread across the Church is evident in his invitation to the then chief rabbi, Dr Immanuel Jakobovits (later Lord Jakobovits), to address the Northern Leaders Consultation at its residential meeting at Scargill. 'By inviting me to participate', Lord Jakobovits has written, 'he introduced me to what was for me an altogether novel experience of Jewish–Christian collaboration, and indeed of the common roots uniting us in our moral commitments.' (Letter to the author, 2 April 1998.) Later, Stuart and Lord Jakobovits jointly chaired the first-ever conference between Jews and members of the Anglican Communion. Stuart also took part in a memorable pilgrimage to the Holy Land comprising both Jews and Christians.

Soon he was to see similar grounds for dialogue with Islam. The Lambeth Conference was not to produce its first pronouncement on such matters until 1988 when it discussed the document *Jews, Christians and Muslims; the Way of Dialogue*. By then Stuart had been retired for five years, but doubtless his influence was among the hidden springs that gave it life.

BROADCASTER

Stuart was a 'natural' for prime-time television slots when they came his way. In 1975 he had been a hit on the Jimmy Savile show, *Jim'll Fix It*, and in September 1976 appeared on the high-ratings *Stars on Sunday*. Here he was invited to talk about prayer, and did so in a way that made it practical, relevant and attractive. 'Prayer', he said, 'is letting the majesty of God, as I see Him in Christ, bear in upon my mind, restoring me and, in some mysterious way, helping to restore others as well. This verse expresses what I feel happening to me when I pray: "And so the shadows fall apart – And so the west winds play – And all the windows of my heart – I open to thy day."' He went on: 'Learn to pray for others, holding them quietly in your mind in the presence of our Father – and expect things to happen.' Referring to a recently produced pamphlet called *Land of Hope and Glory*, he said, 'we really could do with a bit of hope and a touch of glory. This nation could be so different, so much happier, so much more united, so much more influential in the world if we prayed for each other regularly. . . . Here is a prayer we often use in Bishopthorpe: "O God reveal again Thy law, that all nations may bow before it. Reveal again Thy love that we may live together in peace."'

He was also alert to the special importance of local radio, and among his output for local stations was a series for Radio Leicester in Lent 1977. He also recorded tapes for small and special audiences such as the one gathered in a Methodist Home for the Aged. In 1977 he recorded a series of seven talks to be broadcast on Radio Belfast, 29 May–4 June. It was a typically tense time in Ulster, with army reinforcements arriving on 1 May in anticipation of a Loyalist general strike proposed for the following day. In his broadcasts Stuart addressed people on both sides of the sectarian divide by talking to them about people in the Bible: 'We may have to put up with barriers in Belfast for some time to come, but Christians can at least begin to dismantle the inner barriers which created them in the first place.' He then took a number of people from the Bible who crossed inner barricades, among them Philip, Ananias, Barnabas, Peter, and Paul. Referring to Ananias' call to give sight to the blinded Saul of Tarsus – 'it is hard to forgive your enemies but it is Christ's command that we should do so, and he who does not breaks the law of God'. Ananias went, and his first words to the one who had come as persecutor were: 'Brother Saul'.

He continued:

Don't permit barricades in the thoroughfares of your mind. God will not tolerate No-Go areas. The call may come from an unexpected place and lead to unexpected results. . . . The barricades we erect in our streets, the No-Go areas we permit in our mind, are an affront to God Who created mankind to be one community on the face of the earth. So now there are brave souls here and there, amidst a crowd of timid ones, who are not afraid to break with old customs and to challenge old allegiances in the interests of truth and unity. Thank God for them. Thank God for His Church. Thank God for His Spirit. Thank God for His promise that we shall all be one.

HIS PRAYERS FOR THE CHURCH

In April 1977 almost 2,000 people attended a National Evangelical Anglican Congress held on the campus of Nottingham University. Like a similar congress held at the University of Keele ten years earlier, it was part of a process in which the growing numbers of Anglican evangelicals were coming to terms with the responsibilities as well as benefits of their increase in numbers and influence. The older generation of evangelicals in the Church of England had been, and had felt themselves to be, something of a minority group. In the first half of the century a good deal of their energy had gone into defending faith in the inspiration of Scripture against a theologically fashionable liberalism, and to affirming the doctrines of salvation by faith and the need for personal regeneration. They had laboured less at applying the gospel to matters social, economic, cultural, and political. By the 1970s recollection of such a time was fast fading. Evangelicals old and new had for some time been rethinking their approach to such matters. 'NEAC 77' was a carefully prepared focus of that concern and Stuart was invited to give the opening address.

A bomb scare emptied the great hall before he could begin, but when all had safely regathered he told members about his prayers for the Church in such a time of change. He prayed, he said, for four things: '(1) A new generation of "militants" who will study the emergent pattern of things and plan ahead for action based on the Word of God. (2) A new generation of thinkers for "there is no hope for a church which stops thinking". (3) A new generation of contemplatives, for one man of prayer can change the psychology of a whole nation. (4) A new generation of prophets who will hear the word of the Lord and apply it to the issues of the day.' With contributions from a galaxy of diverse luminaries, including Michael Ramsey, Jim Packer, and John Stott, and a closing address from Donald Coggan, evangelicals came away with a great deal to puzzle over and digest. But they also came away with a feeling (new to some) of being mainstream Anglicans carrying socio-economic concerns and national obligations as a necessary concomitant of the gospel and pondering their developing place in the scheme of things.

LAMBETH 1978

Bishops in the Anglican Communion are as various and diverse as their countries and regions. They have different social, cultural, academic and economic backgrounds and have been nurtured in Anglicanism's varied traditions – evangelical, catholic, liberal. Some have the care of huge populations in small areas, others have the care of few people in huge territories. Some have comfortable financial means, some are poor. Some dwell safely, some are daily in danger. For many of them English is their second language. But they belong together in a Church that prizes orthodoxy, reason, and social relevance in ways that have enabled it to take root in the full range of world cultures.

How to benefit from their wisdom and experience? How to minister to their needs? The group dynamics of the Anglican Communion broke surface in 1975 and 1976 when decisions needed to be made about the eleventh Lambeth Conference scheduled for 1978. Although hugely valued by most bishops, questions were being asked. Was it the best way to spend so much money? Was a company composed entirely of bishops appropriate for the sort of trend-setting policy-views most needed by the Church? Should it be enlarged in order to accommodate some assistant bishops? Should it be scaled down and exclude some diocesans? Was Lambeth or Canterbury – or even England itself – the best place to hold it? Such things were discussed when the Anglican Consultative Council (ACC) met in Trinidad in March 1976 and the outcome shaped some of Stuart's later work.

While making it clear that decisions about whether or where to hold the Lambeth Conference rested with himself, Dr Coggan had earlier asked the ACC to give advice. The 1975 standing committee meeting had, by a small majority, favoured an enlarged Conference to which all diocesan and some assistant bishops should be invited. The larger Trinidad meeting, however, tabled other ideas. While one was a call for numbers to be limited to 300, consequently excluding some diocesans, delegates from Africa, Asia, and South America unanimously asked that all diocesan bishops be invited. An alternative location was suggested – the proposal of Canada's west coast possibly reflecting the energy and confidence of a Canadian Church powered as it was with memories of the 1963 Anglican Congress in Toronto. Some delegates reportedly felt the need for a different style of Conference altogether. Also on the agenda was the promotion of 'partners in mission' consultations, taking forward the Anglican Congress principles of 'MRI' (Mutual Responsibility and Interdependence in the Body of Christ).

Dr Coggan concluded that there would indeed be a Conference, that it would be at Canterbury, and noted the clear majority in favour of an extended membership, an option chosen a little later with the effect that membership continued to rise.

These family concerns were not the only ones in the two years left for preparations. What in fact was a bishop's job? And what is the relationship, in spiritual dynamics as well as economic matters, between the churches in rich and poor nations? And underlying all such concerns for the structure and dynamics of fellowship and mission was the deeper theological one that was clearly stated by A. M. G. Stephenson in his book *Anglicanism and the Lambeth Conferences*. Running his eye across the previous decade he noted the deaths of theologians Tillich and Bultmann, Karl Barth, C. H. Dodd, Leonard Hodgson, F. L. Cross, and Austin Farrer. Many giants had left the field at a time when some current thinking had (in 1977) produced *The Myth of God Incarnate*, and in which Professor Maurice Wiles had written 'Christian Believing'. Looking forward to Lambeth 1978, Stephenson wrote: 'Clearly the uppermost question at the moment – and it will clearly remain so in 1978 – is the Christological one. Can the Lambeth fathers of 1978 affirm, like their predecessors of 1867, the Lord Jesus Christ as our Saviour, very God, very man, ever to be adored and worshipped? One hopes they can reaffirm this and yet retain a critical faith in the upsurge of fundamentalism.'

Before leaving Trinidad Donald Coggan outlined his own draft programme proposals, which included a review of twentieth-century theology, the character and organization of the Anglican Communion, and the relationship between Lambeth Conferences and the ACC. It would also give special attention to the understanding of episcopacy and the means of training for it, and would be undertaken with a pervading emphasis on prayer. However, it soon became clear that the outline programme had critics, and during a visit to Canada in 1977 Dr Coggan was invited to add to his engagements a special meeting with the Canadian House of Bishops who had just been discussing it. The Canadians, like others elsewhere, were keen that the Conference should strive to see as deeply as possible into the needs and opportunities of the day and be prepared to speak a word to their contemporaries from the living God. To this end they wanted the Conference to be flexible enough to make it more than an occasion for devotion, organizational review, and learning. Dr Coggan readily agreed and people skilled in matching flexible conference forms with their developing content were involved. The winds of the Spirit were blowing in the provinces of the Communion and the Archbishop was as keen as any good captain to trim the sails of his ship and help it move along.

Overall arrangements for Lambeth were in the hands of Bishop John Howe, executive officer for the Anglican Communion. But there were things to be done by England's archbishops in their own travels. There were fundamental questions at the heart of the enterprise and Stuart was to tackle some of them. He focused particularly on the work of bishops and the doctrine of Christ.

On a trip to New York in the autumn of 1977 Stuart talked to a gathering of American bishops as part of their own advance preparations for the Lambeth Conference and his subject, significantly, was 'Discerning the will of God for the world, the Church, and the bishops'. He began by setting out what the Lambeth Conference now had in view: 'We shall try (1) to describe and evaluate change; (2) identify the hand of God in these changes – regarding change as "an angel of the unchanging God"; (3) renew a vision of the "Kingdom"; (4) loosen our minds from the shackles of upbringing, national conventions, theological fancies and built-in habits ("we have nothing to lose but our chains"); (5) heighten our powers of discernment, which is a gift of God specially needed by a bishop; (6) enjoy ourselves.'

He was in no doubt that the gift most needed by bishops in their work was in fact discernment:

Bishops are invited to discern between options (often legitimate) for the world ('What kind of society? – Collective or privatised?') – for the Church ('Who is on the Lord's side? Radicals, Conservatives, Charismatics?') – for themselves ('What can I or may I do on the way to salvation? Do I lead or follow?'). For ourselves we may ask (1) Where does my life as bishop end and my life as a simple Christian man begin, or vice versa? (2) When does the 'means' render the 'ends' illegitimate? (3) How do I relate personal convictions and the apparent will of the diocese?

Characteristically, in what was a full-orbed and carefully worked lecture, he came quite naturally and with seeming ease to a moment of intimate pastoral relationship with his fellow bishops. Following a section on 'our duty as bishops' he spoke about 'our duty as Christians', making the kind of distinction that is so clear when identified, but so hidden when not: 'We have a soul to save, not just a diocese to run. There can be failures to accept our failures, in addition to regretting or concealing them. We have limitations to live with and profit from by concentration and the setting of priorities.' Here he was pastor as well as teacher.

He concluded by summing up the ten things he believed such discernment required:

(1) A theological knowledge of the Scriptures, as distinct from academic expertise or homiletical skill. (2) The ability to apply historical lessons without regarding history merely as precedent; 'there are dangers in tradition – we must not use last-war weapons for this war's battles'. (3) A predisposition to belief rather than to unbelief (e.g. 'our Lord's opponents were sceptics with the sceptics' instinctive reaction to "enthusiasms"'). (4) A sufficient 'distance' from which to view things. The importance of silence, prayer, withdrawal, holidays. 'The ability to appeal from the verdict of the hour to that of the centuries'. (5) Patience to await the right answer and feel the peace of God upon it, in contrast with 'the sinful desire to get on with the job'. (6) Sensitiveness to the 'common mind' of staff or congregation or diocese. 'As with weather there is a climate'. (7) Responsiveness to 'signs' – the coincidence, the random remarks, the crazy idea (like giving a gift to God at Christmas 2000), the check or the disappointment. (8) Confidence that God is on our side. (9) A friend or two. (10) The gift of the Spirit.

As 1978 dawned Stuart's book of studies in St Mark's Gospel appeared. Called *The Christian Militant*, it was published by SPCK as the diocese of Blackburn's Lent Book in the Golden Jubilee year of the diocese. Meanwhile he was at work on another book to be published hot on its heels on 16 March. Called *The Burning Bush* and sub-titled 'Signs of our Times', it linked people and places characteristic of the day with relevant themes of the Bible, publication being accompanied by broadcasts on Radio 2 and the BBC World Service. Thereafter, as the Lambeth Conference approached, he became increasingly concerned about his own contribution to it. Every weekday morning of the Conference's three consecutive weeks was scheduled to begin with a devotional lecture designed to feed the spiritual life of men spending long hours in discussion and the ordering of thought and resolutions. As with any conference, the passage of time could be expected to produce increasing stress within the dwindling timescale and one of Stuart's tasks was to provide these lectures in the final week. To focus the company's spirituality at this stage was a test of all he believed and of the way he prayed. It had to do with the essentials of life and faith that run beneath all differences of background, circumstance, and culture and before which all members of such a diverse company must ultimately be one.

It is likely that he knew what he wanted to say from earliest thoughts about it. The relationship of a clear Christology to his own workaday needs as a bishop was fundamental to all thoughts of preparation. However deep or complex a bishop's tasks, above all else the work required the true life of Christ in heart and mind. The work had one common foundation. His particular problem was not so much what to say, but how to say it.

This must have been somewhere in his mind during a visit to France in April 1978 that began with an official visit to York's twinned city of Dijon. From there he and Brenda went to Taizé and entered into its life of prayer in a way that prompted the following entry in his diary for 7 April: 'Convicted by this time in Taizé of an essential prayerlessness and a worldly trust in my own powers of organisation, foresight and intellectual grasp.' At the start of a service one day, and wondering where Stuart had got to, Brenda and Bob Lewis suddenly recognized him in the company of the brothers and garbed as one of them in order to give the address.

Hospitality at Bishopthorpe continued to provide much for Brenda to do and she found relocating the dining-room next to the kitchen a distinct advantage. A special guest on 29 June was the Queen Mother, who in planning a visit to Yorkshire had expressed a wish to visit Bishopthorpe. As they accompanied their guest to the dining-room, Stuart and Brenda enjoyed the Queen Mother's exclamation, 'Oh, I've never been down here before!'

'It was a happy occasion,' recalls Brenda. 'The only difficulty was that the staff quite naturally wanted to see the Queen Mother, so I said, "Well, if you line up in the big banqueting hall after lunch I'll bring the Queen Mother up and you can see her as she walks through." And she insisted on walking the length of the hall and speaking to each one.'

On 15 July Cardinal Suenens came to stay for the weekend.

Lambeth preparations may also have been on Stuart's mind when pondering his address to clergy of the diocese of Bath and Wells on 13 June. But they were certainly there later in June when he visited a religious community in Northumberland to speak to the brothers there. In preparation for his visit he had decided to read Irenaeus' book *Adversus Omnes Haereses* (*Against All Heresies*). In one short book this second-century bishop of a small diocese in an unfashionable part of the world was taking on all heresies, including two that were then threatening the course of Christian belief. From his relatively obscure situation, Irenaeus was fighting a battle of the first magnitude that history would acknowledge. The dramatic situation and the spiritual issues appealed to Stuart enormously.

When he knew what to say about a given subject but didn't know how to get it across, he would often take the problem with him on an early morning walk with the dog. Brenda recalls one such day when he set off, dog at heel, and Lambeth lectures in mind. The relaxed stride of the angular figure and scampering dog would not have given the impression of an archbishop at work. But when he returned he said with glee: 'I've got it!' There would be yet one more bishop at Lambeth: he would 'take Irenaeus with him' and he would allow his audience to become aware of their special guest, busily pondering Lambeth's life and business. That dramatic device would provide a way of looking together at essentials.

For the first time in its history the three-week Conference was to be residential. Bishops would be living together and not shuttling to and fro between hotel and meeting place. That alone was to make a huge difference. The West Indian steel band playing at the opening service was immediate evidence of the will to relax and internationalize both the feeling and style of the Conference and also to encourage wider and freer participation by Third World bishops. Family feeling was backed up at evensong on the first night when Dr Coggan himself played the piano for the service. The Conference theme was 'Today's Church in Today's World: with a special focus on the ministry of bishops' and Dr Coggan's opening sermon was on the text 'I will hearken to what the Lord will say' (Psalm 85.8).

The Conference began each day with the Eucharist celebrated by the different provinces in their own languages – Arabic, Swahili, Shona, English, Spanish, and so on. Following the death, during the Conference, of Pope Paul VI, there was also a Eucharist celebrated by the Roman Catholics present. Whereas in 1968 it was six days before a Third World bishop rose to speak from the floor, this time the first speeches from the floor were from bishops from Kenya, the West Indies, and Polynesia. Years later, in an interview, Stuart was to say that 'at Lambeth '78 it was the Africans who made the running'.

The inherent problem was that of attempting work best tackled by two different kinds of gathering – a Council seeking solutions to problems, and a Congress sharing rich experience from many lands. Africans had been pressing for urgent worldwide proclamation of the gospel and Canadians were seeking a culturally and economically relevant word from God to society. In their different ways these pressures expressed the wish of the bishops to be real bishops who had not ceded their leadership to the ACC. According to the agreed principle of flexibility, the programme was reviewed at the point where Stuart began his lectures.

In this crucible of concern he displayed his characteristic way of achieving personal rapport on big occasions. He began:

> We ought not only to be listening to what God will say to us as a Conference but what God will say to us as individual men, Christians, priests, bishops. It is the mark of a skilled wireless operator that he is able, even when deluged with sound, to be nearly always able to identify his own base operator and to read it even though the air is full of Morse. And it could be that amidst all the noise of this Conference and of this coming week, it may be a question perhaps of listening through the noise and hearing what God says to us as individuals.

The prayer that he used then and subsequently before each talk had the same directness of appeal: 'Eternal God, Who tarriest oft beyond the time we hoped for but never beyond the time appointed by Thee, from Whom cometh in due season the truth that cannot lie, the counsel that cannot fail, make us faithful to stand upon our watch-towers and to wait for what Thou wilt say to us.'

Any unease that may have crept into the spirit of conscientious and enthusiastic men was tackled head on: 'Let's face it. We've all made a mess of things.' For any who felt that some bishops were more equal than others he then introduced Irenaeus who, he said, was 'no Prelate living it up on the banks of the Ouse', but a man with 11 clergy, in an unfashionable diocese, struggling with major heresies and possessing an 'unerring eye for essentials'. Much of the Conference, he said, like much of General Synod, was concerned with relatively unimportant things. Irenaeus took issue only on essentials – the heresy of Marcion, for example, which cut the faith off from its Old Testament roots, thus severing the essential link between the doctrines of creation and salvation. And, on the other hand, the heresy of Valentinus, who 'had no time for the flesh' – and consequently made impossible the doctrine of an incarnation. Theology, he said, comes from confronting problems, and a theology that is not capable of becoming a way of life is no theology at all. The essential thing is to be identified with Christ, and he was to speak to them about identification with him in his manhood, in his burdens, in his suffering, and in his vision.

In focusing on Christ's manhood, Stuart considered humanity in terms both of its inheritance and the impact upon it of current events. Human inheritance is that of all mankind 'knowing itself to be outside Eden', yet not outside God's love and purpose. Within that human and theological context the fluctuating times are full of influences to which people are often oblivious. Jesus was born into manhood such as this, and Christians are called to identify with him in it. For 'this little Jewish man was King of Kings – He is the Word made flesh'. Political thinking, he said, was 'thin and insubstantial' in comparison with the 'audacity of Christianity'. Christianity is a new evolutionary process within the story of mankind. It was no escapism, but a correction in the balance of busy minds coping with the world as it is. His concluding prayer was: 'God help me to know the deep truth within: "for me to live is Christ".'

In his second lecture laughter greeted his explanation of Conference business to an intrigued Irenaeus. It was a welcome approach to distinguishing between what in their business was important and what was essential. Without downgrading 'important' matters, he insisted that the Church's essential concern is for mankind's rebirth in Christ, the New Adam. Greek ideas about the difference between God and humanity had created difficulties that Christian theologians had struggled with down the ages. Humanity and God, however, are not incompatible and Christ's manhood is accessible: 'He became what we are so that we can become as He is'. In the intellectual struggle between faith and culture there are no ready-made answers and this is nothing new. Our theological labour is not over. However, in sharing common cause with Christ his followers are not identifying themselves with the world, but with Christ in the world. Identification with Christ in the burdens he bore is the key to Christian involvement in human need. This reveals the spirit in which to care for the world and its troubles.

On Wednesday his third address was about suffering. No ideology can claim attention, he said, unless it attends to suffering. He spoke about the 'sheer perversity' of it and hinted at personal experience when speaking of 'a pain in the mind reactivated from long ago'. Jesus exemplified the human condition and in it made a creative response to the Father's will. Suffering for him was the inevitable consequence of conflict with evil: 'All the experience of mankind, recapitulated in Christ, and pumped through a human heart provided an objective event in the spiritual world to be rested upon.' Jesus saw the travail of his soul. Christians are called to identification with Christ in his suffering; mankind can know that a 'heartache on earth would strike a note in Heaven'.

On Thursday his theme was identity with Christ in his victory, but began with an account of Jesus' seeming failures: these appeared to be with his own family, with areas of unbelief, with the Pharisees, with Judas, and with Peter. 'How would you think and talk about Jesus', he asked, 'if He were a cleric on your diocesan staff?' Then he went on to review Christ's victories: over demons, despair, and prejudice. For Jesus, there were victories in defeat: 'The moment of defeat is to cease to rely on God.' With this in mind, Stuart spoke of false success, alluding to the way in which the world was invading the Church in terms of courting the attentions of television, looking for popularity, and for the important 'seats at the synagogue'. Our eternal and significant victories arise out of our failures. There is a victory for a broken man with no spirit in him. 'The Church must be of God,' he said, 'if, being so bad, it has lasted so long.'

He concluded the series on the Friday morning by speaking of identity with Christ in his vision. Again Irenaeus proved a helpful ally. He was a man located in time between the Fathers and Athanasius – that is to say, between the authentic authority of the teaching of the early Church and the full-orbed dogmatic expression of it fashioned by the great Councils. Given the theological debate in which Irenaeus was engaged, he 'was our sort of bishop in our sort of church with our sort of theology'. He could not appeal to the Councils of the Church and their Creeds. He was concerned to create a theology that could be lived by a new humanity in the second creation. 'We must not be mesmerised,' he said, 'by our image of the Catholic Church.' 'Our sort of vision' is of our new humanity in Christ. We must beware preoccupation with unimportant things. In appraising church work we must 'judge the temperature' by what the Church is doing. For the Hebrews, vision comes in terms of command. Vision is not a thing to lose but a thing to learn, and it is learned by following Jesus.

The lectures made a deep impression to be taken to all parts of the Anglican Communion where they were to be remembered for decades to come. In the short term they inspired a group of American bishops on their return home to form 'The Irenaeus Fellowship'. At the end of the lectures one American bishop said to Bishop Morris Maddocks that it was now obvious who would be the next Archbishop of Canterbury.

Soon to be known was the identity of the new Pope. He took the name of John Paul, and on 1 September during his first week in office Stuart had an audience with him, being the most senior Anglican representative at his enthronement on 3 September. To worldwide consternation, the 65-year-old Pontiff died on 30 September after only 33 days in office, thus Stuart was the only Archbishop of the Church of England to have met with him as Pope. On that day, having in the meantime addressed the Church Missionary Society (CMS) Northern Congress, Stuart was flying from Manchester for a six-day visit to the Republic of Ireland. Brenda, however, feeling far from well, had had to drop out of the journey. After a range of meetings, and having already conducted a day conference for clergy, Stuart attended a meeting for Jewish Christian Understanding being held in Cork. Returning home there was a meeting of the House of Bishops to attend in London while Brenda went to hospital for tests and subsequently began to recover.

'The great day in Liverpool' was how he noted 25 October. This was the service to mark the completion of Liverpool Cathedral. It was attended by Her Majesty the Queen and Stuart preached the sermon, proclaiming that 'the stones cry out'.

Reflection on the Lambeth Conference was on the agenda of General Synod in November, and for Bishop John Howe's report Stuart took the chair, saying, 'I was at the 1968 Lambeth Conference, and the 1978 Conference, was, from my point of view, an entirely different experience. There are ecclesiastical experiences I could well do without, but this was not one of them, and I came back from it refreshed and invigorated and certainly with a very much deeper concern and sense of pride in the Anglican Communion as such.' John Howe, significantly, spoke of the direction in which the Anglican Communion was going and saw it

as a steady transition from the situation where the Church of England was, as it were, some would say the head office or the Mother Church, and the Provinces and the dioceses the branch offices or the daughter Churches, to the situation where the Anglican Communion sees itself as one worldwide family of equals. ... Over the last ten years the Anglican Communion has quietly, gently, crossed an important watershed towards which, I believe, the great mission endeavour of the Church of England has long been looking forward. .... I think I am in general agreement with one of your own bishops who wrote to me after the conference and said: 'I felt I was in at the rebirth of the Anglican Communion – a kind of recapitulation with a long evolution ahead'. By nature I am a little more cautious than that, but on the whole I would not disagree.

As the year drew towards its end Stuart's next book was nearing completion, and by 18 November he had completed the ninth of its 12 chapters. It was one in which he wished to show the link between law and freedom, and was to be called *The Trumpet in the Morning*.

The great year ended with domestic adventures. A new dinghy had arrived at Bishopthorpe and on Boxing Day Stuart was afloat in it and clearing the Palace pond. By the 29th the river had risen, the Bishopthorpe cellars were flooded, and Stuart's diary records: 'Dinghy used to collect wood, etc.' The occasion brought a much recounted telephone conversation with an official at the electricity company. In reply to Stuart's question about what to do about the underwater fuse boxes, the reply was: 'Well, your Grace, on no account attempt to walk on the water.'

A VACANCY AT CANTERBURY

As the retirement of Donald Coggan approached there was a portentous look about Stuart's schedule for the coming year. A month-long tour of India and Sri Lanka was planned for the spring and a heavy programme in Canada arranged for the autumn. Accompanied by Brenda he visited Sri Lanka from 8 to 14 February, preaching, lecturing, and making pastoral visits before an onward flight to India. From 14 February to 6 March they visited the Mar Thoma Church in Kerala where, at two conventions, Stuart preached daily for two weeks on a dried-up riverbed to congregations of 100,000 people, and Brenda – invited to speak to a 'women's meeting' – found herself addressing a gathering of 40,000. Rounding out the programme were engagements with the Church of South India. It was a month of much travelling and speaking in very high temperatures. Stuart was at the height of his powers as a speaker, but for a 61-year-old the schedule was physically punishing.

Returning home they were hosts to a three-day conference of bishops' wives at Bishopthorpe, with mid-March bringing heavy snowfalls in Yorkshire and a sense of change all round. At the end of March Prime Minister James Callaghan called a General Election for 3 May and on 4 May 1979 Margaret Thatcher came to power.

On 5 June, while Stuart was fulfilling engagements in Jersey, Donald Coggan announced his retirement. At once speculation began about his successor. Would it in fact be Stuart? He would certainly have been a popular choice. Someone asked him directly what he thought about the job, and his reply had significant undertones. Without his usual twinkle he said that he had other and more important questions on his mind, including the 'salvation of my immortal soul'. It was not easy to judge whether this was a fairly light-hearted remark, sufficiently highly coloured to fend off further enquiry, or whether it was admitting a current sense of frailty. Word of a seemingly ambivalent attitude got about and he found himself strongly urged to be open to accepting the post, with one influential correspondent writing to him plainly about the ground-swell of public opinion set in his favour. But whatever the truth of the matter, something seems to have been troubling him for on 8 June he wrote: '"Why are you so full of heaviness, my soul?" (Psalm 42.6). There is a kind of heaviness not entirely due to speculation, public or personal, about the next Archbishop of Canterbury but to the onset of "dread" at the issues of life and death in one's own person. We are strangers and pilgrims on the earth.'

The high-profile success of his work, peaking spectacularly in the previous 12 months, together with the prospect of another demanding tour in Canada, was of an order that can take over-exposed public figures to their limit. It is also likely that the terminal illnesses of two of his bishops in the north, Gordon Fallowes of Sheffield, and Douglas Sargent, were weighing upon him personally.

Would Stuart have been the right man for the job? One who worked with him most closely and regarded him most highly was his lay chaplain David Blunt. In Stuart's first years at York, David thought Stuart was undoubtedly destined for Canterbury. His estimate of him could not have been higher: 'I think if he had been physically stronger and perhaps a bit less modest he would (or could) have had some of the public acclaim given to the Pope.' He retained the latter view, but modified the former one. He came to believe that the Canterbury agenda would prevent Stuart from fulfilling the kind of role he had developed from his base at York, and would deprive him of the time needed to do the things he did best and that were needful in Church and society.

The uncertainty continued. On 16 July 1979 Stuart's diary records without comment: 'Interview with PM.' What passed between him and Margaret Thatcher is not known. On the following day he and Brenda attended a garden party at Buckingham Palace followed by a meal with chief rabbi Immanuel Jakobovits. August brought an interrupted holiday at the cottage in Marloes, with trips to London and to Sheffield for the funeral of Bishop Gordon Fallowes. And on 25 August shock waves ran through the nation as Earl Mountbatten was killed on his yacht by an IRA bomb, and 18 soldiers died.

It was on 7 September that Robert Runcie's appointment to Canterbury was announced. Stuart's diary notes: 'At Auckland Castle. Returned for lunch. Institution at Hedon. Announcement of Bob's appointment to Canterbury.'

On 14 September he wrote: '"Forsake me not O God in my old age when

I am gray-headed till I have shown the strength of your arm to future gener-ations" (Psalm 71.18 – Liturgical). Not a plea for a great old age but for effective witness influencing the course of future history (a message for the next five years in York?!)' On 23 September he preached at a reunion service of the Green Howards, reflecting on Mountbatten's murder and taking the theme 'Be strong'. His diary entry for 27 September was: 'The lament of every child of man at some point in his life – "why did I not perish at birth?" And the answer must be that God in his inscrutable love has some purpose for us in this painful pilgrimage to self-knowledge and self-oblation.'

On 14 November, again accompanied by Brenda, he set off for Toronto and Vancouver. The programme included a meeting with the Prime Minis-ter, the receiving of an honorary doctorate at Toronto, and a series of social occasions in influential circles. In his lectures his principal concern was to deepen Christian faith and understanding, and to strengthen people in the work of the ministry. Among his lecture titles was (at Wycliffe Theological College, Toronto) 'Our Lord as Pastor, Teacher, Prophet and Evangelist'. For Wycliffe alumni, significantly for men who were 'at the coal face' of min-istry, his subject was 'Christ in the Wilderness'. In Vancouver (26–28 November) his theme was 'The Bible in Preaching, Counselling, Prayer and Study'. Characteristically, each occasion had its own lecture.

He was impressive among archbishops not only for his lecture output, but also for managing to write so many books while in office. In his four years at York he had published three, and would write two more before retirement – all extra to a workload too heavy for most. Moreover, his mingling with people on or after public occasions was never perfunctory. He liked to estab-lish a real and felt contact and there is a price to be paid for such openness. He was apt to be drained not so much by speaking to large numbers en masse, but by exposure to too many individuals. Some public figures cope with con-tinual over-exposure by developing an inner sheath to protect their natural vulnerability. This he seems never to have done. As with his curacy days, and as with his care for his family and immediate colleagues, it was Stuart's nature to carry them in his heart. It seems he paid this price in Canada, and the long flight home from Vancouver seems to have driven home the sense of exhaus-tion that had been building up.

A TIME OF EXHAUSTION

As the busy year drew to an end he was clearly drained, and early in the new year his body told him what his mind had been neglecting. He awoke one morning to face the usual round of duties only to realize that all at once it was for the moment beyond his powers. He was suffering a form of burn-out and had no option but to take time off.

This was a double blow. It had physical effects that were debilitating for some time, making him shaky and uncertain, and introducing for a while an occasional stumble in his speech. But it came also as an affront. In order to guard against exhaustion he had been careful to build proper rest periods into his daily routine, and proper holidays into his year, and had taught others to do likewise. But the care with which he did so indicates the level of stress to which he was accustomed, and signs of it are scattered throughout his diaries. On 25 June 1970 he had written, 'Tension and overstrain are the "sufferings" through which God calls me to inner obedience, quietness of spirit, a yielding mind, independence of the "world" and its judgements.' On 15 May 1971 he had written, '"The cool twilight I longed for has become a terror" (Isaiah 21.4) "Twilight and Trembling", Ainsworth p. 138. The cry of many a retired man.'

He saw the doctor for a complete physical check-up and was told to stop work immediately. On 25 January John Habgood, Bishop of Durham, was able to undertake the consecration of David Lunn to be the new Bishop of Sheffield, an arrangement that did not, however, stop Stuart and Brenda from providing the usual hospitality to the future bishop on the eve of the consecration. Reports of his indisposition appeared in the press. On 23 January *The Times* carried the headline 'Archbishop Exhausted'. 'This is not quite how it is,' he wrote in a letter to Edward Patey, 'but there is no doubt that I shall have to cut back on public engagements. This would not be at all a bad thing if it gave me a little extra time for study, reflection, thought and prayer which I have always thought to be ingredients of the ministry. All this leads up to the point that I fear I shall not be free on Monday March 10th though I would like to be there.'

There is no doubt that this was a daunting experience for him. As is the way of the world, some people looked for its cause in the possibility of concealed inadequacies. For others, his time of exhaustion was to provide a faulty lens through which to study the man and his work, shifting the focus from the achievements that preceded and followed it. While he did not regain his maximum powers for the administrative and organizational drudgery of high office, he was in other respects to continue to learn and grow.

Stuart was not of course without his faults, but within the wide spectrum of his life the criticisms are confined to a remarkably narrow sector. Some people felt that in confronting problems he was too 'laid back', and that in personal meetings would go too far in encouraging them to solve their own problems. Most, however, came away strengthened and refreshed by the degree of his empathy and understanding and of his confidence in their ministry. Often the problem remained, but did so in a different spiritual context – one in which they had a new attitude and the upper hand. Both as a child and an adult, Tim Blanch says that he was able to talk over personal problems with his father. In terms of transactional analysis, he reflects, Stuart was nearly always 'adult to adult', a role that also characterized his approach to his clergy in their own problems. Thinking in Myers-Briggs personality types, Tim sees him as 'absolutely an intuitive – a perceiver'. In confronting difficult issues between people, he believes his father was brave: 'He wouldn't shy off talking about difficult things.' He was not, though, very good at expressing anger: 'It came out – you knew it was there – but it wasn't very open. He'd never shout. Not even in the family.' Nevertheless, 'he carried quite a strong emotional charge'.

There was also a view that his radical thinking was not always backed by practical plans for translating it into action. Maybe this was the downside of a teaching ministry designed to open the doors of imagination for others he prayed would be called and gifted for the various tasks involved. But even here one could not be sure that there was not a method in his manner. Tim Blanch recalls a typical incident when 'I spent a few months at home driving him around – I think Joe was ill – and so I remember sitting through a meeting when I knew precisely what he wanted of it and at the end they all agreed it, but all thought it was their idea.'

Stuart didn't go away during this perod of exhaustion, but stayed at Bishopthorpe, dealt with his mail, cut out all public engagements for a month, and thereafter reduced the number of his speaking engagements. There was an immediate review of his way of working, involving his staff at Bishopthorpe. The response to invitations changed from 'Is it possible?' to 'Is it necessary?' And as he began to get back to public occasions the family and chaplains developed a strategy for helping him to leave after-service gatherings more quickly, nudging him gently towards the door for reasonable departure times.

The first time many church leaders saw him that year was at the Northern Consultation for Mission overnight conference at Scargill. Here he was clearly not yet himself, while equally evident was Brenda's strength as she unobtrusively took some of his usual quiet initiatives. As the party gathered for the concluding prayer it was she who suggested they stand in a circle to join hands and pray together – something they had never done before at that gathering.

Most people in most jobs would surely have taken more time off, and it is likely that it would have been better for him to have done so. But it was a learning experience and may well have made him even more sensitive than usual to the fears of one young couple who came to see him with their baby. Anxiety about nuclear warfare was running high and he discovered from this young couple how their generation was powering the resurgence of the Campaign for Nuclear Disarmament (CND). Later in the year, when Stuart was asked to discuss these concerns in a north Yorkshire town, he took with him two nuclear scientists whose calm description of the effects of atomic warfare chilled the gathering of 300 people. Then – and on further occasions later – he said that peace is 'one and indivisible', that no international programme can preclude the possibility of nuclear war, that mankind will have to live for ever with that threat, and that the Christian's problem is not just how to cope with that, but also with the fear itself. It was a point he was to make the following year in General Synod's debate about the nuclear bomb when he was the only speaker to set the issue in the framework of Christian eschatology and the sovereignty of God.

Although still feeling his way back to health, he remained in the public eye and an aside made while preaching in the Minster triggered media interest. He had wondered whether it might be wiser for news editors to include at least one item of good news in each bulletin. In *Living by Faith* (p. 33) he reports:

> I was pursued for interviews with the press that evening, rewarded with a splendid cartoon by Giles the following morning, and almost at once plunged into controversy with the news department of the BBC. My comment was not intended as a criticism of the BBC, although it was inevitably regarded as such. It was an attempt to expose the risks we face in society when we touch the tender nerve of fear . . . the correspondence with the BBC was carried on in a most friendly spirit, but was brought to a grinding halt by the suggestion that every applicant for a post in the news-room should be asked whether he had read Kierkegaard's *Concept of Dread*. That was indeed a somewhat flashy remark on my part, but there is truth in it. Kierkegaard said of himself, 'everything frightens me, life itself frightens me'. What then is the Christian response to the universal experience of dread, to whatever passing fear it may be attached?

Stuart continued to write. He did work for Transworld Radio, and wrote an article for the Sheffield diocesan paper *The Anvil* – the latter showing signs of the deep resources he had been finding in the doctrine of creation. He was also writing another book. It was a writing-up of a series of talks about the Ten Commandments which he had broadcast in America, and *The Ten Commandments* was to be its name when published early the following year. Despite the setback at the turn of the year, he was steadily building up strength for another important trip abroad that was scheduled for the summer.

ISRAEL

From 11 August to 8 September 1980 Stuart made an official visit to Israel. At the time, special interest surrounded the fact that the Anglican Bishop of Jerusalem, the Rt Revd Faik Haddad, was an Arab. The first Arab to be an Anglican bishop in Jerusalem, Najib Cubain, had been consecrated in 1958 to serve under the then Archbishop of Jerusalem, Campbell MacInnes. Faik Haddad, however, was the first Arab diocesan. This was a significant development. Many Arabs numbered themselves among the land's most ancient Christian people, proud of direct links with New Testament times. Many immigrant Jews and Palestinian Muslims were surprised by their presence, and it was important that Bishop Haddad's position in the world Church should be identified and affirmed in a way that furthered good relations all round. Stuart's comfortable understanding of the Jewish community, his recognition of Jews as spiritual colleagues in secular society, his gifts of diplomacy, and his standing in the world ideally equipped him for the task. He had other tasks too.

Coexisting with the special problems between Israel and its neighbours, and the deeply layered tensions between Jew and Arab, were all the complexities of the Christian scene in the Holy Land. These were not confined to the jigsaw of major denominations only partially portrayed by their composite occupation of the Church of the Holy Sepulchre. Anglicanism itself was represented by several strands. The work of the Church's Ministry among the Jews (CMJ), dating back to the 1830s, had helped create the Anglican bishopric in Jerusalem, a development so far from being simple that for some years an Anglican had alternated with a Lutheran as bishop of the one see.

Later work by the Church Missionary Society (CMS) among the Arab population helped lay the foundations of the diocese, while – under the influence of the Oxford Movement – the Jerusalem and the East Mission made its own major contribution. In Galilee and the West Bank many parishes owe their origin to the work of the CMS, while in Jerusalem, Christ Church, Jaffa Gate, is the descendant of CMJ forebears, and St George's Cathedral has spiritual links with the Jerusalem and the East Mission. Towards the end of the twentieth century Christ Church had become evangelical and charismatic, and St George's liberal catholic in an English broad church tradition. Further refinements of complexity reside in the fact that although Christ Church is part of the diocese of Jerusalem, much of its property and funding is owned by the Israel Trust of the Anglican Communion (ITAC) by which CMJ conducts its ministries and holds its properties in Israel – properties that also include a hostel and study centre in Tel Aviv and a fine conference centre on the slopes of Mount Carmel. Within this brotherhood of faith Stuart had engagements with each group and lectures to deliver.

Judaism itself is far from having a monolithic form, and its varieties – orthodox, liberal, progressive, and indeed secular and atheistic – are all well represented in Israel, while Islam's varieties are also there, though more apt to be seen under the one blanket of political alignment with the Palestinian cause.

Stuart was able to relate with seeming ease to every group largely because of his theological understanding of each, and his unerring concern to meet individuals at their centres of self-understanding. But he felt the need to rest and tune in afresh to the life of that wonderful and troubled land.

Earlier in the year Stuart and Brenda had discussed with Israel's London ambassador, Schlomo Argov, their wish to have a fortnight's private holiday in Israel before embarking on their official engagements. They wanted time for rest and preparation in a place where they could absorb in greater measure the feel of the land and its history ancient and modern. Consequently Mr Argov made special arrangements for them to stay at Israel's oldest kibbutz, Degania Aleph, a working community on the southern shore of Galilee. The birthplace of Moshe Dayan and other founding figures of modern Israel, it was not normally open to residential guests. Here they stayed in the congenial care of Alan and Yona Shapiro, Yona herself being a child of the community. This proved to be a wonderfully happy arrangement.

As the Blanches arrived in pitch darkness one hour after midnight – Stuart in clerical garb – the Shapiros were at first uncertain about how to entertain an archbishop and his wife. Next morning, however, Stuart appeared in shorts and open-necked shirt, and throughout the following fortnight long hours were spent in expansive conversation on the patio of their single-storey house, in the shade of a magnificent bo tree and looking out across the hot glitter of the great lake. For Stuart it was a wonderfully restorative and happy time, one when he absorbed from their hosts and their community a fresh impression of Judaism as a living religion. For his part, Alan Shapiro would later recall how Stuart made them see the Bible and their own land in a new light. Stuart and Brenda were to return the hospitality in the future when the Shapiros came to stay with them in Bishopthorpe.

Later on in the trip, Stuart's official engagements included visits to the President of Israel, the Speaker of the Knesset, the Mayor of Jerusalem, and the Greek, Armenian, and Latin patriarchs, and a round of visits to the ecclesiastical and civil authorities on the West Bank with Bishop Faik Haddad. At Jaffa he opened the new Study Centre at Immanuel House, where he lectured on 'Jesus as Teacher of the Law'. At Christ Church, Jaffa Gate, in Jerusalem, he lectured on 'Jesus as Prophet and Evangelist'. At St George's he conducted a quiet day for diocesan clergy where one of the Arab clergy present, Samir Kafity, ultimately became the Bishop of Jerusalem. Twenty-five years later, with no prior notice of the question put to him, Bishop Kafity was still able to recall the headline points of Stuart's talk. He spoke about ministry, referring once more to Irenaeus and saying that ministry equals servanthood and is always exercised in a special place and context. In this case it was in the Holy Land in the 'here and now'. In this part of the world the biblical imagery of servant-ministry has its original impact: shepherd, farmer, healer, reconciler in the context of the Israel/Palestine crisis. The situation signalled the importance of the role of the Christian Church in its ministry of reconciliation, justice, and peace. The three go hand in hand. You cannot speak of one without the other. Such was Bishop Kafity's instant recall in 1995 of a quiet day conducted by Stuart a quarter of a century earlier. 'It was clear', said Bishop Kafity, 'that he had had more contact and interaction with the Jews than with the Arabs, and this was one of the few times he encountered Arab Christians.' He was, he said, sympathetic and attentive when 'he knew who and what we are and what we stand for'. He gave the Arab Christians an 'active hearing'. The following week Stuart was back in Jaffa to conduct a quiet day for CMJ staff at the school, and their final weekend was spent in what Stuart called a pleasantly relaxed atmosphere at Stella Carmel near Haifa with nearly all the members of the CMJ staff.

MATTERS OF UNITY

A major feature of life at this stage was that of getting used to a different colleague at Canterbury. With Donald Coggan in office there had been what was for the Church of England the unusual combination of two evangelicals in its two top posts. But while sharing a kindred spiritual and theological formation, Donald and Stuart were none the less men of different temperaments and ways of working. With Robert Runcie, matters were reversed. They were clearly of different traditions, but in personality had a good deal in common. It was to be a good arrangement. As a new primate Robert Runcie consulted widely, acquired a team of advisers, aides, and (something Stuart would never have contemplated) speech writers. A warm friendship developed between them. In their distribution of responsibilities one task that came to Stuart was that of chairing a national Partners in Mission (PIM) consultation.

General Synod wanted to 'open the books' of the Church of England to Anglicans from other countries. They wanted to learn from Christians from lands where hardship was partnered by spiritual growth. The plan was to invite 17 people from around the world to engage with 56 'home partners' in looking at the central structures and voluntary bodies of the Church, and at 17 selected dioceses, to see how well the structures involved served the Church's primary role. The task was much to Stuart's taste and sense of what was important in life and it came in a year when the effect of not accepting so many invitations gave his programme a relatively uncluttered look. For the first time in his episcopate he passed a whole year without developing and presenting a new lecture, although his sermons were as fresh and well worked as ever and 1981 saw the publication of his book *The Ten Commandments*. He also began to speak more frequently in General Synod.

His years at York had paralleled the life of the Churches Unity Commission. Set up in 1974 to develop proposals for a covenant for unity between Anglican, Methodist, and URC churches, it was due to present its report at General Synod's February sessions prior to their being sent to the dioceses for consideration. Within the provisions of ten propositions addressing the complex situation of reunion there had emerged the idea of a covenanting service in which participating churches would receive each other's ministries with prayer for God's healing grace with a future commitment to episcopacy. However, a dissentient report had been presented by some members who believed such an arrangement to compromise the character of the historic episcopate, and Stuart had a point he wished to make:

> I honour the tradition which is represented here, and that tradition, both in its theology and in its spirituality, contributed very largely to my own ordination; but I do find, not the content of the report, but the tone of it, surprising. It has a kind of certainty which I think can hardly be justified by the evidence before us. It speaks, for example, of the 'invariable practice' of episcopacy, it speaks about the 'fundamental principles of Catholic order', it speaks of the 'historic

threefold ministry'. These are perfectly reputable, well rehearsed opinions, but they fall short by far of any kind of certainty.

It was a belief, he said, that 'certainly not believed "ubique, semper, ab omnibus" and there is not the slightest evidence that it was ever so'. He quoted with approval a letter written by Professor Hanson to *The Times* a few weeks earlier saying, 'No denomination should claim that its ministry is superior to others simply on the grounds that the ministry derives in a direct line from Christ. That is quite incapable of proof and for many centuries in the life of the Church it has not even been attempted to be proved.'
He concluded:

> We are not just in the position of inheriting by the grace of God a system of ministry which is rich and well proven and to which we adhere. We are not simply offering that to other people as an act of grace. . . . I believe that the movement towards unity and all that that implies is absolutely essential to the mission to our country. Therefore I would hope that we shall . . . accept these motions in the belief, not simply that we shall be offering something which others lack, but that we shall be receiving something which we ourselves lack (*GS Synod Report*, vol. 12, no. 1, pp. 215–19).

Work on PIM continued through the year and its concluding sessions were held at Scargill House from 29 June to 3 July, with members going on to join the summer sessions of General Synod, held as usual on the campus of the University of York. At the General Synod's Sunday morning Eucharist in the Minster, Stuart devoted his sermon to the PIM experience. We need 'Pauline zeal,' he said, so that 'the Church by law established might be by Gospel renewed'. Revival in the Church could revitalize the nation: 'I look for a revived Church of England in a revived England – nothing less.' The afternoon gathering was not a formal session of Synod, but a conference in which the PIM partners participated. Speeches – warm, colourful, and blunt – spoke of opportunity and resources, of things that the Church could do with and do without. In due course the report of the consultation was published under the title *To a Rebellious House*, which Stuart presented to Synod in November of the following year. In an exercise so much needing a balance between challenge and support, Dr Runcie said he had never heard the mixture so well put.

RIOTS AND ROYAL WEDDING

Ironically it was on the evening of that particular day that serious rioting broke out in the Toxteth district of Liverpool, the first in a sequence of inner-city riots in other places. Synod members, like the rest of the nation, were startled by the scale of the violence and thoughtful about its implications. The attention of the world, however, was increasingly being focused upon the wedding on 29 July 1981 of Prince Charles and Lady Diana Spencer. Never-theless, for many English cities the hot month of July was rife with unrest. The Toxteth riots continued sporadically for several weeks, and 10 July was labelled in the press as Britain's 'night of anarchy' with rioting in parts of London, Wolverhampton, Birmingham, Reading, Luton, Chester, Hull, and Preston, as well as Liverpool where, at the height of the troubles, its Bishop, David Sheppard, and Roman Catholic Archbishop Derek Worlock, at some risk to themselves, took to the streets together to appeal for restraint.

On the eve of the royal wedding television was presenting a powerfully evocative programme of panoramic aerial views of the British Isles accom-panied by music and poems chosen by Poet Laureate John Betjeman. On the same night in Liverpool, a 22-year-old man was struck and killed by a police personnel-carrier being driven along a pavement to clear rioters. Unem-ployment, poor housing, and racism were root causes. 'But there are signs of hope,' wrote a Liverpool vicar in his journal that day. 'Not just in the very good work of the local churches in Toxteth but also in the presence at the wedding of the Dean of St Paul's, Alan Webster. As he read the introduction to the wedding service today I had in mind his words at General Synod earlier this month – speaking about coloured people and immigrants he said that they are part of our past who are now part of ourselves, and that we have to "die to our Englishness", in the sense of an "Englishness" which is exclusive of any who are citizens of the realm.'

For Dr Runcie, still in his first year as Archbishop of Canterbury, the act of presiding at the royal wedding was to make him instantly recognizable worldwide. His engaging manner in the conduct of the service was greatly enjoyed and the world press echoed his words: 'This is the stuff that fairy tales are made of'. To Stuart on that day came the task of broadcasting a special *Thought for the Day* on Radio 4. He spoke of the need for privacy in shared lives which, like those of the Prince and Princess, were to be lived in the full glare of world interest. His concerns and his prayers were accurately focused, and sadly prescient in their implications.

Long-distance travel returned towards the end of the year with a trip to

New Zealand when, accompanied by Brenda, Stuart represented the Archbishop of Canterbury at the centenary of Christ Church Cathedral, taking with him the special burden of a section of Minster glass for Christ Church, and noting on 28 October 'the missing day' aboard a flight via Honolulu. A full round of engagements went well, though a light aircraft flight over southern glaciers left Brenda feeling unwell. From there they went on to Australia to stay with a former parishioner from Eynsham before flying on to Sri Lanka where, at a meeting with clergy in Colombo, Stuart spoke about 'Sources of Mission' and later preached in the cathedral on the theme 'Hallowed past: dynamic future'.

At the end of the year his diary indicates something of his thoughts and prayers at the time: 24 November: '"I saw heaven standing open" (Rev. 19.11). "He sits enthroned above the circle of the earth" (Isa. 40.22). The great visionaries inhabited a high plateau from which they viewed with mingled horror and hope the frantic activities of men on earth. It is the plateau experience, not the peak experience, which we need'; 3 December: '"Do not dwell on the past. See I am doing a new thing" (Isa. 43.18,19). It happens insidiously – we dwell on the past (imagined adequacy, high spirits, long horizons) to the disadvantage of the present (less confident, apprehensive, cautious). But the new thing may be born within that unwelcome experience.'

One new thing coming to birth was yet another book. It was to be called *Living by Faith* and in its aim and content was itself something new. It was to be the most autobiographical of his books, and his writing began to show new powers as this essentially private man openly delved into the deeper places of his inner life. His style was frank and informal. Coming to terms with his period of burn-out and finding resources for his inner pilgrimage was a process bearing its own kind of fruit. The book, when published, was to be a boon to many. George Thomas, Speaker of the House of Commons, was to keep a copy of it by his bedside to the end of his life.

THE YEAR 1982

The deep mid-winter brought heavy snowfalls, and Stuart's and Brenda's post-Christmas break in Marloes found them completely snowed in at the cottage, with Stuart unable to get to London for a meeting of General Synod standing committee. They eventually made their escape when the harbourmaster picked them up from Dale Fort steps in his launch.

Plans were afoot for the Pope's visit to Britain later in the year. It was to be a busy winter. Back in York, Stuart installed David Watson as a provincial canon and started work on his 'charge' to the Minster, a substantial document that he would not deliver until the autumn. On his sixty-fourth birthday he delivered a lecture to the annual Christian Local Broadcasters' Association conference at Swanwick, his theme being 'Communicating with God'. A few days later he shared in an ecumenical confirmation service, and quickly followed that by hosting a 'Feed the Minds' concert at Bishopthorpe, after which came an Anglo-Israel dinner attended by Israeli Ambassador Schlomo Argov and his wife. A busy month ended with an enjoyable trip to speak to newly qualified RAF navigators at RAF Finningley.

With the approach of the Pope's visit, feelings were running high in some quarters. On 10 March Robert Runcie, making an extended visit to Liverpool, was shouted down by a group of protesters as he began a midday Lent address in Liverpool Parish Church. On 29 March the final report of ARCIC was published and Stuart noted 'a somewhat euphoric press conference'. The euphoria was not to last, though. Two days later he wrote, 'Living in the wake of the ARCIC Final Report and the fierce reactions to it.' On 2 April he wrote: 'Surprised by my own revulsion against the excitements roused by the unhappy coincidence of the Pope's visit and the publication of the ARCIC document.' That proved to be the day when Argentina invaded the Falkland Islands. Two days later the British task force dramatically set sail for the South Atlantic. For war veterans – service and civilian – there was the dread sense of being at war again. Arrangements for the Pope's visit, meanwhile, were put on hold because of Vatican links with Argentina. The mixture of emotions was complete.

On 9 April, which was Good Friday, Stuart was clearly feeling the absence of the family, for he wrote, 'Good Friday. Susan, Tim and Angie at Marloes, Al at Inverness with Bill, Hilary at Little Garth, Tim in London. It has been a strange Lent unduly preoccupied with ecclesiastical affairs and the Pope's visit in particular.' Good Friday, he noted, 'gaunt and cold', stands over against such lesser matters. On 14 April he was busy preparing a pamphlet entitled *What the Church of England Stands For*.

April took Stuart and Brenda to warmer climes on a four-week tour of the Gulf States. On 24 April Stuart laid the foundation stone of a new church complex in Abu Dhabi and on 1 May he rehallowed St Christopher's pro-Cathedral in Bahrain, making a formal visit to the Emir of Bahrain the following day. On 4 May they flew to Cyprus where he made an official visit to Archbishop Chrysostomos and gave Bible readings at a five-day clergy conference. They returned home on 15 May to a state of uncertainty about the Pope's visit.

The embarrassing on-off situation was resolved in time for the visit to proceed, and it is thought that Derek Worlock, the Roman Catholic Arch-bishop of Liverpool, played a key role in the final decision-making process. On 20 May British troops landed on the Falkland Islands, and while the battle raged the Pope began his tour of Britain. And on 29 May, two weeks before the end of the Falklands War, the Pope and Robert Runcie knelt side by side in Canterbury Cathedral to pray at the tomb of Thomas à Becket – a moment of spiritual depth that was also a massive media event. Nowhere was the Pope welcomed more warmly than in Liverpool which he visited next day. It was Whit Sunday. Here a crowded cathedral erupted with joy as he made his crowd-delayed entry 45 minutes behind schedule, and where he and David Sheppard embraced before processing along Hope Street for a similar event at the Catholic cathedral. On Whit Monday, in the continuing sunshine of the holiday weekend, the Pope went by helicopter to York where 210,000 people had gathered in festive mood on the Knavesmire and where, to great applause, Stuart also warmly bade him welcome.

On 4 June Stuart and Brenda received the shocking news that their friend, the Israeli ambassador Schlomo Argov, a recent guest at Bishopthorpe, had been gunned down in London. They had enjoyed a warm and fruitful acquaintanceship with both him and his wife and felt his death deeply. It was an event followed, on the next day, by Israel's invasion of Lebanon, coming only a few weeks after Israel had handed back the Sinai peninsula to Egypt and so cutting short all feelings of progress towards peace. Stuart's diary for 4 June reads: 'Schlomo Argov shot in London and critically ill – a bitter expe-rience, the product of the unruly wills and sinful affections of men. . . . The voice said "Cry".' It was also at this time that a future king was born: on 21 June Prince William was born to the Princess and Prince of Wales.

The July Synod of 1982 was not at York but Westminster. It brought the long-awaited debate and vote about covenanting for unity with the Methodist and URC Churches, churches whose governing bodies had already signalled a willingness to proceed. A necessary hernia operation pre-vented Stuart's attendance, though he had earlier made known his support for a scheme that, though 'not perfect', was 'good enough for him'. Having been approved by 36 of the 43 diocesan synods, the scheme now required of General Synod a two-thirds majority in each House (Bishops, Clergy, Laity). The final vote did in fact secure such majorities in the House of Bishops and the House of Laity, but in the House of Clergy the figure showed only 61.9 per cent in favour, and so the scheme failed. The sticking point continued to be a particular view of the historic episcopate deemed integral to unity. It was a sad day, with opponents of the scheme insisting that they too were seeking unity while some of those who had worked and prayed for the success of the scheme felt physically ill at the outcome. One senior bishop returning to Church House for the next day's business found that he had to walk round the block before he could bring himself to re-enter the building. There was sadness upon sadness when the well-loved David Brown, Bishop of Guildford, who had lived with the scheme for so long and had presented it to Synod, died of a heart attack the following week. It seemed that within the terms of current ecclesiology the Church still lacked the power to heal itself.

Still recovering from surgery, Stuart once more invited John Habgood, Bishop of Durham, to stand in for him at the consecration of two new bishops on 22 July. As usual, though, the new bishops, Bill Persson and Donald Tytler, along with their wives, were among the eight overnight guests entertained at Bishopthorpe before the service.

Following 1981's lack of newly written lectures, Stuart's 1982 records list eight new titles. One was his charge to the community of York Minster, and typically it was about mission. In it he said, 'Effective mission does not depend upon tidy organisation and coherent structure alone; it will depend upon the extent to which members of the staff feel themselves part of an organisation committed to the Christian faith, concerned with mission to their world, and aware of a common overriding objective. Mission is always the product of enthusiasm.'

Much on his mind was the care of his suffragans, and one of them, Morris Maddocks, Bishop of Selby, was exercising an increasingly effective ministry of healing. Bishop Maddocks recalls how Stuart

> encouraged me in the writing of my first book *The Christian Healing Ministry*. He allowed me a month off other work to complete it and wrote a gracious foreword. He was kind enough to say that it was one of the best things I had done and talked of it as the standard textbook on the subject. He was always interested in the work of our fellowship of healing prayer groups kept together by a monthly prayer leaflet and an annual gathering on the vigil of Pentecost. When our prayer and work led to the founding of Spennithorne Hall in Wensleydale he came to preach and open it on Easter Monday 1982. Later on that year he saw that my work was increasing owing to the demands to speak all over the country on the healing ministry and wisely sent me on a sabbatical. Anne and I spent it at Burrswood and came to the vision of what we had to do. We returned to report to Stuart. He had been at his prayers about it, as we discerned, and given it much thought. After carefully listening, which he always did, we told him that we felt called to

this ministry full time but we did not know how to go about it. He said: 'Well, I've got a job for you: you can be adviser to Bob and me on the ministry of health and healing. That's the good news. Now for the bad news: there's no money!' We replied that the Lord would provide and we would work at it. This is how the Acorn Healing Trust was formed. Stuart gave us his full support in our setting out. He suggested we get in touch with John Bickersteth [Bath and Wells] and eventually I became an assistant bishop to him when we began our work in April 1983. He and Cantuar gave £1000 towards our setting out.

And so the year was running its course. On 19 October Stuart chaired the House of Bishops' consideration of first reactions to the ARCIC report and the Pope's visit. And as the year drew to its end so too did the final chapters of *Living by Faith*. December brought a special delight with a visit to Liverpool for the opening on 7 December of the new Archbishop Blanch School, a union of two former grammar schools for girls, and an overnight stay with former Archdeacon Eric Corbett and his wife, Sylvia. This time the whole family were home for Christmas, with Stuart having recorded a BBC programme for transmission on Christmas night. On New Year's Eve he appeared on Yorkshire Television's programme *Seven Days*. It was to be his last Christmas as Archbishop of York.

THE LAST MONTHS AT YORK

Stuart reached the age of 65 on 2 February 1983. It was the year in which he played his last game of squash, and in which he was to put into effect his plan to retire. But there was still much to do. Synod's debate about nuclear warfare was scheduled for the February sessions and on 20 January Stuart wrote: 'It is evident that the early church took its bearings less from the past than from the future (Matt. 24 etc.) and I find myself adjusting to that truth as I cope with the steady flow of CND letters. The "end" envisaged by the world is not the one envisaged by the Christian believer.'

On 25 January he notes: '"You will be bound so that you cannot go out among the people. I will make your tongue stick to the roof of your mouth" (Ezek.). Some such experience seems to be inseparable from the prophetic (and apostolic) office – a reminder that it is God who gives the word and may withhold it.' Next day he wrote: 'House of Bishops' acceptance of deed of resignation.' One day later he was involved in a breakfast television programme from 6.30 a.m. to 9 a.m., prior to a further meeting of the House of Bishops and a return to York.

The 'Church and the Bomb' debate took place in General Synod on 10 February when Stuart brought his own well-rehearsed perspective to bear upon it. Five days later came a press conference in London to make public his resignation, an exercise repeated the next day in York. On the day following he had a staff conference at Bishopthorpe with the theme of 'Renewal', a day that brought two long interviews with the media for Brenda, and for Stuart an evening game of squash. Next day (18 February) he was reading Genesis 21 and wrote: 'In a desert place, a slave without a home or family, bitter, desolate, with her only child dying in her sight – and then a well of life-giving water. This is a message repeated over and over again in Holy Scripture and in the life of the believer.'

March brought his last attendance at the Northern Consultation for Mission (NCM) at Scargill. His mind must have gone back over the years to 1969 when such ecumenical gatherings of bishops and other church leaders began at Bishopthorpe. The gatherings had bridged most of his years both at Liverpool and York, their themes ranging widely and including the following: in 1977 – The Christian's Role in Public Affairs; in 1978 – The Educators (Family, Church, School, Media); in 1979 – Freedom and Law; in 1980 – The Church's Aims and Objectives in the 1980s; in 1981 – Young People; in 1982 – Shared Ministry. In 1983, the subject was Marriage and Family Life. Among his memories would have been the chief rabbi's contribution on freedom and law in 1979; the warm spirituality of Cardinal Suenens in 1981, who, with his brief to understand and care for charismatic experience in the Church, led informal devotions in the chapel; and Gerald Priestland's reflections in 1982 about his major radio series on contemporary English Christianity. But what he seemed most to enjoy was the continuum of friendship and the collegial spirit of church leaders learning together. Sessions had more than a little flavour of the 'Little Chapter' at Rochester Theological College and teatime at the House of Lords.

One visitor to the 1981 Consultation who also came as a guest on the two subsequent years was the first local government ombudsman in the north, F. P. (Pat) Cook. Soon after his appointment to this new and little understood post, Stuart had asked him to tea, invited him to address York diocesan clergy, and then to address the NCM. The ending of Mr Cook's talk to the church leaders is a happy gloss on their gatherings: 'We share a concern about the alienation of any citizen from society . . . we share the pursuit of justice, itself an aspect of love. But what you alone can add (hopefully in unison) is the clear call and distant vision. . . . My impression is that people are listening.'

The planned departure of Morris Maddocks for his work with the Acorn

Trust had created the need for a new suffragan bishop, and this was met in the following way. Clifford Barker moved from being Bishop of Whitby to succeed Morris Maddocks at Selby, and for a new Bishop of Whitby Stuart looked – as in the case of his chaplains and chauffeur – to Liverpool. Gordon Bates, Precentor of Liverpool Cathedral, recalls receiving a phone call from Stuart: 'Gordon, I've just decided how you can spend the next 16 years of your life!' And when the future Bishop of Whitby, on a preliminary visit to Bishopthorpe, was seen gazing at a map of the diocese indicating his area of oversight, Stuart cheerfully said: 'Don't look at that yet. It will only make you nervous!' To announce the planned departure of Morris Maddocks to lead the work of the Acorn Healing Trust, Stuart called a press conference at Bishopthorpe on Easter Monday.

His last trip abroad as Archbishop of York came in May when, following a bomb scare at Heathrow, he flew to New York where appointments included an ecumenical lunch and addressing a clergy conference. He returned home on Ascension Day in time for a religious communities' service marking the 150th anniversary of the Oxford Movement.

It was a time of special concern at what proved to be the terminal illnesses of three senior colleagues: Bishops Stuart Cross of Blackburn and Geoffrey Paul of Bradford, and also, after marvellously fruitful remissions from cancer, of Canon David Watson. Stuart took such concerns to heart – 27 May: '"Is the Lord's arm too short?" (Num. 11.23). Moses' understandable rage at what was being expected of him is part of the lesson. The lesson that life is always too much for us and that the Lord's arm is never too short. (Geoffrey Paul in hospital, Stuart Cross persistently unwell.)' Gordon Bates's consecration was on 9 June, and on 11 June Stuart wrote: 'Announcement of Life Peerage.' (His diary records no comment, but he was the first Archbishop of York to be so honoured and it clearly gave him much pleasure.)

He also made the following diary entries:

(16 June): 'I heard a voice I had not known saying I eased your shoulders of the burden and your hands were freed from the load' (Ps. 81.6) – a mysterious verse, variously translated. There is always something unknown, unfamiliar about the voice of personal revelation which invariably surprises him who hears it; (17 June): 'You love the most important places in the synagogues and greetings in the market place' (Lk. 9.43). The unerring shafts against all enjoyment of honours ecclesiastical and secular! We love the praise of men more than the praise of God; (24 June): St John the Baptist. 'When I was brought low He saved me' (Ps. 116.6–10). Geoffrey's illness, C.'s sudden collapse, D.'s protracted problem with her back, plus the

pressures of retiring. 'I was brought very low but He saves me'; (8 July): 'I waited patiently for the Lord' (Ps. 40.1). There are some issues in life in which there is no resolution. The psalmist does not suggest that the Lord answered but that He inclined His ear and heard. He knows our sorrows – and in that knowledge there is a kind of peace; (10 July) [Stuart's and Brenda's Ruby Wedding]: Trinity VI. Early service at St Andrew's – taking us back to Bibury church 40 years ago – when things were simpler! Geoffrey Paul's death reported a.m.

GENERAL SYNOD'S FAREWELL

From 11 to 15 July General Synod met at York. Its business included its farewells to the Archbishop. During the course of that Synod he wrote – 12 July: '"My soul truly waits still upon God for of Him comes my salvation." The willingness to wait when all hope seems to dissolve is the mark of the real man of faith (Bishops dinner)'; 14 July: '"Cast me not away in time of old age" (Ps. 71.9) – a series of farewells, the growing consciousness of how much we shall miss this place and these people, not altogether untouched by "existential" doubt about the future – all this, like every other period of my life, a summons to faith in the goodness of God.'

The last day of Synod was 15 July, and the occasion of affecting farewell speeches by Robert Runcie, Peter Boulton, and J. D. McLean. In the morning, however, Stuart was writing: 'Saul's career is a "tragedy" in the Hebrew mode – the story of a man richly endowed by God and "baptised in the Spirit" who repeatedly falters at the last step. And so even his natural virtues – courage, magnanimity – fail him. His tragedy was the tragedy of the man called to the ultimate "sacrifice" [who] tried to be content with less.'

There could be no doubt of the affection that surrounded the farewells expressed in Synod itself. Robert Runcie spoke of the

quality in him which we all love – his ability to travel light, uncluttered by pomposity and uncorrupted by ecclesiastical clobber. He always seemed to me . . . to carry about with him a sense of being a layman in Holy Orders, surprised to find that God has put him there, and this means that he has been the friend of mayors and mechanics. He would even find something to talk about with a mermaid – well, so would I! But that is not something superficial. It springs from something deep within the heart of the man, the one thing necessary, because his life is rooted in the quiet time and daily Bible reading of his evangelical background, and all his scholarship combined with that has made him in books and sermons a teacher of our faith beloved throughout the world, a hero to generations of students, a personal friend and pastor to clergy and their wives, and an encouragement to any parish, a breath of fresh honest air for the puzzled seeker, and a gentle rebuke to the cynic.

The other source and mainspring is his marvellous family life, because Brenda, who is with us this morning, has been such a wonderful partner who has accepted houses small or immense and turned each of them into a ministry of welcome.

I, as you all know, am an old soldier. He was a sky pilot. He is a converted evangelical in background. I am an unconvinced Anglo-Catholic, but what I want to say – and this is a personal contribution – is that I could not have had a more generous and Christian colleague in the responsibilities we have held together. To put the Archbishop of York in his place is to put him at the heart of our affections. Whenever he is here, whether speaking, rarely but always pointedly, or by his presence, there is something reassuring about it.

Canon Peter Boulton, Prolocutor of York's Lower House of Convocation, included in his speech a reference to Stuart's skill as chairman which has 'made the Synod a friendlier and less anxious place in which the church makes its decisions, and your personality has made it more capable of reconciliation after hard fought debates'. And of his teaching he said: 'When the gales of laughter have faded away you have always brought our debates gently and firmly back to the larger canvas of God's work in creation, redemption and final consummation, your transparent faith that God is in charge. Out of this we have heard your doctrine of the church – the servant of God called to proclaim and foreshadow the Kingdom in joy and without fear.'

Professor J. D. McLean, vice-chairman of the House of Laity, recalled Stuart's prophetic voice in Church and nation, adding, 'for Stuart, the North and indeed the whole world is a great place for mission'.

In his seemingly unprepared response, Stuart bade his own farewell to Synod with a special tribute to those faithful members who read their mountain of papers, did their thinking and their praying, made their decisions, and recorded their votes without ever having made a speech. The day ended with Church House staff repaying Stuart's and Brenda's hospitality over the years by entertaining them to dinner.

And so the days passed, as Stuart's diary records: 18 July: 'Geoffrey's funeral at Bradford'; 19 July: '"The Battle is the Lord's" (1 Samuel 17.47). It would have been a help to have been more vividly aware of it in Liverpool and in York. It would not have made it any less demanding but it would have qualified the stress with a sense of God's responsibility for the outcome. He must reign'; 27 July: 'Royal Garden Party'.

～ 6 ～

Wisdom:
An Active Retirement

AN END AND A BEGINNING

Stuart's diary entry for 31 August 1983 is as follows: 'Last day as Ebor: David and Dorothy and Su for lunch. Barograph descending rapidly.' So he noted the friendly informalities of his last day as primate, observing the drop in atmospheric pressure which was signalling an end to the hot weather. Next day his morning readings from Scripture included the story of Solomon and the Queen of Sheba. As he rose to begin his retirement years he noted: 'It is a heathen monarch who expresses the most impressive admiration for the wisdom of Israel in the person of Solomon – no more spirit left in her. There is a wisdom which has universal appeal even when not associated with the region which gave rise to it (1 Kings 10).'

Glad that they had got used to feeling at home there on holiday trips over recent years, they moved to 'Little Garth' in Bloxham and the rest of 1983 and much of 1984 was occupied with the multiple adjustments of early retirement. Prayer and study were part of an unbroken chain of life in which new strength gathered and new tasks emerged and Stuart settled down to write. One task was calling for his immediate attention. Following the success of his book *The Ten Commandments*, which had appeared in 1981, he had been invited to write a companion volume on the Beatitudes that he was to call *The Way of Blessedness*. He tackled it straight away and it appeared in 1985. 'The book on the Ten Commandments,' he commented, 'began as a series of broadcast talks for American radio where instant communication is the order of the day. This book permits of a more leisurely treatment.' He was on favourite ground, as keen as ever to emphasize the creative balance he found between Old and New Testaments, and pointing to the 'clear connection between the law given to Moses on the mountain in Sinai and the new law given by Christ on a mountain in Galilee'.

While busy with *The Way of Blessedness* he was also invited to compile an anthology of Amy Carmichael's work. It was another project near to his heart, but one that he couldn't tackle within the timescale proposed. Brenda, however, provided a happy solution by volunteering to be the anthologist and, with a foreword by Stuart, the book appeared in the same year as *The Way of Blessedness*. It was a wonderful way to begin retirement years together.

Stuart was, however, soon sought out as a speaker. In March 1984 he lectured in St Martin-in-the-Fields as part of the Bishop of London's Lent course. The theme of the series was 'Power and the Cross' and his subject was 'Jesus and the Tradition', the subject mirroring much of what concerned him throughout his ministry. Tradition, he pointed out, was one of the sources of power unable to make room for the radical theology of Christ. Nevertheless, it is Jesus who said, 'not one jot or tittle shall pass from the law . . .' (Matthew 5.17–20). Education therefore has a dual task – to preserve and transmit the tradition and at the same time to make room for radical reinterpretation of it: 'Jesus was crucified on a Cross made for Him by the heirs of a great religious tradition slavishly devoted to the past and unwilling to change.' Embedded in Stuart's message was a typically terse and memorable saying, weighted like a proverb and signalling much more to come from his marriage of orthodox faith and prophetic spirit: 'Tradition without innovation is dead: innovation without tradition is ephemeral.'

Personal experience gave him understanding of times of darkness encountered by people who are much in the public eye and constantly open to the trouble of others. This understanding was nowhere more apparent than in an address he gave on 17 March 1984 when he returned to York Minster to preach at a thanksgiving service for David Watson. David Watson had pioneered and presided over the remarkable life of St Michael-le-Belfrey in the shade of York Minster where a very large eclectic congregation had sprung up and become the seed-bed of much Christian work around the world. David Watson's last book, *Fear No Evil*, gave an inspiring account of wonderfully fruitful life and work while struggling with terminal cancer. News of his illness had been noted in Stuart's diary and he had prayed for him regularly.

Stuart's text was 'he was a burning and a shining lamp and you were willing for a season to rejoice in his light'. Likening David Watson to John the Baptist as one sent to prepare the way of the Lord, he said:

David, of course, had to pay the price: he had to grow less. There is a sense in which every minister of the gospel is diminished by his ministry. If he has any self-knowledge at all his ministry makes him less confident in himself, less assured, less doctrinaire, and therefore sometimes less secure. . . . Every John the Baptist has his own 'Machaerus', that grim forbidding fortress in the Judaean desert, the place of fear and doubt and spiritual imprisonment. But through it all David never proposed for himself anything other than the will of God. Of course he was occasionally, as everyone else, mistaken about what the will of God was, but he never sought to evade it and he never ceased to seek it. The cost of discipleship of that kind is very high; there is no cheap grace. . . . His study was not of the academic kind, removed from life. It was a struggle to understand the inexplicable, the struggle to express the inexpressible: the struggle to penetrate the ineffable mystery of Christ. . . . Burning and shining is a costly business and it took its toll. . . . There are times when the dazzling outward success only deepens the sense of inner depression and despair.

This was undoubtedly the voice of experience. Others might well have said the same about Stuart. Certainly he was in an area of human experience that he knew well.

TRAVELLING AND WRITING

Another trip to Israel came in the summer of 1984 and 1985 brought an increase in work. Engagements included two working trips, on the first of which, 15–20 February, he gave two lectures in Belfast entitled 'The New Reformation'. In them he traced the roots of the 'old' Reformation back to divisions in medieval theology, outlining papal rivalry during the great schism, the availability of vernacular scriptures, and the search for authority. He then listed comparable features of contemporary Christian life: dissatisfaction with the Church ('we are all Lollards now'), an interest in and dependence on the Bible (12 major translations between 1946 and 1985), a hunger for spiritual experience, and the lack of a theological view of the world. Today's reformers, he said, were not yet identifiable by name but were representatives of movements in contemporary church life, and he saw evidence of their work in liturgical reform, the development of new forms of ministry, and the search for acceptable authority. He ended by saying that 'Faith in the God and Father of our Lord Jesus Christ (experienced, felt, articulated as best we may, and shared across the denominational boundaries) is the only convincing authority available to us (and the only source of unity). It follows that today's reformers in this field are those painfully committed to the pursuit of unity, struggling individually and in groups to recapture the authority of Christ within the doctrinal and institutional bedlam of today's church.'

The period of 22 April–16 May 1985 brought another trip to America, where in Newark, New Jersey, he repeated his lecture on the New Reformation, and in Washington lectured on the role of cathedrals.

A week after returning from America, and almost two years after his own retirement, he was invited to tackle the subject of retirement before a gathering of retired clergy in Pimlico. In so doing he summed up his own approach to it, and under 'theological aspects' drew upon Canon W. A. Vanstone's book, *The Stature of Waiting*, which traces in Christ's ministry a transition from the activity of teaching and healing to the passivity of accepting what was done to him upon the cross. This was the movement in life from being a person who made things happen to being one to whom things happened. It was in this 'passive' state (upon the cross) that Christ accomplished his greatest work. Retirement, Stuart said, brought a challenge to long-accepted attitudes together with an opportunity for glorifying God in weakness rather than in strength. Here was a shepherd of the shepherds who knew for himself what it is like to need a shepherd's care. By 24 October 1985 Stuart was delivering the Josephine Butler Memorial Lecture at the Birmingham Institute, his theme being 'Morality, Politics and Theology'.

On 11 January 1986 he set to work on a new book, noting in his diary: 'Began sample chapter on "Encounters with Christ".' This account of life-changing one-to-one encounters in the Gospels was to be his last book and appeared in 1988 as *Encounters with Jesus*. A passage in which he discusses the transfiguration of Christ has its own illumination:

Some of the most important things that happen to us are those that happen within, out of sight, without perceptible consequences, and with no permanent record outside the private diary of the person concerned. I have, for example, for the greater part of my career, been involved in public life . . . but I know that this outward life, which seems to dominate us most of the time, was nothing like as important as events, perceptions and impressions in my inner life which shaped and controlled my feelings and attitudes, my hopes and fears, my shames and my gratifications. The Hebrew mind at its best would never have surrendered to a view of life which exalted the seen above the unseen, or the outward above the inward. When Mark recorded this incident he recorded what he took to be the crucial event in the life of Peter, James, and John, and of Jesus himself. . . . History for him was the outward expression of the activity of God in the human soul (*Encounters with Jesus*, p. 115).

179

Stuart's diary indicates some of his preoccupations of the time. On 19 January he wrote: 'The steady erosion of familiar delights and long standing interests could just be the process of weaning from this world and preparation for the next' (Psalm 119.19); 21 January: '"If only you would hear his voice today" (Venite) – if only for two minutes what a difference it would make to the whole inner life and outward ministry'; 24 January: 'Francis de Sales – "The devout life takes many forms", and I have to rediscover my own in circumstances different from the past. A listening ministry?' 1 February: 'The balanced life – listening, abiding, trusting, hoping, rejoicing. It is the real agenda for life beneath the appearances'; 3 February: 'To London for Lords and Centenary of the House of Laity'; 4 February: 'Heavy fall at Paddington Station in which I was "strangely" preserved from harm.'

15 February: 'Eric Atkins died at age of 79. How much I owe to that man for all that I now value. Funeral 21st – where would I have been without him?' 19 February: 'Painfully learning to listen – not so much for "guidance" as for the still small voice around which my life may be re-orientated. But it is difficult to identify that voice amidst the noise in my own mind, plans, projects, sermons, lectures'; 20 February: '"That you may be filled with all the fullness of Christ" – by the inescapable process of joy and pain, light and dark, happiness and unhappiness, anxiety and peace'; 23 February: 'I listen not just for guidance but for understanding and direction (orientation)'; 25 February: '"The things that are seen are transient" – all of them, nature, people, heaven and earth, stars and dust. It is obvious to the most casual observer but we are slow to take it on board. Richard Hamper [his Baptist friend and colleague at Eynsham] died mid-day'; 1 March: 'St David's Day. As in human relationships it is not just a matter of hearing the word but reading the mind of the Lord, which is itself the product not of a flash of inspiration but of a long companionship'; 3 March: 'To Watford for Richard's funeral – in spring-like weather. Back in memory 30 years to Eynsham and our creative, sometimes hilarious ministry.'

Stuart continued to broadcast from time to time – 28 January: 'Several letters, mostly friendly, re "influences" broadcast. How unpredictable the response to "casual" broadcasts of this kind. A lot of fertile soil around if we knew how to sow.'

Not all holidays were working ones though: 14 July–15 August 1985 was happily spent in Norway, and there was another holiday in Guernsey from 27 April to 4 May 1987, but in November that year he lectured in Bermuda on the theme 'God, the World, the Church and the Christian'. However, the year 1987 also brought the strange experience of fainting while in the House of Lords, something that he mused upon in a diary entry made some two years later on 17 June 1989: '"When death comes let God put His hand beneath our head to lift us up and hold us" (Claudius, quoted by Thielecke, p. 70): a reminder of my experience when I fainted in the House of Lords, alarming but heartening at the same time.'

SHENINGTON

After a while Stuart and Brenda looked for a quieter spot to live, a little deeper into the surrounding countryside, and eventually came upon a house on the fringes of Shenington where visitors to 'Bryn Celyn' found a physi-cally less active man surrounded by, and delighting in, a formidable personal library that occupied floor-to-ceiling wall-space in a room that was by no means the smallest in the house. Though reduced in scale it was the library of a working scholar and included in the ranks of its many titles a nine-volume theological dictionary of the New Testament, Robertson Nicoll's four-volume *Expositor's Greek New Testament*, James Strong's *Exhaustive Con-cordance of the Bible*, Harold Smith's six-volume *Ante-Nicene Exegesis of the Gospels*, Hastings's five-volume *Dictionary of the Bible*, Alford's five-volume *Greek Testament*, a two-volume *Dictionary of Christ in the Gospels*, Smith's and Wace's five-volume *Dictionary of Christian Biography*, seven volumes of Driver's, Plummer's and Briggs's *International Critical Commentary*, four volumes of the Old Testament in Greek, five volumes of Schurer's *The Jewish People in the Time of Christ*, and Tillich's three-volume *Systematic Theology*.

From Bryn Celyn he would set off to help the local rector by taking ser-vices and preaching in the village church down the road. There were five churches in the parish and the Revd Alan Lancashire greatly appreciated his services. Enduring the usual shortage of organists, the congregation and their minister would often have to make do without musical assistance. Whenever possible Brenda would play the organ and the small congregation would gather contentedly within the unrendered red-brick walls of the old church to share their lives with God and each other. It was in this quiet spot that Stuart was invited to contribute to the current concern about the stormy waters of adversarial politics. David Edwards, then Provost of Southwark, was editing a book in which 15 prominent people were invited to share their thoughts about the relationship between religion and politics in an increas-ingly polarized society. Stuart was the only bishop among the contributors. Published in 1990 under the title of *Christianity and Conservatism*, it carried a preface by Margaret Thatcher.

181

In his foreword David Edwards said: 'I have felt the force of the popular suspicion that despite the entertainment value of the gladiatorial fights in the Commons (now featured on TV) the great economic and social problems of a new age may require a different treatment. A wisdom may be needed of which no one party has the monopoly, even if one does not agree with all the low opinions which politicians proclaim about their adversaries.' Stuart's task was to offer an answer to a question once put by King Hezekiah to the prophet Jeremiah: 'Is there any word from the Lord?'

In his article in the book he wrote:

> Secular, pluralistic, we may be, but we remain the inheritors of a tradition which took its rise in the Sinai desert some three thousand years ago. In that sense we cannot undo the past and we would be wise not to ignore it. . . . The question I am asked to address . . . is whether this episode in the life of an ancient Middle Eastern people is of any significance in the decision making activity of a modern government, grappling with the intransigent problems of a society uncertain of its direction, with heavy international responsibilities, and exposed to persistent political and social problems at home. We might put the question in a slightly different way . . . : 'Is there any source of authority outside our political and judicial structures to which we can appeal . . . ?' (pp. 80 and 81).

After providing a brief, almost epigrammatic, statement of the way Old Testament thought is wedded to making sense of the vagaries of history and guiding the people involved, he made the following five points: 1. Serious concern for society requires serious attention to the Bible because of (a) the range of its experience, (b) the character of its law, (c) the effect of its interiorization within human life. 2. Every politician has a proper need for a sympathetic group of praying, believing, thinking friends with whom to share his or her dilemmas, and the Church has a responsibility to provide such. 3. Christians should be ready to hear or to be a Bonhoeffer or a William Temple – exemplars of sacrificial allegiance to moral absolutes in the face of tyrants, and able to think through the goals, structures, and relationships of society in a Christian way. 4. They should learn to recognize and address the sense and awareness of law in the non-religious man. 5. They should be open to God.

In such thoughtful company as that provided by his fellow contributors, he did not flinch from making the point that he alone had made in the General Synod debate about the atomic bomb, and setting the whole debate within the framework that Christ envisaged and taught – namely, the ultimate coming of God's kingdom in power and glory. 'Of course,' he added, 'the belief defies description. The kingdom to come lies above and beyond any views we may entertain about the ideal society. It follows that we shall have to be content with strictly interim political and social institutions, and forswear ideological bigotry' (p. 98). Stuart saw the battle for the faith as lying deep beneath the issues of his own day and every other era too.

On 31 January 1989 Stuart and Brenda set off for what was to be their last visit to Israel. Later in the year Brenda began work on an anthology of Evelyn Underhill's writings designed to mark the fiftieth anniversary of her death in 1951. Stuart's tasks, meanwhile, included preparation for a lecture tour in America scheduled for 22 February to 22 March 1990, where he was to note a wide interest in Underhill's life and work. It was his last working tour abroad, the topics reflecting those of the oldest of the Gospel writers – the ripeness of his own mind somehow resonating with that of the aged John. At Charleston he lectured to the Irenaeus Fellowship, founded in response to his lectures at Lambeth 12 years earlier. His subjects there were St John himself, Nathanael, Nicodemus, and the woman of Samaria. He also spoke about Ephesus. The work was enjoyable, but he found the physical demands of travel and the social exposure of hospitality increasingly exhausting and this may have caused him to miss one event in 1990 that would have given him more joy than most: a major event in the religious life of York that owed much to his years as Archbishop.

The twelfth-century massacre of Jews in the city's Clifford Tower had cast a long shadow that had been of special concern to Stuart, and he had hoped for a way of publicly dealing with that memory. He was delighted to hear of a project called the Clifford Tower Commemoration which came to remarkable fruition in 1990. Closely involved in its events was Canon Geoffrey Hunter who, during his years as Rector of Heslington (1976–99), had seen a good deal of the Archbishop. He writes: 'The initiative for it came from Geraldine Auerbach of the Benai Berith Music Festival. She and I and Rabbi Walter Rothschild of Leeds became co-chairmen of a steering committee. I was at the time Chairman of the York Anglo-Israel Friendship Society, which had good links with Stuart. What emerged was an amalgam of lectures, services, and concerts, all built around the theme of commemorating the massacre at Clifford Tower on Palm Sunday 1190.'

This was a tremendous achievement requiring close and courteous diplomacy. Canon Hunter continued:

Even the title was a difficulty: 'celebration' was too jolly for such a sombre event! Despite that, a memorial gathering in the Tower began the proceedings; old and new music reflecting the theme was performed in various places; lectures were delivered; synagogue services were observed in a school. And the highlight was the final service entitled 'Expressions of Heritage and Hope' in the Minster, which was packed with a congregation of Jews and Christians, almost all of whom at the end paraded up the cathedral to light a candle at a replica of the Tower, until the replica almost caught fire in the heat. When at the end the shofar was blown there was an electric feeling running down the church, and one of my fellow-committee members, a Jew, embraced me in tears. If only Stuart had been there. But already he was in poor health and did not fancy the journey from Oxfordshire. Archbishop Habgood gave the commemoration full support and attended both the opening and the closing ceremonies.

Stuart was now settled into a life divided between study, writing, helping his local vicar, and the delights of a large and varied garden with its view of a rolling tree-studded landscape over its hedges. Here he continued to keep his customary daily record of the weather and feel the closeness to the soil that was the stuff of childhood memories. And here, too, Brenda completed her compilation of Evelyn Underhill's writings, which was published in 1991, again with a foreword by Stuart, under the title *Heaven a Dance*. Requests to lecture, however, still arrived and some he was able to accept. Among these was one from the Oxford Ministry course to be delivered at their summer residence at Cuddesdon. The required subject was episcopacy. He gave the lecture at Cuddesdon on 5 August 1991, and again on 3 October, at a meeting of Stepney Evangelicals. He called it 'Bishops in the Vision of the Church' and it lay behind the booklet he wrote on the subject for publication by Latimer House, Oxford. He also accepted an invitation to speak about moral rearmament – a subject close to the heart of his old college principal, Canon Thornton-Duesbery. He also kept up to date with the current interest in 'New Age' religion – reflecting on its current significance, its source, character, and appeal.

In September 1991 his five-year diaries had shown him in a questing mood in which it seems he was making fresh discoveries. On 24 September he made the following entry: '"I can only find if I know what to seek" (Bonhoeffer, p. 441) – the importance of the Bible for him and for me. My problem in retirement, I suppose, is being uncertain what I seek when it used to be so obvious.' Three days later, on the 27th, he wrote: '"We are theologians who ask the question of our ultimate concern, the question of God and His manifestation . . . and we are able to receive spiritual knowledge" (Tillich – *Foundations*, p.

122). So I have been a "theologian" from childhood, yet only now able to receive spiritual knowledge.'

In this rural idyll, however, he soon had cause to call on his old political and public-relations skills. Having so recently written theological reflections on politics and society on a global scale in *Christianity and Conservatism*, he was now caught up in some parish pump politics which would have supplied Radio 4's *The Archers* with a good, long-running storyline as an 'everyday story of country folk'. Infill plans for the local quarry and intentions to excavate motorway construction materials nearby filled local residents with alarm. The parish council appointed an Environmental Issues Group to look into the matter and Stuart became its chairman. That particular danger averted, Stuart's committee sprang into action again to protect villagers from the noise of go-kart racing – action resulting in well-disposed organizers building a sound barrier bank between the racetrack and the village. And when a planned increase of gliding activity at a local airfield brought fears of increasing powered flight overhead, together with extra traffic through the village, Stuart was contacted by 30 local residents to take up the cudgels again and there were committee meetings in the picturesque Bell Inn, which managed to arrive at an accommodation of interests.

Such events were part of life in the years 1991–3, years that also brought sorrow. On 1 November 1991 his diary noted a major event in just eight words: 'Will died at 8 p.m. – with very little warning.' Will was the beloved elder brother who had been a quiet giant of his childhood years, and a wise friend and discreet counsellor in the pattern of changes into adult life. 'Requiescat in Pace,' he wrote. Later he conducted Will's funeral, taking as a text for his address the words of Isaiah 40 – 'Comfort ye, comfort ye my people, saith the Lord' – and going on to say 'We all need comfort today.' Will, however, was full of years, and death – though unexpected – held no tragic note. Darker times lay ahead. In the meantime, though, the days passed, with his diary noting events of the day that caught his attention: 6 November: 'Death at sea of Robert Maxwell'; 18 November: 'Terry Waite released'.

Then, striking the deepest recesses of the heart for Stuart and Brenda, came news that their eldest daughter Susan had developed cancer. In helping them and the family come to terms with that knowledge, Susan played a magnificent part. A talented and popular teacher of music with a wide circle of friends, she coped with her illness and the approach of death with a radiant and courageous spirit that was an inspiration to all who knew her. In the most taxing of all spiritual and emotional journeys, Stuart and Brenda shared the pilgrimage of her last months. There is no doubt that she made her journey in a way that brought much love and light to family and friends and she was at her spiritual best some months later when Stuart and Brenda spent time with her on 21 April 1992: 'Lunch with Susan and detailed discussion re funeral arrangements, etc., etc., conducted with ease and humour.'

There is no doubt that Susan's death was a heavy blow, long and deeply felt. There was nothing easy about the courage and faith in which it was borne by Stuart and Brenda. But her funeral was an outpouring of love and creativity involving many friends, and she was laid to rest in the churchyard at Shenington where visitors are able to look out across an open, rolling land-scape. In later years Stuart was himself to be laid to rest alongside her.

As Stuart progressed into his seventies, his back gave him increasing trouble and he acquired a stoop. His voice retained its winningly attractive timbre, but occasionally words were slurred and momentary pauses would interrupt the customary smooth flow of his speech – although not enough to create difficulties for the listener.

The evidences of age brought different requests for his services, and the editor of one periodical invited him to write an article on 'Age'. However, this manuscript was not published; perhaps it was not what the editor had expected. The text does, however, say a good deal about his own experience of ageing:

I apply myself to the detailed study of the Hebrew and Greek texts of the Bible. I find in this respect at least that increasing age is not a handicap. I have more time. I am in some senses more alert to nuances of the text than I used to be. But it is true that on the practical side I sometimes feel at a loss. The first time I used my cash card it disappeared into the bowels of the bank, and no money appeared in the tray. So I had to appeal to a friendly cashier in the bank, who observing my age, recovered my card and came out and did the transaction for me. . . . I avoid departmental stores which overwhelm me with the sheer variety of the goods on offer. I was taken aback last Christmas, when pressed into service in the village choir, that I could not remember the harmonies which used to be second nature to me . . .

Many travellers to Israel are surprised at how narrow the river Jordan is. It is deep and sometimes turbulent but it is never far to the other side. . . . I end with an old man's prayer. 'Now that I am old and my hair is gray, do not abandon me O God. Be with me while I proclaim your power and might to all generations to come' (Psalm 71.18 TEV) . . . Every society, so it is said, has to be judged by its attitude to the old and weak.

～ 7 ～

Gospel:
Light in Darkness

HIS LAST SERMON

On Sunday, 23 January 1994 – the third Sunday after the Epiphany – he set off for Shenington Church to conduct the service and preach at evensong, his sermon carefully prepared as usual on a sheet of lined quarto paper, folded to provide four octavo-sized pages of notes. His text was John 6.5: 'When Jesus looked up and saw a great crowd coming towards him he said to Philip, "Where shall we buy bread for these people to eat?"' – a question Stuart had encouraged today's disciples to confront throughout his ministry. His distinctive script in strong black ink set out the course his talk would take.

With minimal editing this is what he said:

The feeding of the 5,000 is the only miracle recorded in all four Gospels, therefore it is highly significant in the early Church. It is not just a miracle, but a parable about a chaotic world pointing to an inadequate Church and the all-sufficient Christ. A chaotic world is seen today in public life: displayed night after night on TV. It is marked by astonishing technological progress but is still a dangerous 'wilderness' where misfortunes abound, as for example the recent earthquake in Los Angeles, persistent failure in Bosnia, the confusions of the government's 'Back to Basics' call. At a personal level, even when exempt from dramatic disasters we all have our 'wilderness' moments, for example a sense of isolation, fear of the future, persistent illness, dread of unemployment, breakdown of relationships. This wilderness of ours is not a comfortable place once the romantic view of life is punctured and 'success' challenged.

An inadequate Church was evident in the response of the disciples. Philip did not know what to do; Andrew had an absurd suggestion; Peter was silent. They did not know how to provide bread in the wilderness, with crowds getting restive and darkness coming on. They were helpless. The disciples do not get a good press in the Gospels. They quarrelled with each other for Christ's favour, Judas betrayed Him, Peter denied Him, they all forsook Him, and they were slow to believe in the resurrection. In the rest of the New Testament Paul quarrelled with Barnabas, Mark deserted the mission, Peter compromised with Jewish zealots, and the early Church was bitterly divided. Never speak of 'reunion' – unity has yet to be experienced.

Today we have a partisan church, marred by divisions, preoccupied with trivial arguments, helpless in the face of the real needs of the world, unable to cope with the problems of this 'wilderness', offering five loaves and two fishes in a ludicrous gesture. But our faith is not in the Churches, but in Christ and in the 'holy catholic church' which is an ideal we have yet to experience. Our faith is in the all-sufficient Christ.

In His ministry then He was adequate to every situation, the 5,000 in the Wilderness, the sick child, the madman, the mortally sick, the leper, the cripple. He healed them all without distinction and without reserve. That is the message of the New Testament exemplified by the feeding of the 5,000 in the wilderness. But that is past history. What about us now in this 'wilderness', fearful of the future, hampered by past mistakes, haunted by our fears. I remember my mother – if you had a cold she saw the undertaker at the door! What about now? I can only speak for myself. Despite what some people think – like the organist at the Minster who spoke of a 'sunny temperament' – I am not by nature a sanguine person. But I am learning slowly, and not before time, to stretch out a feeble hand to Christ in time of need in my particular wilderness experience – which is something we all have. We all have to learn, as a nation, as a Church, as a parish, to trust God in this 'wilderness'. He fed the 5,000 then, He can feed the chaotic millions now – if He can find a few disciples to take the bread around. Fear not, God has the whole world in His hand.

Stuart replaced his notes between the hard covers in which he carried his papers to and from church, went home, clipped them into the metal spring clasp of his current collection of sermons, and wrote at the head of its first page the number 1424. Of course there are many other sermons not recorded or included in that particular count. But sermon number 1424 was to be his last.

FINAL DAYS

The beginning of the end was unexpected and sudden. It was a winter's day that had left patches of ice on the paths and Stuart was busy with his usual odd jobs in the garden. Hearing a cry for help Brenda came out to find him lying where he had slipped and fallen. His hip was broken and he could not be moved without help. Bringing him blankets, she called for the ambulance that took him to the Horton General Hospital in Banbury.

With hip repaired Stuart was allowed home, and seemed to be recovering until some cardiac problems took him back to hospital again. For a while he experienced drug-induced hallucinatory experiences that he found deeply distressing, but as his mind cleared articulate prayer became possible once more. It was a great struggle, but the habit of a lifetime surfaced when he resorted to the well-tried ways of writing down his thoughts. Having asked Brenda to buy him a new exercise book he managed to write a prayer and a meditation. The writing was in a shaky hand eloquent of physical as well as mental difficulty, but the words revealed great humility and the special power of a spirit exercising faith bereft of feeling. The prayer was written on 3 March 1994, some of which was hard to decipher:

The difficulty of concentrating and a disheartening [?] sense of hopelessness make prayer seem like conversation without a listener. But the Lord knows my need and will respond to my prayer. I believe – help my unbelief, open heaven's gate and help me to feel again . . . [Here he mentions some names.]

Not a matter of persevering, but of openness to the Very God who can [?] make life real again. All that has happened is that my usual defence [?] viz [?] prayer, study, correspondence, public esteem, past achievements, social status, mean nothing, and I am naked to my enemies and very vulnerable. Lord speak to my condition with words of love and mercy.

On 6 March he wrote:

The feeling of helplessness and dependence is a reminder that this is how it is all the time. Hence we build our own structures (spiritual and physical) to make us feel secure in an insecure world where accidents do happen day in and day out, from which there is no protection, which leave all things [?] feeling insecure and needing human and divine support as a guarantee against disaster. My defences have certainly been shown for what they are – towers of Babel inviting collapse.

Following a further spell at home in Brenda's care, Stuart developed a blockage in the bowel and, during a third spell in hospital, cancer was diagnosed and surgery followed. The day after the operation the surgeon asked to see Brenda to say that he had only a week to live. Stuart and Brenda talked together, and Stuart said that he didn't want to die in hospital. At the surgeon's suggestion, Brenda visited the hospice at Adderbury, not realizing that Stuart was its patron. He was admitted to the hospice and spent his last days lovingly cared for in a quiet and spacious room.

In the wilderness experience of those days he had no sense of the lasting contribution he had made to the family of Church and society. In illness it seems these things were hid from him and his praying had to go on without benefit of vision, assurance, comfort or warmth. Stripped of all but faith, it was consequently the truest of prayer and, significantly, was not confined to his own need. He spent much time praying for others. On the reverse side of the page bearing the prayer and meditation quoted above he wrote the names of people on his mind. There were no fewer than 180 of them – family, friends, and colleagues. So we are left with a picture of a man of prayer deep in the wilderness and praying for his people.

Happier states of mind and sensation did, however, return in his last few days, and when Bishop John Bickersteth came to visit him there was laughter and happy reminiscence as well as prayer. Bishop John recalls how, 'he was perfectly conscious but in great discomfort – moistening his gums with a small sponge on a stick because his mouth was so dry. I remember the intercession lists lying on his bedclothes, and the laughs we had. "Tea and cakes on the sofa", I remember him saying, "you often blew in around that time, and Brenda would join us in a 20-minute threesome. I'm sure a lot of our problems looked less intractable as we chatted together over those cakes."'

A regular visitor in his last months was Dr Anthony Russell, Bishop of Dorchester:

> I found ministering to Stuart in his last months a deeply moving experience; his gentleness, his profound trust in the goodness and grace of God, his concern for those around him and his total absence of any sense of grandness was to me deeply moving. His faith had a simplicity and a humility and his life had a singularity of purpose all of which I found very moving. He was a lover of peace and quiet and the house in Shenington suited him very well. He found being in the Horton General Hospital in Banbury very frustrating, largely because of the noise and sense of activity and movement which seemed to go on all the time. He relaxed completely in the Hospice. There I had the privilege of praying with him, anointing him, and giving him his last Communion on Sunday, 29 May, with the chaplain, the Revd Jeffrey Chard. Brenda and Alison were there, as were some of the staff, and although Stuart was very ill he was aware of the prayers around him and held my hand throughout the short

service. This was the last occasion on which I saw him alive but his serenity, calmness, and trust were deeply touching, even at this very advanced stage of his illness.

Two other visitors noted the impression he left upon them: 'He is completely spiritually healthy – radiant, expectant, and at peace.'

John Bickersteth also visited again at this time: 'I went into his large room (room for two or three other beds) and Brenda was sitting on an upright chair, quite calm, up near his pillow. He was sitting up in bed, thin and near to death; he couldn't speak, but he smiled. They both looked so firm in faith it almost seemed an intrusion to pray with them.'

He died on 3 June 1994.

To Brenda from Dohnavur, India, 17 May 1945:
'My hut is perched at the top of a flight of stone steps and the view from the verandah is through the tops of the trees; the wind is fresh and clean and the sun dances and dazzles on the leaves. By day a place of earthly delight but by night, so I have found, a lonely silent place which strips the mind and spirit of its trappings and holds them up naked to the eye of God. The precipice yawns at our feet again, as it has done before, and we look up from its depths, helpless, to the mercy of God and the homely companion-ship of His Son. Deep cries unto deep.'

RAF Heaton Park, Christmas Eve 1942:
'A day of reading and prayer, timeless – a symphony, transient across the still deep music of God. So will it always be now until I have learnt to accept Christ and to live in Him in the world in my stead. . . . I am dead now, waiting for the shudder of a new life, deep in the womb, awaiting birth. I have knocked and await now the drawing back of the bolt, the silent opening, the step into the darkness, the blinding of the light, then, pray God, the warmth of a family, children's laughter. . . . "In my Father's house are many mansions, if it were not so I would have told you".'

Books by Stuart Blanch

The World Our Orphanage: Studies in the Theology of the Bible (Epworth, 1972)
For All Mankind: A New Approach to the Old Testament (Bible Reading
     Fellowship/John Murray, 1976)
The Christian Militant: Lent with St Mark's Gospel (SPCK, 1978)
The Burning Bush: Signs of Our Times (Lutterworth, 1978)
The Trumpet in the Morning (Hodder & Stoughton, 1979)
The Ten Commandments (Hodder & Stoughton, 1981)
Living by Faith (Darton, Longman & Todd, 1983)
The Way of Blessedness (Hodder & Stoughton, 1985)
Encounters with Jesus (Hodder & Stoughton, 1988)
Future Patterns of Episcopacy: Reflections in Retirement (a pamphlet) (Latimer
     House, Oxford, 1991)

Books Referred to in the Text

Note: references in notes in the text to the work of Baron Friedrich von Hugel do not include the titles.

Alison, Michael and David L. Edwards (eds), *Christianity and Conservatism*, Hodder & Stoughton, 1990.

Chambers, Oswald, *My Utmost for His Highest*, Simpkin, Marshall, 1927.

Church Assembly Report, *Towards the Conversion of the Church of England*, 1945.

Farrer, Austin, *The Brink of Mystery*, SPCK, 1976.

Fosdick, H. E., *The Meaning of Faith*, SCM Press, 1915.

Glover, T. R., *The Jesus of History*, SCM Press, 1917.

Golding, William, *The Spire*, Faber, 1964.

Gore, C., Henry Leighton Goudge and Alfred Guillaume, *New Commentary of Holy Scripture*, SPCK, 1928.

Heaven a Dance: An Evelyn Underhill Anthology, compiled by Brenda and Stuart Blanch, Triangle, 1992.

Hick, John (ed.), *The Myth of God Incarnate*, SCM Press, 1977.

Kafka, Franz, *The Castle*, Martin Secker, 1930.

Lambach, Frank Charles, *Letters of a Modern Mystic*, Lutterworth Press, 1950.

Learning of God: Readings from Amy Carmichael, compiled by Stuart and Brenda Blanch, Triangle, 1985.

Macquarrie, John, *The Principles of Christian Theology*, SCM Press, 1966.

Maddocks, Morris, *The Christian Healing Ministry*, SPCK, 1981.

Nicodemus (Melville Channing Pearce), *Midnight Hour*, Faber and Faber.

Orwell, George, *Animal Farm*, Secker & Warburg, 1945.

Poulton, John, *Dear Archbishop*, Hodder & Stoughton, 1976.

Robinson, J. A. T., *Exploration into God*, SCM Press, 1967.

Robinson, J. A. T., *Honest to God*, SCM Press, 1963.

Sayers, Dorothy L., *The Man Born to be King*, Gollancz, 1943.

Stephenson, A. M. G., *Anglicanism and the Lambeth Conference*, SPCK, 1978.

Temple, William, *Christianity and Social Order*, Penguin, 1942.

Vanstone, W. A., *The Stature of Waiting*, Darton, Longman & Todd, 1982.

Waddell, Helen, *Lyrics from the Chinese*, Malvern Publishing Company, 1913.

Watson, David, *Fear No Evil*, Hodder & Stoughton, 1998.

Winslow, Jack, *The Lee Abbey Story*, Lutterworth Press, 1956.

Index

Index